MW00975707

ADVANCE PRAISE FOR

White Fatigue

"The concept of white fatigue is an important contribution to creating a more nuanced understanding of the challenges of educating white students about racism. *White Fatigue* offers helpful context and pedagogical considerations for supporting the development of white allies for racial justice."
—Diane J. Goodman, Trainer, Consultant, and Author of *Promoting Diversity and Social Justice: Educating People from Privileged Groups, Second Edition* (2011)

"In direct and explicit language, Joseph E. Flynn, Jr. pulls no punches in his challenge to teacher educators to dig deep into the layers of white fatigue. Such accounts are critically necessary in a moment where some whites feel emboldened to act on deeply-seated racial hatred. Where such overt acts are considered the norm, Flynn brings us closer to the subtleties that are often ignored in the current social, political, economic, and educational moment."
—David Omotoso Stovall, Professor of African American Studies and Educational Policy Studies, University of Illinois at Chicago

"With this accessible and engaging work, Joseph E. Flynn, Jr. makes a critical contribution to social justice education. He offers insight into a recognizable exit point for many White teachers on the journey toward more racially-just teaching—fatigue—and considers how it might be addressed. This book will be invaluable to both current and future teachers and those who educate them."
—Robin DiAngelo and Özlem Sensoy, Authors of *Is Everyone Really Equal? An Introduction to Key Concepts in Social Justice Education, Second Edition* (2017)

White Fatigue

sj Miller & Leslie David Burns
GENERAL EDITORS

Vol. 8

The Social Justice Across Contexts in Education series is
part of the Peter Lang Education list.
Every volume is peer reviewed and meets
the highest quality standards for content and production.

PETER LANG
New York • Bern • Frankfurt • Berlin
Brussels • Vienna • Oxford • Warsaw

Joseph E. Flynn, Jr.

White Fatigue

Rethinking Resistance
for Social Justice

Mom,

But not for your fierce sacrifice and
support, and the moral foundation you laid,
this book would not have been possible.
I love you Mom. Happy birthday. May the Lord
bless and keep you.

Joseph Ernest 3/21/2018

Don't forget to check the
bookmarked pages. These
are my favorite passages.

PETER LANG
New York • Bern • Frankfurt • Berlin
Brussels • Vienna • Oxford • Warsaw

Library of Congress Cataloging-in-Publication Data

Names: Flynn, Joseph E. (Associate professor), author.
Title: White fatigue: rethinking resistance for social justice /
Joseph E. Flynn, Jr.
Description: New York: Peter Lang, 2018.
Series: Social justice across contexts in education; vol. 8
ISSN 2372-6849 (print) | ISSN 2372-6857 (online)
Includes bibliographical references.
Identifiers: LCCN 2017043225 | ISBN 978-1-4331-5026-5 (hardback: alk. paper)
ISBN 978-1-4331-5027-2 (ebook pdf) | ISBN 978-1-4331-5029-6 (epub)
ISBN 978-1-4331-5028-9 (mobi)
Subjects: LCSH: Multicultural education—United States.
Race relations—United States.
Racism—United States.
Social justice—United States.
Classification: LCC LC1099.3 .F58 | DDC 370.117—dc23
LC record available at https://lccn.loc.gov/2017043225
DOI 10.3726/b12016

Bibliographic information published by **Die Deutsche Nationalbibliothek.**
Die Deutsche Nationalbibliothek lists this publication in the "Deutsche
Nationalbibliografie"; detailed bibliographic data are available
on the Internet at http://dnb.d-nb.de/.

The paper in this book meets the guidelines for permanence and durability
of the Committee on Production Guidelines for Book Longevity
of the Council of Library Resources.

© 2018 Peter Lang Publishing, Inc., New York
29 Broadway, 18th floor, New York, NY 10006
www.peterlang.com

All rights reserved.
Reprint or reproduction, even partially, in all forms such as microfilm,
xerography, microfiche, microcard, and offset strictly prohibited.

Printed in Germany

Dedicated to
Jacob (Poot),
my eternal hope for the future …

In memory of …
Don Moore
David Lustick
Kevin Basmadjian

Table of Contents

Acknowledgements

Writing a book is an intense labor of love (and sometimes hate) that takes a considerable amount of time, energy, sacrifice, and sanity. Equally important is the amount of collaboration that happens, even for a solo-authored project such as this. Although I can probably never name all the people that have some fingerprint on this project there are a few I must name.

The first person I must thank is my colleague and friend, Dr. Leslie David Burns, co-editor of this series. Les and I have been talking about the ideas of race and racism since our days in graduate school back at Michigan State University. Over the years those conversations have been a strange mixture of freewheeling, critical, emotional, considerate, challenging, and *always* punctuated with humor. Through the drafting of this document Les was always there to help me tackle problems, offering a source, turn-of-phrase, or just an ear that unstuck me in that moment. His support of this project was crucial and his friendship is indispensible.

I also wish to thank the scores of theorists and researchers that literally changed the way I see the world. Some of these folks I know, and some I do not. Some made their marks in academic disciplines and some from outside academia. Some are here, and some are here in spirit. In no specific order, the roll call: Rev. Dr. Martin Luther King; the Honorable Minister Malcolm X; Barack Obama; W.E.B. DuBois; Carter G. Woodson; Don Moore; David Lustick; Paulo Freire; Gloria Ladson-Bilings; James Banks; Christine Sleeter; Geneva Gay; Sonia Nieto; Lisa

Delpit; James Baldwin; Eddie Moore, Jr., Tim Wise; Gary Howard; Stan Howard; Peggy McIntosh; Kevin Kumishiro; Cleo Cherryholmes; Lynn Fendler; Dorinda Carter; Chris Wheeler; Jay MacLeod; Kimberlé Crenshaw; Derek Bell; Ta'Nehisi Coates; Ernest Morrell; Henry Giroux; Franz Fanon; Pauline Lipman; Stephen Haymes; Sandra Jackson; Amira Proweller; Chuck D; Barbara Sizemore; Chris Dunbar; Jean Anyon; K. Wayne Yang; Zeus Leonardo; David Kirkland; sj Miller; Gil Scott-Heron; Bob Dylan; William Ayers; David Stovall; Cornell West; Spike Lee; Hunter S. Thompson; Michael Eric Dyson; David Simon; Kendrick Lamar; George Carlin; and Richard Pryor.

I must also extend thanks to my colleagues at my home university, Northern Illinois University. Although I have had many conversations about this book with colleagues, there are a few that I must recognize for their ears and advice: Patrick Roberts; Amy Stich; Rebecca Hunt; Michael Manderino; James Cohen; Patricia Kee; Amelia Gould; Kerry Burch; Sarah Militz-Frielink; and LaVonne Neal.

Occasionally any one of us can get the chance to be plugged into a community that invigorates and pushes your thinking. The American Association for Teaching and Curriculum (AATC) has been such a community for me. There are so many people in AATC to thank, but there are a few member, friends, that are crucial: Drew Kemp; Michelle Tenam-Zemach; William White; Bradley Conrad; Richard Biffle; Pamela Thompson; Chara Bohan; Ruben Garza; Shelley Harris; Christy McConnell; Derek Gottlieb; Kate Kauper; John Pecore; Matt Spurlin; David Flinders; and Dan Conn. Thank you all for your friendship, ideas, and support.

I also wish thank my students. Everyday I teach I realize something new that makes me a better teacher and that is a direct result of their questions, discussions, and after class conversations. I have been lucky that many of my students—especially my doctoral candidates and students—have been interested in both my opinions about racial issues in education, society, and popular culture and the development of this book. Those conversations and concerns directly influenced this project.

In full truth though, this book would not exist had it not been for the development of friendships that are now more than twenty-five years old. I have sat with these guys for countless hours talking about the spectrum of life, and race was/is a recurrent topic: Ronnie Herman; Lance Hochmuth; Christopher Conrad Legan; John Brillhart; Todd Utz; and Brent Goers. No matter how near or far, each of you will be an eternal influence in my life.

I must also thank my folks: Julius, Lisa, Dad, and Mom. Their support and encouragement of me throughout my life has been indispensible and their understanding, open ears through the process of writing this book has been a true blessing. Julius' daring spirit and the stories of his travels around the globe helped me consider the meaning of diversity and a beloved world. Lisa's steadfastness and quiet intellect was always an inspiration. Dad's lust for life and work ethic showed me how to struggle through and get it done, come what may. And with that, Mom is my original teacher. She taught me to always remember my faith and Creator. Moreover, she taught me what a life of selflessness looks like. These four people … I love and thank them.

No disrespect is intended to any of my extended family members, but the role of my aunt, Shirley Bradley, is paramount. Aunt Shirley exposed me to a world of art, music, and literature, unlike any other person, and she not only planted the seeds but also nurtured my intellectual curiosity. When I was young on our annual trips down to Memphis, she took me to colleges and universities; she took me to libraries; she shared with me her music collection (that any DJ would die for); she suggested books for me to read; she encouraged me to *look* at art; she created a space for me to explore and I will be eternally grateful for that. Much love, Aunt Shirley.

Last and most definitely not least I must express my sincerest love and appreciation to Jacob and Gena, my son and wife. This book was also inspired by watching Jacob grow and begin to develop his own ideas about justice, friendship, and love. He is a role model to me and I hope this work makes him proud. And finally, to Gena, my beautiful and brilliant wife and partner. For twenty years, she has been by my side, offering support, guidance, encouragement, time, patience, an ear, and so much more. My respect for her required me to do the best work I could, for her acumen and prowess never cease to amaze and inspire me. This achievement is not solely mine, but ours. We have been talking about these ideas in various permutations since we were back in Dr. Howard's class (she knows what that means), and we have developed a community of friends—our "chosen" family—that reflects the kind of world I have always wanted for my family: intelligent, critical, diverse, and understanding. There are no words to fully capture my respect, gratitude, and affection for her. G, I love and thank you, for everything. This work would have been impossible without you.

Foreword

BY LESLIE DAVID BURNS

It is a rare and exhilarating experience to see a scholar produce new knowledge. It is intellectually thrilling to be in dialogue with a scholar and witness the conception, development, and realization of a crucial pedagogical construct that has such potential to advance the project of teaching for social justice across diverse contexts. It is an honor to work closely with a public intellectual who has shed new light on a problem that has rightly troubled our profession from its inception in U.S. society. This has been my experience serving as editor for Dr. Joseph Flynn's first solo-authored book, *White Fatigue: Rethinking Resistance for Social Justice*. Using theories and research from Multicultural Education, Critical Studies, Critical Race Theory, and Second Wave Whiteness Studies, Dr. Flynn has done nothing short of identifying what may be one of the most confounding challenges to anti-racist education today: White fatigue.

In this book, Dr. Flynn illustrates that racism is, fundamentally, a structural and institutionalized system that instigates, exacerbates, normalizes, and perpetuates hegemonic systems of practice and power relations. By design, racism often renders its most insidious manifestations as twisted caricatures of a "common sense" that attains the level of habitus. In other words, systemic and institutional practices tend to create norms that become hardwired in our collective consciousness, rarely to be questioned or critiqued. In this state of being and perception, social structures and elements of power, discourse, and social interaction become assumed to the point of invisibility. In the unquestioned state of habitus (fully explained by Dr. Flynn in Chapter 5 of this book), racist systems, structures, instruments, practices, and behaviors can not only manifest but thrive based on the false presumption that they are simply "the way things are" rather than "the way we have constructed things to be." In such a context wherein systemic racism is too often invisible or unremarked, the capacities for individuals to recognize, identify, and respond in just and inclusive ways are too often constrained by their personal psychological dispositions and experiences. While they are able to recognize and acknowledge many racist attitudes, acts, and behaviors, they are less able to identify the deeper systems and structures from which those more overt racist elements manifest, knowledge essential for anti-racist theorizing, action, and reform. As a result, many people learning about racism (let alone considering how to acknowledge, resist, and eliminate it) find such learning difficult at least. This is acutely the case for those who benefit most from racist systems, White people.

The point is simultaneously simple and complex: racism functions by normalizing systems of power through institutional practices that promote a racial hierarchy in which individuals—depending on their designation—occupy and reproduce roles in the system, oftentimes unconsciously. Dr. Flynn points out that despite the deep knowledge base we have in multicultural, social justice, and anti-racist education, students are nonetheless exposed more often to uncritical lessons on diversity, promoting human relations and tolerance rather than broader explorations of the hows, whys, and whatfors of racism. Uncritical examinations of racism do not get at when, how, and why—for example—Whiteness was created and constructed as the norm, let alone the consequences of that normalization.

As such, and especially with regard to educating White folks who seek to serve as educators in our nation's schools, anti-racist education is not merely a project of highlighting responsibility and culpability for their privilege and complicity in racist systems. It is also a project of critically examining how systems and institutions function to promote and sustain a racial hierarchy. As Dr. Flynn notes, the vast-majority of White people typically recognize racism as a negative and serious problem. Many Whites enter studies of race and racism with strong desires to help end racism, or to lead others in resisting racist practices. Unfortunately, many current and ongoing discourses of White Privilege position Whites in ways that require them to not only acknowledge and take responsibility for their privilege and power in racist systems. They also, perhaps inadvertently, require them to maintain identities of Whiteness that render them always, inherently, and inescapably racist, simply by the fact of their own genetics. Positioned as such, countless potential White agents of anti-racism are, at best, offered limited and subordinated roles as allies, as though White folks have no skin in the fight against racial oppression. In the extreme unhealthy cases, they are rejected or excluded from the discussion altogether.

The generalized and ascribed racism projected onto White students in contemporary arenas of anti-racist education often demonize Whites categorically. When this sort of essentialization occurs in any context, the project of anti-racist education becomes immediately fraught with paradox. This is especially so in the fields of teaching and teacher education, where over 80% of the workforce is comprised of Whites who are responsible in turn for educating a student population that is over 50% non-White and growing in diversity.

Confronted with their inescapable privilege and power as White people in a society that systematically and institutionally maintains their status, significant numbers of White learners fail to understand why they are positioned as such, often conflating White privilege with economic privilege. At a basic level, many Whites can become tired of learning about racism simply from the intellectual challenge and complexity of the subject matter. Others become cognitively frustrated by persistent messages that they must learn about racism, including their own, but can never alter or escape the racist identities they have acquired—whether earned, presumed, or ascribed. They become fatigued by deficit model approaches to anti-racism in which they are constantly expected to atone for their privilege when they have had little guidance or opportunity to assume new positions or intersectional identities that they might otherwise seek to use as tools of change for doing so. Having entered into study with good faith, significant numbers of White people learn from their engagements with anti-racist education that they are not just part of the problem but are the problem itself. They often get taught that due to their status and position in racist systems, they may only assist, follow, and comply with the leadership of non-Whites, or at best help non-White leaders from positions of limited allyship. This reinforces a binary oppositional construct that dictates struggles against oppression are solely the province of the oppressed and flies in the face of the underrepresented historic interracial struggle against racial oppression. Facing what seems to them a scenario in which they are damned if they do and damned if they do not, many Whites disengage, sometimes completely but other times only momentarily. Dr. Flynn ultimately begs an essential question: Should we confront all forms of resistance with the same contempt even though we know that systemic and institutional racism function by a design that tacitly reinforces a racial hierarchy?

It is an understandable temptation to consider the supposed plight of White learners in anti-racist education contexts described above to be largely if not entirely matters of classic White resistance, White privilege, White fragility, White guilt, and willful ignorance. There is certainly considerable anecdotal and

scientific evidence that White racism and White maintenance of racist social practices and structures is all too common. In this age, where Black children are labeled
as struggling or even cognitively disabled in wild disproportion to their White
peers in schools? In this age of mass incarceration for non-Whites, especially
Blacks, based on a notoriously and historically racist legal system? Where Latinxs
are still marginalized for speaking their first language? Where Asian Americans
are still constructed as model minorities and permanent outsiders, masking the
social, educational, and economic struggles of that community? Where Indigenous cultures are still facing deeply entrenched poverty and annexation of protected and sacred lands? Where LGBTQAI people are actively and even legally
discriminated against out of fear and ignorance? In the contemporary climate of
racial tension in which citizens' peaceful protests are met with violent police, government, and civilian suppression, sometimes encouraged by charismatic political
leaders? Many readers, especially those who are non-White and knowledgeable
about racism in American society, might understandably respond with skepticism,
even derision. But such responses highlight a missed opportunity for all who seek
to challenge and change racist systems and ameliorate their effects.

Dr. Flynn's conception of White fatigue is not offered as an excuse for White
people, and is most certainly not offered as a shield for them to use in defend-
ing themselves or deflecting the facts and repercussions of their privilege. Rather,
Dr. Flynn demonstrates that White fatigue is an important, unexamined phenomenon we can no longer afford to ignore or dismiss out of hand. It is in some ways a
manifestation of resistance and should be treated as such. But serious examination
also presents opportunities for anti-racist educators to open new spaces and avenues
for understanding and educating White students more successfully as they navigate their own racial identity development and experience the processes of learning
about systemic racism and how to resist it in schools, society, and everyday life.

The conceptualization and theorizing of White fatigue generated by Joseph
Flynn in this book provides important pedagogical considerations for all anti-racist
educators to explore, expand on, and implement in their collective work. Anti-racist
education is absolutely a project of teaching for social justice. Social justice is
absolutely a project of inclusion. Given these, Dr. Flynn sets a productive course
for anti-racist education across contexts, especially contexts pertaining to teaching and schooling. White fatigue requires explicit, honest, grounded inquiry and
dialogue that informs and includes all learners. It also offers the crucial means to
understand and support participants in anti-racist projects to not just orient or
ally themselves in those projects, but learn how racism operates far beyond the
levels of individual psychology and interpersonal discourse. Understanding White
fatigue enables anti-racist educators to position all learners, especially Whites, to

go beyond examinations of their privileges to become full members of their communities, including as leaders. And if teaching for social justice is truly our intent; if inclusion and success for all and not just some is our mission? Then understanding White fatigue is not just worthwhile. In a society where a significant majority of all teachers are White and most students are not, acknowledging White fatigue and managing it is an imperative.

We present Dr. Flynn's work with tremendous gratitude for his important contributions to our field. In this book, readers will find a passionate, powerful analysis and critique of Whiteness, Multicultural Education, Diversity Studies, and Anti-racist Education framed by both sociopolitical matters of the day as well as intimate narratives that humanize the challenges, work, and complexities of racism in our lives. It is rare to find such innovation, intellectual advancement, and forceful yet productive and compassionate discussion of social justice in one volume. With open eyes, a kind but firm hand, and a deep set of insights borne of long thought and hard experience, Dr. Flynn has created a book that can change minds, lives, and ways of thinking about how to address key challenges of Whiteness and racism in our schools and society. It is my honor to stand with him and invite all readers to join him in his work to resist racism in our lives and educate ourselves for true—and truly inclusive—teaching for social justice.

Introduction

Notes on My Relationship
With White Folks

I am not racist; some of my best friends are White. Nor am I a sell-out, for that matter. I was raised in the church (Friendship Missionary Baptist Church in Peoria, Illinois to be exact), and from the time I was a little boy to a young man striking out on my own, my mother and pastor ingrained into my conscience a few key Bible verses. "Judge not, lest ye be judged" (Matthew 7:1). "He who is without sin cast the first stone" (John 8:7). And, "Do unto others as you would have them do unto you" (Matthew 7:12). These three verses—essentially communicating the virtues of fairness, humbleness, and graciousness—have grounded not only my spiritual beliefs but also my sociopolitical and pedagogical beliefs.

Growing up in a city like Peoria is nothing particularly special. It is a conservative second-tier city with a few claims to fame: Caterpillar, Betty Friedan, Dan Fogelberg, and ... my man Richard Pryor. Groucho Marx used to ask, "Will it play in Peoria?" Not because we are a mecca of arts and entertainment, but because we are milquetoast, run-of-the-mill. If it can play in Peoria it can play anywhere! Peoria is the prototypical Midwestern city: politically and socially conservative, industrial, and pretty White, approximately 65% White according to the 2010 U.S. Census. For the most part though, like many other working and middle class Black kids, my childhood was filled with great memories and friendships across racial borders. It was rare for me to feel attacked or marginalized, and if I did, usually there was a White kid behind me offering support, whole-hearted compassion, and shared frustration.

So, in the spirit of not judging and doing unto others, I learned from a very young age to try to see beyond our skin and embrace the humanity in all people, while also knowing and representing the history and culture of my folks—all of it. I brought those values into my career as a teacher educator and I chose to focus on multicultural and social justice education, with an emphasis on race. This book is about race and social justice. Specifically it is about the ways in which White folks respond to learning about race and racism, in the effort of building community and helping White folks develop habits of mind that promote social justice for all groups.

Before continuing there are some points that must be put on the table. First, what is contained in the coming pages is in no way an attempt to appease White folks or give them a free pass on dealing with and learning about racism, nor their responsibility for addressing racism. I am in no way claiming that there are no unrepentant racists who would prefer a world in which only White people exist, separate and/or superior to the more "melanin rich." This book is not about the willfully ignorant; those who choose to turn away despite any compelling arguments. This book is not about those who wallow in a false sense of entitlement, inconsiderate of their positioning. This book is not about those White people who jeer and mock protests and demonstrations against racial injustice. This book is not about those people. Rather, this text's focus is on the millions of White Americans that feel racism is wrong but nonetheless displays frustrations with conversations and education about racism.

Second, it is essential that we consider language for a moment. I do not believe in the essentializing of groups. If essentializing—painting an entire group with a monolithic brush—is unsound and offensive for one group then it is for all groups. However, when talking about macro phenomena it is common and convenient to use the name of groups: White people, Black or African American people, Indigenous cultures, Latinxs, Asian Americans, etc. Using these macro descriptions is not meant to essentialize those groups. At times I will use adjectives and adverbs like many or some as a way of warding off essentializating.

Third, the audience of this book is an important issue. Principally, this book is written for teacher educators generally, and those who identify themselves as multicultural and/or social justice teacher educators specifically. This text is also aimed at those who identify themselves as educators generally, especially in the Kindergarten through secondary education ranks, and by educators I include both teachers and administrators. I believe that all of these actors can find this book edifying. Throughout the text I will shift between teacher educators and teachers. I do this because the teacher educators I know see themselves as *teachers*, first and foremost. Additionally, teachers at all levels who are concerned with the challenges of teaching about race may find the contents of this book useful. At the end of the day, we are all teachers and based on the research (to be explored in the coming pages) there are serious challenges, intellectually and practically, to teaching children, youth, *and* adults about race and racism. This book is also for students and the general public. I do not believe that the knowledge we discuss in graduate programs (nor in the Ivory Tower for that matter) ought to be occulted knowledge accessible by a handful of individuals. I hope to speak past the confines of teacher preparation programs and education graduate programs in order to encourage more critical conversations about race for us all.

Finally, this book will use both narrative-style prose and academic-style prose. I shift into a narrative, colloquial voice as a way of positioning myself. Much of this introductory chapter and the first chapter are written in a narrative, looser style as I offer personal testimony that can help the reader get inside my thoughts. I think it is important for us academics to try to be accessible to a broad range of readers. Although I recognize the importance of "bringing the theory," I do not want to be too esoteric, lest I alienate readers, and building a bridge from the layman's to the academic's register is fundamentally important if we want our discussions to go past the Ivory Tower.

What this book hopes to do is point out that there are and have always been White allies, accomplices, and leaders in the fight for racial justice, and equally important there are millions more that know that racism is wrong but do not necessarily understand the hows and whys of racism. Beyond theory and books I know this from decades of experiences. Most importantly, the intention of this book is to advance a conversation. But before I go on, please allow me to introduce myself. ...

Beginnings

The year was 1970. I was born in Peoria, Illinois to a Black mother from Memphis, Tennessee and a Black father who was also from Peoria. We were a working class family; Mom worked for Hiram-Walker, a liquor distillery, and Pops worked for Caterpillar, a manufacturer of construction vehicles. In my early years, we lived in predominantly Black neighborhoods and attended an all-Black church. Most of my parents' friends that I remember were Black as well. However, there were a few White folks that came around from time to time, friends my parents made at work, parties, whatnot. The White folks that came around never seemed "out of place," but it was clear that they were different, visually at least. Regardless, those picnics and cookouts, card games, and random visits never seemed tense, and in more recent discussions with both my parents, they still speak of those White friends with warm reminiscence. For all intents and purposes I lived in a Black world with occasional White visitors. During this era of my life, that reality extended to the composition of my own friends who I mostly knew through church and school.

The Move

The year was 1976. I was in the first grade. As I began the early years of elementary school I attended a racially and economically diverse school. I was never "the only" Black kid in class. After all, some of my friends at school also attended my church. This was also the first time I had a significant number of White peers in my world and I developed my first real friendship with a White kid, Charles. Like they always say, kids don't care about race they just want to play, and Charles and I got along like nuts and bolts.

But then, in 1978, a disruption. My parents decided to rent a house in a suburban neighborhood on the other side of town. Like many other Black families at the time, my parents wanted to move to a "better" neighborhood to offer us kids (I also had two older sisters and later a little brother) a different experience and more opportunities.

In the fall of 1978 and a fifteen-minute drive across town I suddenly found myself in a school where I was one of "the onlys" and in a classroom where I was *the* only Black kid. Initially, that was an inconsequential fact of my reality. You see, as a second grader new to the school, my new White peers received me warmly. I never felt like an outsider. I was never blocked from playing with the others. No one called me any racial slurs, well not yet anyway. Equally important, the other kids on my block welcomed me with open arms, inviting me to play with *Star Wars* figures, a rambunctious game of whiffle or kickball, and run rampant around the neighborhood like the little kings we thought we were.

Now, it was not idyllic by any stretch of the imagination! Of course there were growing pains, but it was rare that my peers used my race against me or made me feel like my Blackness was an issue. I say rare because there were a few instances in which marginalization smacked my young face in brutal ways. In third grade one of my White peers took to kicking the back of my chair, whispering "nigger, nigger, nigger" repeatedly in my ear. Eventually I got tired of the verbal bullying, and when I loudly ordered him to stop, our White teacher reprimanded me instead of him. When I protested and tried to explain my outburst neither my teacher nor my principal would let me speak, literally silencing me. As punishment my teacher "isolated" me from the rest of the class by having me move my desk to the front of the room, near the chalkboard and next to her desk, like a pet. I was insulted, silenced, and dehumanized. All the while I had watched my White peers do far worse often with little consequence. The White boys could just be boys, but we Black boys were incorrigible, unless we were on the basketball team, of course.

More than my peers, it was the adults in school (my principal and some teachers) that reminded me I was Black and not like everyone else, oftentimes resulting in my mother showing the titan she was by reading them the riot act when necessary. As I progressed through my elementary school years, I noticed the *unfair/inequitable/contradictory* treatment I and other Black kids received in relation to our White peers. Many of us boys were "squirrely" but it seemed like I was marked for reprimand more often than my White friends. My principal could be especially brutal. This was a time when corporal punishment was still routine in public schools, and he seemed to take a particular joy in giving me and other Black students "swats" with a wooden paddle, the same kind you see hanging on the walls of fraternity houses. While he "averaged" three swats with the White boys, I would get five or more. More importantly, many (if not most) of my teachers never defined me as curious, inquisitive, or precocious—which is how the folks at my church talked about me. On the contrary, teachers would label me as inattentive, lazy, unfocused, etc. Again, I displayed the same kinds of behaviors as many of my other classmates and rarely heard them disparaged as such.

Idyllic?

The year was 1981, the beginning of the Reagan era. As children we were to be seen and not heard. So I often stood or hid back in the cut eavesdropping on my parents' phone calls and listened to half of the heart-wrenching conversations of my parents' friends who were losing their jobs, questioning how they were going to make ends meet. "Oooo girl, I know it's hard … Uh-huh … Uh-huh. … Something will come along; just trust in the Lord … Uh-huh. … It'll be alright …" Eventually, I got to hear the other side of those phone calls as my own parents began lamenting losing their jobs by no fault of their own. Hiram-Walker, the distillery where Mom worked, relocated to a southern state (Arkansas as I remember), and Caterpillar, where Pops worked until his retirement, went through a decade of strikes and layoffs. I listened to both of my parents, especially my dad, commiserate with friends about how "we always be the last hired and first fired," or how the foreman on the line "don't give a damn about what's goin' on wit us," or how "we always getting passed over," or how "the union don't give a shit about us except for a vote."

Sometimes Mom would recount stories of growing up in Jim Crow Memphis, Tennessee. Most frequently she spoke of the good times and the warmth and tightness among her family. She also spoke of the comfort and pride in the fact that her father, Granddad, worked hard as a mechanic. He bought the land and built their home with his own hands—the home we still go down to visit. She also recounted stories of being spit on for no reason and called outta her name by White kids riding school buses while she and her siblings walked. She would say, "Just when we feel like we about to get ahead, something happens." She said it was what it was; you just knew where you could and couldn't go, how to speak to people, how to act around people.

For his part, although Dad rarely ever talked about overt racist experiences, he occasionally lamented how his high school teachers and coaches disregarded the needs of Black students. Pops was an athlete, a state level competitor. He always encouraged me to get on my grades because I wasn't all that athletic, and he wanted me to be sure that my future was in my own hands and not of gatekeepers like coaches. His coaches literally discouraged him from pursuing a higher education. They traded his academic success for their win columns, making sure that he stayed eligible even though he had periods of academic struggle. All the while those same coaches demanded academic excellence from their White athletes and encouraged their higher education opportunities. My parents made sure we knew and understood that we were Black and even though we had White friends, there were real difference between the two experiences.

Formative Years in Black and White

My family was the first line of learning about Black culture and identity, like many other young suburban Black families. My Mom framed this for me as a defense mechanism. "You ain't like all those White kids," she would say. "You might get along but you gotta work harder to get the same credit and that still might not get you nothin'." "Remember son," she would say, "don't trust nobody but Jesus." At the time all my friends in the neighborhood were White and we all seemed to get along fine. I honestly do not have many memories of strife or slights. Not to say that it didn't happen or there were no kids in the neighborhood that had animus toward Black folks, but the kids that occupied my immediate orbit didn't make me feel ... lesser. The reality in my young life was that I was hassled (or at least teased) about race far more by kids from the old neighborhood, my church, and other spaces outside school. It was other Black kids that made fun of the way I talked "proper," my obsessive love for *Star Wars* and science fiction, the way I dressed like a "little White boy," or *some* of the music I liked. I often felt like a hybrid of identity. Although some could be "bullies" I knew that most of the teasing was out of love and culture. I later learned those moments of teasing was reflective of our racial identity development and our understanding of what it meant to be Black. At home and in those places my parents made sure we were connected to (church, Saturday bowling leagues, down at the Urban League, etc.) I was immersed in Black culture, including strategies to resist and thrive through racism. While outside home in the neighborhood and at school I was learning elements of White culture: language, dress, mores, art, music, etc. Some called us Oreos for that, which can be frustrating, but I would rather be called an Oreo than a nigger any day. Know what I mean?

These "lessons" were not the sole providence of Mom and Pops. My sister, Lisa, was the first to ever tell me about lynchings, and she would regularly drop knowledge about Black luminaries that got no play at school: Medgar Evers, Malcolm X, Madame C. J. Walker, Ida B. Wells, Marcus Garvey, Stokley Carmichael, Angela Davis … My aunts and uncles talked to me about the beauty and depth of Black culture: art, music, film, and literature. My aunt Shirley always encouraged me to read, watch, and listen to the many facets of Black culture and life. My family fostered in me a respect for the ways in which Black folks made these gorgeous cultural creations that challenged our oppression: the blues, gospel, jazz, spoken word, the Black Arts Movement, and on.

Decades later, armed with life experience and theory, I have had the chance to critically reflect on my childhood, growing up as the only or one of the only Black kids around, and realized some subtleties that smacked of racism and marginalization. I recognize that one can easily make the argument that I may not have always been aware of when I was being victimized by covert racist practices. That would be fair. I always wondered why all the other kids could regularly go into a certain kid's home to play Atari, but I could not join them because there were "too many kids already." Or why I *always* had to be Lando when we played *Star Wars*. Or why all my White friends hated that "rap shit" but never thought once about whether or not I liked Rush, Loverboy, Billy Joel, or Judas Priest. Or the hazing from some of the boys when a White girl from the neighborhood and I had an innocent summer romance. One of the boys would ride up behind us on his Huffy singing, "Black and white, its an Eskimo Pie …" Or being the first questioned by police about neighborhood vandalism. Or never being complimented by any of my White teachers, except for Mr. Randy Steuve, my seventh and eighth-grade science teacher. He was the first teacher to tell me I was really smart. Or never being exposed to anything about Black history or culture in the curriculum, except for the obligatory nods to Martin Luther King, Rosa Parks, Frederick Douglass, Crispus Attucks, and George Washington Carver—as though they were the *only* relevant Black people in the history of America. Or that Africans were slaves, and that was that, no resistance, no force, they just were.

In the final years of elementary school, a few other schools were closed and those students were funneled into my school. Suddenly there were a lot more of us. We Black kids were tight too—the boys and the girls; we knew there weren't many of us. Although I lived in a White neighborhood, most of the time we left the house my family and I were going to predominantly Black spaces, back to a large network of friends and acquaintances that spanned the spectrum of Black culture. From perpetually broke brothers and sisters struggling in the housing projects down on the south side of Peoria to the Black intelligentsia and professionals scattered across Peoria's cityscape. But more important at this time was my homeboys: Tobi Davis, Lamont Williams, and Chris Lamon. There was also Jason and Clinton Stewart and Anthony Richmond. Although Jason, Clinton, and Anthony were not in my grade, their move into my subdivision was profound, as I began to revel in the safety of having a partner (or partners) that shared my identity—working class Black kids trying to thrive out in the boondocks. Man, we were thick as thieves; they were my brothers. They made me feel a connection I could not understand at the time, but as I matured I realized that it was that sense of a shared identity and experience, for even though I didn't get hassled much by my White peers I knew I was not like them, nor treated like them by the adults at school. There is legitimacy to the notion of comfort among those that share identity and experience. Learning those lessons of experience can be hard, and when we were together we felt invincible against any slings and arrows that could come our way.

Despite the influx of Black students into my school, all us kids took it in stride. There were no racially charged fights on the playground or during lunch. Again, I don't mean to make it seem like there were no challenges, but the general tenor of my environments was kind and inclusive. Perhaps that was reflective of the idea that kids just want to be kids and do not foreground animus. Perhaps I blocked some more challenging events, leaving them in the dustbin of my memory. One thing I can say for sure, we Black kids *always* had "cool" White kids around us and it was rare that any of us felt put upon by any of our White peers. It was a great time to be alive.

Turning Point

The year was 1985 or '86. I had moved to a new high school in Peoria. Like my last high school it was predominantly White, but there was considerably more racial, ethnic, and class diversity than at *any* of my previous schools. While attending that high school I got involved with the music department. After the fall musical, a group of fellas and I were driving over to the cast party at a classmate's home. We were a good eight deep packed into one of those late '70s Pontiacs, you know, the kind you could launch airplanes off the hood with four-in-the-front-four-in-the-back seating. Since I was small for my age, I was sitting in the back, on the "hump." As we rode the streets of Peoria smoking cigarettes trying to act grown, some of the guys started telling jokes. Simple jokes at first, one-liners like Redd Foxx or Rodney Dangerfield. Then, one of the boys told a nigger joke. As the other boys began a round of timid laughter, waiting to see how I was going to respond, the joke-teller looked back at me and said, "No offense, Joe." I nodded and said, "Okay," uncomfortably laughing it off. I thought that was the end of it, but then another came, and another, and another. Before or after each "joke" "no offense, Joe" was offered as pittance, and the phrase was said so often I thought it was from the book of Proverbs. Each joke began to feel like one of those thousand little cuts (i.e. microaggressions), after all, these were supposed to be my friends, but I swear I felt like I was in hostile territory. Sitting there on that hump, a good five minutes left until our destination, "What do you call a nigger when. ... How many niggers does it take. ... There was a Jew, a Polack, and a nigger ..." My blood boiled. My closest friend at the time, a White kid named Bobby, was sitting next to me, and our eyes communicated the discomfort and pain I had and the embarrassment and growing misery he had upon recognizing that this was going way to far. After one more "No offense, Joe," I bellowed, "Oh yeah, but what about my momma, or my sisters, my brother? What about all the people at my church? My mom's friends at the beauty shop or the guys that hang out with my dad?" The jokes stopped, faces turned from revelry to shame, and the only sound heard was the full-blast of the heater and the roar of the V-8. Slowly but surely, they all apologized, and I graciously decided to not take the derision into the party.

As painful as that was though, what I remember most was the look in Bobby's eyes, a look of regret and embarrassment at not knowing what to do. Yes, the obvious thing was for him to say "guys cut it out," but that is easier said than done when an adolescent, a time when you are not really sure of much. No matter what I knew where his heart was, and for the record, he didn't tell a single joke.

That car ride was not the norm of my high school experience, but the event forced me to accept that my White friends could be ill about race and sensitivity. The experience forced me to ask a question, what does it mean to be racist? How do I know someone is racist? And, what does it mean if people do not see themselves as racists but do things that could be interpreted as racist or have racist repercussions? It was one of those watershed moments that pushed me onto the path of multicultural and social justice education, for I wanted to be a part of the vanguard of teaching how to deal with a situation like that and to understand the broad range of dynamics at play.

Launch

The year was 1991. I attended Eastern Illinois University. Have you ever heard the term PWI (predominantly White institution)? Well EIU was an OWI, an *overwhelmingly* White institution in an *overwhelmingly* White, Midwestern town!

Although I had a lot of White friends, I also began to encounter, or at least became much more aware of, instances of racist treatment. It was a struggle to find a part-time job off campus. It was rare to see a Black person employed at any of the near-by off-campus establishments: restaurants, bars, stores. If it wasn't for the university Black student unemployment would have been around 97%. I was often the only Black student in class and oftentimes assumed to be the "Black representative." Bars resisted catering to Black folks by not playing R&B or hip hop, and when fights between White and Black patrons would break out at the only establishment that regularly played dance music, management would reprimand the Black community by banning hip hop and R&B music, even when the source of the scuffle could be traced directly back to a White person (which was typical). There were no Black beauty shops or barbershops. There were few Black professors, administrators, or staff members. And, every February there was an incessant stream of letters to the editor of the school newspaper lamenting Black History Month and questioning why there was not a White History Month. All the while I still made substantial and lasting friendships with a number of my White peers, and I developed an important network of White university employees that were truly invested in my (and other Black students') success.

My White friends and I did not shy away from race. We shared a lot. When issues would erupt, like the release of Nelson Mandela from Robben Island or the Rodney King beating and subsequent Los Angeles riots, we discussed them at length. Walking home from a night's festivities, I could talk to them about feeling marginalized, isolated, and targeted at bars and parties where I was the only Black person around. We talked about literature and ideas we all were learning in our classes and social interactions. While some of my White friends were turning me on to Jack Kerouac, Ken Kesey, and Hunter S. Thompson, I was turning them on to James Baldwin, Malcolm X, and Toni Morrison. While they were encouraging me toward the Grateful Dead, the Clash, and Nirvana, I was encouraging them toward Billie Holiday, Public Enemy, and Parliament/Funkadelic. (And vice-versa to be completely honest. A dude named Jeff was the first White cat I ever met who listened to P-Funk; I was twenty-two at the time)! We were just as likely to gather together to watch *Pink Floyd's The Wall* or Stanley Kubrick's *A Clockwork Orange* as we were to watch Spike Lee's *Do the Right Thing* or Gordon Parks' *Shaft*.

My dear friend Todd and I would talk a lot about the connections between hip hop and punk rock, and since he was a music aficionado he exposed me to hip hop I didn't know anything about. My dear friend John gave me my first copy of Toni Morrison's *The Bluest Eye*. I remember the look of sorrow and confusion on the face of my dear friend Lance when someone yelled "nigger" at us from a speeding pick-up truck as we walked home from the library. My dear friend Brent shared a great deal about growing up in his small town and the racist attitudes that swirled through the air of that community, and when I was hassled at a party in his home-town he made no bones about letting everyone know if they had a problem with me they had a problem with him. My core group of friends, which was predom-inantly White, was open and we communicated with one another on substantial and deep issues, including race and racism. We bonded and provided each other a space of safety to talk about things. Safety does not mean lack of argument; rather, we knew we cared about each other and hoped our discussions lead to growth rather than cheap shots or "gotcha" moments. To this day we are still close, no matter how much or how little we get to talk.

This is not to say that my White friends understood everything about race or never said anything that would hint at their own latent or dysconscious (King, 1991) racism, rather they were open and receptive to understanding. They were engaged. They recognized *my* challenges, too, never denying the legitimacy of my experiences. They appreciated having someone of a different racial background with whom they could explore ideas and advance their own growth. This was crucial in the wake of the 1992 Los Angeles riots that erupted after four White officers were acquitted of beating unarmed Black motorist Rodney King, an event that had reverberations on college campuses across the nation. What arose from that era, in part because of these discussions, was my decision to commit myself to being an educator dedicated to the empowerment of oppressed groups, and the promotion of racial equity and social justice.

A profound experience was meeting Donald Woods after a lecture he pre-sented on my campus. Donald was a White British journalist and close friend to anti-Apartheid activist Steve Biko. In 1977, the South African government killed Biko while he was detained for his protest activities. Since Donald was his friend, Donald was placed on house arrest. After Biko was murdered, Donald managed to escape South Africa and wrote a blistering article detailing what happened to Biko and the true nature of Apartheid rule.

After his lecture, I decided I was going to talk to him and we sat and smoked a cigarette together (I smoked back then). After talking for a few minutes about the events of the day and his travel plans, I asked him "What was Biko like." He said, "Steve was the kind of guy who could drink ten pints (of beer) and come back for more! He loved life. He loved to laugh. And he loved people." He went on to ask me what my plans for my education were. I said I didn't know. He said, and I will never forget this, "You wanna know what Steve would say? Earn your doctorate. We need more Black doctors." Biko and Wood's story encouraged me to recognize that strong relationships, at root platonic, can blossom into a powerful vehicle for changing the world, and the struggle for racial justice is just as much about the hard work of non-White activists as it is for White activists.

Confrontation and Self-Proclamation

The year was 1993. The "scene" from my life that forced me to really think about my racial identity, the nature of my interracial friendships, and my sense of social justice occurred in a senior seminar on the Black woman. We had a Black female instructor and an overwhelming Black student composition, with a few White students present. I walked into class that day, as I did most days, with headphones on, that day listening to Pearl Jam's *Ten* on full blast. As class progressed, we began to discuss the notion of sell-outs, questioning exactly what a sell-out is. As the discussion ensued, a particularly radical young brotha accused me of being a sell-out because I hung out with White people, did not go to a lot of house parties, and listened to rock music.

I was insulted. I challenged him and asked him what he actually knew about me? Did he have any knowledge of my history, family, or politics? Had he ever had a conversation with me about ideas? Did he know that I listened to A Tribe Called Quest and Public Enemy as much as I listened to Pearl Jam and Nirvana, and Miles Davis and Billie Holiday? Did he know that I actually had consistent conversations about race with my White friends and challenged them to think more critically about their understanding of race? Did he know that days before, I was followed—no, stalked—in a bar by a drunk White guy who clearly had a problem with me being around? Did he know that I too struggled to find a job in that town, and that I too had been called a nigger while on campus? I ultimately opined that it takes much more than being friends with White people and listening to rock music to make one a sell-out. After all, there is more than one way to be Black, and as we hunt for who is a sell-out and who isn't, we ultimately become crabs in a barrel, disregarding the spectrum of our own humanity, a tip of the hat to not essentialize.

These encounters provided me with what I used to think was a unique experience with race. As I have met an ever-increasing number of suburban Black Gen-Xers, I have come to realize that many of us had similar experiences with race and racism. We know that things are not like they were for our parents and grandparents, but we are also aware that a rift persists in the ways in which we think about and engage race across our different groups. The reality of that rift does not necessarily mean that we *never* see eye to eye, nor that White folks are always on "the other side." Rather, our social world is far more complex than simple binary distinctions rooted in essentializing practices and the construction of an American racial hierarchy. Nationally we are in the midst of a cultural shift in our racial relations, and as with any shift, there are some that are going along for the proverbial ride while others are caught in antiquity, obstinacy, and/or willful ignorance.

Transition: Today's Issues and A System of Advantage

Allow me to be blunt. For those that may be in denial, racism is real. In this case I am not speaking toward notions of individual racism or actions of prejudice and discrimination perpetuated by individuals (Sensoy & DiAngelo, 2012a). Rather, I am speaking about racism as a system of advantage based on race (Sensoy & DiAngelo, 2012a; Tatum, 2003; Wellman, 1993), and will be for the remainder of this book. It is essential to focus on the system of advantage based on race as its manifestations impact all our lives in complex ways and is far more challenging to understand and ameliorate. The systemic and attendant institutional manifestations of racism create a sociopolitical and economic context and worldview (Smedley & Smedley, 2012) that shapes our values, perspectives, and experiences. Although promoting respect, tolerance, community, and cultural competence are important, those actions alone can only set the stage for dismantling racism. It is essential that our society understand how racism as a system of advantage based on race functions in order to more effectively create an egalitarian anti-racist society.

Along with the statistics a number of events in this decade alone have reminded us, once again, that the problem of the color line remains a problem well over 100 years after W.E.B. DuBois made that prescient declaration, despite pronouncements of a post-racial America: The murder of Michael Brown by Officer Darren Wilson, and the protests in Ferguson, Missouri; the death of Freddie Grey while in police custody, and the uprising of Baltimore; the death of Eric Garner at the hands of New York City police officers and the unconstitutional "stop and frisk" policy; the death of Sandra Bland while in police custody; the killing of Tamir Rice by the Cleveland police; the death of Laquan McDonald, shot in the back by a Chicago police officer and covered up by the district attorney's office; the resignation of Timothy Wolfe, former president of the University of Missouri after students protested his lack of response in the face of heightened racist incidents on campus; the revelation of and reaction to Rachel Dolezal, a White woman "passing" for Black; repeated attempts to disenfranchise African American and Latinx voters by republicans and the repeal of a key provision of the Voting Rigths Act in the Supreme Court's *Shelby County v. Holder* decision; a xenophobic immigration debate that demonizes Mexicans; the mass incarceration of African American males and the construction of the school-to-prison pipeline; the disregard of protests from Indigenous cultures against the Dakota Access Pipeline (another slight in a long line of the marginalization of the Indigenous); the rise in domestic terrorism against Muslims and Jews; and, a young man named Dylan Roof murdering nine African Americans in a South Carolina church. Ultimately, the racially charged tactics of Donald Trump's presidential campaign further revealed the fissures of understanding around the relationships between race and class, oppression and marginalization, social justice and personal gain. These acts of racism are more than misdeeds or misappropriations by a handful of White folks. They are bell-weathers of larger systemic and institutional challenges that have grown out of racism and other forms of oppression.

Since racism is real, by extension White privilege is also real. White privilege is largely defined as the unearned advantages White people receive through a system of advantage based on race (Irving, 2014; Jensen, 2005; McIntosh, 1988; Sensoy & DiAngelo, 2012a; Wildman & Davis, 2008). Wildman and Davis (2008) illuminate White privilege in this way:

> When we try to look at privilege we see several elements. First, the characteristics of the privileged group define the societal norm, often benefiting those in the privileged group. Second, privileged group members can rely on their privilege and avoid objecting to oppression. Both the conflation of privilege with the societal norm and the implicit option to ignore oppression mean that privilege is rarely seen by the holder of the privilege. (p. 112)

Many of my colleagues and I are constantly interrogated about the legitimacy of White privilege. Oftentimes White students will say that they struggle just like everyone else and that is proof that they are not privileged. I ask them, "Is racism real?" To which most of them respond affirmatively. Then I ask, "If racism is real, who benefits from it, cumulatively?" And then I have them look at a bevy of statistics, from incarceration rates, to death penalty sentences and exonerations due to DNA evidence, unemployment rates, the number of White CEOs in the Fortune 500, life expectancy rates, foreclosure rates, composition of federal and state governments; graduation rates, etc. The simplest way of *proving* White privilege is to have students look at the larger picture and once they see the picture ask, "Either minorities are inherently inferior to White folks to always finish behind White folks in virtually every measure we can find, or there is something else going on here. Which do you think, and why?"

All the vignettes recounted in this introduction made me wonder how do we resolve the fact that there are many White folks who know racism is morally bankrupt and hope to move past this social hurdle, while at the same time there seems to be a consistent misunderstanding of or disregard toward systemic and institutional constraints on non-White folks? These instances and many others made me seriously question my role in the exploration and amelioration of racism in the United States, especially in light of the fact that my experiences with different communities have allowed me to see the humanity in all of us? After all, I have had nearly an entire lifetime of productive, caring, and loving transracial friendships that have been and are indispensible. In the process of learning about racism for decades (interpersonally and intellectually) I have always tried to strike a difference between the trends of a group and the trends of individuals within groups. Those questions and concerns bring me to this book.

Purpose: Considerations of Privilege, Resistance, and the Preparation of Teachers

The year is 2017. After seventeen years as a teacher educator, this book is an attempt to *expand/recast/deepen* the conversation on teaching about race and racism by recognizing essential nuances in our social relations and the ways in which we learn about race and racism, both formally and informally. The fundamental assumption of this text is that learning about race and racism is a long-term project that invariably challenges long-held assumptions, values, mores, messages, and representations. In short, critical examinations of race and racism challenge deep-seated worldviews (Smedley & Smedley, 2012) and there is a range of ways in which individuals can respond to what can often be a cognitively and spiritually disruptive conversation. It is essential to ferret out differences in locations in the process (or project) of learning about race and racism and recognize the struggles for White folks embedded in that process.

We often talk about resistant responses about racism from White folks. Noted anti-racist and social justice educator, Diane Goodman (2011), says, "When people are resistant, they are unable to seriously engage with the material ... resistance is not about people's specific views, but their openness to consider other perspectives" (pp. 51–52). I used to get quietly angry when students would ask questions like, "Why am I being blamed for things that happened a long time ago," or "Why is it racist to not have sympathy for a Black kid that goes to jail for selling drugs, after all he had a choice about committing that crime?" I used to get angry when I felt like my White students just did not care about the readings, the ideas, or my perspectives. Those were my assumptions, and at the time I was unwilling to see that there were many iterations of resistance. We often talk about White guilt (Leonardo, 2004; Tatum, 1994) or more currently White fragility (DiAngelo, 2011), ideas discussed more fully in Chapter 2. Although these forms of resistance are important and essential to consider, I argue that they are not all encompassing of how we can talk about White resistance. Alongside that notion, terms like guilt and fragility—let alone the term resistant—can be alienating.

This book comes from the perspective of a person that has been exposed to multiple racial contexts and experiences, and over time I have ebbed and flowed in the advancement of my own knowledge and understanding. Just because there is a structure and system to racism, that does not mean it is static. To the contrary, racism is dynamic and complex. Although we may encounter resistant or guilty or fragile White students, those labels do not always accurately encapsulate students' struggles. As a teacher educator dedicated to social justice, I am principally concerned with the humanity of all my students, and our current era could not dictate a more crucial calling.

According to the National Center for Education Statistics (NCES, 2011a), culturally and linguistically diverse students comprise 44% of our nation's K-12 students. Concurrently, NCES (2011b) also shows that 83% of the teaching force is White. No matter what strategies teacher preparation programs or school districts use to recruit and retain more culturally and linguistically diverse teachers (and administrators), the imbalance of representation will continue for some time. Helping our largely White preservice and practicing teachers understand how race and racism function—especially in relation to schooling—is essential in today's multicultural present and future. If we are to advance our practices, and if we are truly committed to the mission of social justice, then we must be willing to challenge existing frameworks and consider how the discourses we further may marginalize the very people we are trying to engage in a process of unlearning and learning. In other words, we need to rethink the way we talk about the challenges White students face when learning about the complexities of racial oppression in the United States.

When talking about White students (White people in general) and their willingness to engage with and learn about racism, we tend to focus on privilege, resistance, fragility, and allyship. These labels *are* indispensible. However valuable these terms are, they can also paralyzes discourse and cage dialogue, creating scripts that result in the production of the same results again and again—White folks are racist no matter what, and the best they can do (and what they deserve) is to be confronted with their racism as their personal failing, whether ignorant, willful, or both. For White students, who are largely negatively constructed in our divisive, binary discourses on racism, it is sensible that as they progress through the development of their racial identities, they will tire of rhetoric that discursively pins them into a corner in which, no matter what, they are agents of racism. That discursive half nelson oftentimes results in fragmentation of the class community and by extension our collective community. More importantly, that half nelson can bring about a fatigue for students, even when they are consciously aware of the immorality and destruction of racism.

The concept introduced in this book, *White fatigue* (Flynn, 2015), attempts to identify another dynamic—in addition to White guilt, White fragility, and White resistance—that recognizes the challenge of transmuting one's worldview. More-over, White fatigue attempts to recognize the humanity of those that engage in this process but find frustration in it. These challenges are common, but our field also tends to marginalize folks by constructing them as simply guilty, fragile, or resistant. That is not to say those constructs do not have validity; it is to say that, perhaps, there is more going on. It is my hope that this book will encourage rec-ognition of the fatigued and remind us all to vigilantly seek out the humanity of others, especially those in midst of struggle and progress.

White Folks: Possibilities of Allies, Accomplices, and Leaders for Social and Racial Justice

Throughout this book I will be talking about White people. I am understanding of the fact that any statement cannot be a blanket statement to represent all people of a certain group; if essentializing is not good for one group it is not good for any groups. However, common experiences and trends do exist for different groups. For example, African Americans are incarcerated at a much higher rate, by propor-tion, than any other group (Alexander, 2012). Now, I know not *all* African Ameri-cans are incarcerated, but there is a trend nonetheless. When talking about White folks I am speaking about general trends and not necessarily making indictments or criticism of each individual, discreet White person. It is important to point this out when talking about macro phenomenon, as a matter of social justice, which brings me to the next terms which needs defining. What is social justice and what are allies, accomplices, and leaders for social justice?

Social justice has been defined in a number of ways, but when I consider it, if there is any definition that is most closely aligned with my own perspective it is that of Özlem Sensoy and Robin DiAngelo (2012a). They offer the idea of a critical approach to social justice that recognizes the basic idea that society is structurally and systemically stratified. As they say:

> A critical approach to social justice refers to specific theoretical perspectives that recog-nize that society is stratified (i.e., divided and unequal) in significant and far-reaching ways along social group lines that include race, class, gender, sexuality, and ability. Criti-cal social justice recognizes inequality as deeply embedded in the fabric of society (i.e., as structural), and actively seeks to change this. (Sensoy & DiAngelo, 2012b, pp. 379–382)

What captures me most about their definition is that it foregrounds the impor-tance of examining the ways in which society, through the laws, policies, accepted daily social practices, and other means can privilege and marginalize groups.

In short, real live, flesh and blood human beings are directly impacted by the functions of systems and institutions. Our lives are always framed by larger contexts and the factors of those contexts can impact us all in different ways, depending on the intersection of our identities. However, that does not mean any of us is better or lesser than the other, and we all ought to see the humanity others. Like the National Council for the Teachers of English's Conference on English Education points out, "all students should be treated with human dignity, that all are worthy of the same educational opportunities, and that the contract they enter into with schools must honor their sociocultural advantages and disadvantages" (Glaser & Strauss, 1967, cited in Conference on English Education Commission on Social Justice, 2009, Belief 2, para. 1). This belief/value ought to be sacrosanct in the most human of all endeavors: education. Education's role in promoting social justice, especially at the younger grade levels can set the stage for the cultivation of more allies, accomplices, and leaders in the struggle against racial oppression.

Allies, Accomplices, and Leaders

In *We Can't Teach What We Don't Know*, noted anti-racism educator Gary Howard (2006) made a statement that stands for not only White teachers but also White folks generally. He said, "When White educators acknowledge both our (White folks') insecurity and our privilege when dealing with issues of race, and when we begin to question the influence of the dominance paradigm in our work with students, we actually gain credibility with our colleagues and students from other racial and ethnic groups" (p. 75). This is the root of being an ally.

By definition an *ally* is a person who helps or cooperates with another; a supporter, an associate; a friend (Oxford English Dictionary Online).[1] One who cooperates or considers oneself a supporter is open to recognizing the challenges of their ally. One who is an ally stands supportive of their ally's struggle. Allyship can be displayed in small ways, like correcting someone's language, or vocally expressing support for their ally's causes, or voting for candidates that express policies supportive of their ally (especially when it is not in their own self-interest), or marching alongside their ally in a protest, or continuing to learn more about the struggles of their ally. However, allyship can also be incidental. An ally can be supportive for sure but can also see herself or himself as not an active "warrior" in the fight against racial injustice. Being an ally is not necessarily a bad thing at all, but allyship does denote a juxtaposition in the fight. Allyship says "I am with you but I am not quite of you."

On the other hand there is the *accomplice*. An accomplice is a partner in some undertaking; an associate (Oxford English Dictionary Online). The main difference between an accomplice and an ally is that accomplices align as being knee-deep in the fight for racial justice. Accomplices understand that the fight against racial justice is just as much about assisting in the liberation of historically marginalized groups as it is about reclaiming the humanity lost from Whiteness as a result of the furthering of systemic and institutional racism. Accomplices recognize the damage racist practices do to society writ large and stand in solidarity with their historically marginalized sisters and brothers, to stand for higher ideals of equity, justice, and liberation. Accomplices don't want to just recognize the reality of racism and/or White privilege but intend to dismantle the system of advantage based on race and intend to actively struggle in the name of that cause. Before one can be a leader, one must first learn to be an ally, and then be an accomplice.

A *leader*, by definition, is one who guides others in action or opinion; one who takes the lead in any business, enterprise, or movement (Oxford English Dictionary Online). The question of whether or not White folks can be *leaders* for racial justice is a curious question, sort of like whether or not White folks can teach Black, Latinx, Asian American, or Indigenous histories. These are important questions too, no doubt. After all, it seems sensible that there is a feeling in the public space that issues of racial justice are the domains of the historically marginalized. However, as will be explored later in this book, the notion that our White brothers and sisters were either never part of or played secondary roles in the fight for racial justice in the United States (and other struggles for that matter) is a gross misrepresentation of history, and, I argue, a vestige of systemic and institutional racism. What better way to keep racial groups divided than to privilege discourses that proscribe racial minorities as agents of racial justice and White folks as passive observers or strident detractors?

Of course White folks can be leaders in the struggle for racial justice and they always have been. Depending on the age and experience that leadership can appear in a number of ways. It can be as simple as being the only one in the classroom to correct a teacher that makes a disparaging statement. It can be stepping up to stop the racially based harassment of someone. It can be chastising someone at a party for telling a racial joke. It can be forming an organization at her school for racial and/or social justice. It can be leading a White Greek organization and crossing borders and boundaries to form coalitions with Black Greek organizations to foment policy changes at a university. And, it can be lobbying or litigating for social and racial justice. White leadership for racial justice is possible and can appear in an infinite number of ways.

However, the issue is how they come to the table. If they come to the table without humility and a genuine sense of caring for both the human beings struggling through oppression and a sense of the higher ideals of justice and equality for all then that leader is missing the point. Freire (1970) identified an essential point about members of oppressing classes joining forces with the oppressed in struggles for liberation. He stated:

> ... the fact that certain members of the oppressor class join the oppressed in their struggle for liberation, thus moving from one pole of the contradiction to the other. Theirs is a fundamental role, and has been so throughout the history of this struggle. It happens, however, that as they cease to be exploiters or indifferent spectators or simply the heirs of exploitation and move to the side of the exploited, they almost always bring with them the marks of their origin: their prejudices and their deformations, which include a lack of confidence in the people's ability to think, to want, and to know. ... The generosity of oppressors is nourished by an unjust order, which must be maintained in order to justify that generosity. Our converts, on the other hand, truly desire to transform the unjust order; but because of their background they believe that they must be the executors of the transformation. They talk about the people, but do not trust them; and trusting the people is the indispensible precondition for revolutionary change. (42)

Freire's point is fundamental. He is not promoting the idea that those from oppressing groups cannot join in the struggle against oppression but that those from oppressing groups must alter their understanding and assumptions about the oppressed. A critical education that challenges long-held assumptions about the superiority and centrality of Whiteness is crucial in altering consciousness, and an education that shows models of those once aligned with oppressors who shifted their position to stand with the oppressed can offer moral choices about how to use Whiteness (in this case) for liberation and not oppression.

Similar to Freire's point are the ideas of Kwame Turé, formerly known as Stokley Carmichael. In their magnum opus, *Black Power: The Politics of Liberation in America* (1967/1992), Carmichael and his co-author, Charles Hamilton, speak to the issue of forming coalitions. Although they recognize problems with creating coalitions, they are not dismissive of the role White folks have in the promotion of Black Power and by extension racial justice. In the Black Power movement, Carmichael and Hamilton argue that there had never been a push to dismiss White folks in the struggle, but their role should be supportive. Their issue is not the presence of White folks in the movement but their motives and privileges.

> It is our position that black organizations should be black-led and essentially black-staffed, with policy being made by black people. White people can and do play very important supportive roles in those organizations. ... All too frequently, however, many young, middle-class, white Americans, like some sort of Pepsi generation, have wanted to "come alive" through the black community and black groups. They have wanted to be where the action is and the action has been in those places. They have sought refuge

among blacks from a sterile, meaningless, irrelevant life in middle-class America. They have been unable to deal with the stifling, racist, parochial, split-level mentality of their parents, teachers, preachers and friends. Many have come seeing "no difference in color," they have come "color blind." But at this time and in this land, color is a factor and we should not overlook or deny this. The black organizations do not need this kind of idealism, which borders on paternalism. White people working in SNCC have understood this. There are white lawyers who defend black civil rights workers in court, and white activists who support indigenous black movements across the country. Their function is not to lead or to set policy or to attempt to define black people to black people. Their role is support. (Lack of capitalization of Black in original text) (Carmichael & Hamilton, 2008, pp. 186–187)

Their initial point, especially at that time, reminds us of the importance of the oppressed doing the work of liberation. At the same time though, Carmichael and Hamilton promote the idea that White supporters should be taking the lead in educating other White folks about these issues:

One of the most disturbing things about almost all White supporters has been that they are reluctant to go into their own communities—which is where the racism exists—and work to get rid of it. ... They should preach non-violence in the White community. Where possible, they might also educate other White people to the need for Black Power. ... Across the country, smug White communities show a poverty of awareness, a poverty of humanity, indeed, a poverty of ability to act in a civilized manner toward non-Anglo human beings. The White middle-class suburbs need "freedom schools" as badly as the black communities. Anglo-conformity is a dead weight on their necks too. All this is an educative role crying to be performed by those Whites so inclined. (pp. 185–186)

White folks so inclined in this case are more than simply allies or accomplices. They too are leaders, as they take the risk of promoting the understanding of oppression and marginalization to those who may be flatly resistant to the challenging information. The essential underlying trait of a White leader for racial justice is an understanding of the ways in which historic racial oppression has shaped our society coupled with a profound belief in our collective humanity. This fight is not trivial; it is humane, and haughtiness or arrogance should be checked at the door.

If they come to the table understanding of the issues, the history of racial oppression, recognition of the brilliance and strategic deft of marginalized groups, and a genuine sense of community, shared sacrifice, and positional understanding then that is a leadership footing. Finally, if they come to the table understanding of their own privilege, what that means in a system of advantage based on race, and willing to use that privilege as a tool to dismantle systems and institutions of racial oppression then that is a leadership footing.

Any of us from historically marginalized groups have every reason and right in the world to be angry and skeptical. No doubt. But, we should also be careful of who and what is the focus of our derision. We should be less angry with White folks—especially if they are showing a willingness to learn, engage, and promote issues of racial justice—and more angry at a system that at every turn attempts to construct White people as the norm and renders them unexamined, unquestioned, and uncritiqued.

A Road Needing to Be Traveled

It is 2017, and there are reasons to doubt White folks in our nation when it comes to race. We all often hear the refrain that things have gotten so much better in terms of race relations, and we perfunctorily offer credence to the declaration in order to curtail animosity and hopefully prepare a launch pad for dialogue. As we have seen scores of unarmed African Americans on the bullet-end of police brutality, the continental Indigenous continuing to battle land annexation up in Standing Rock, and Latinxs continuously vilified as illegal immigrants stealing good American jobs, we have also heard victim-blaming coming largely from White folks. As racial minorities promote sustained engagement through movements like #BlackLivesMatter, we also hear many White folks lamenting police officers second guessing their actions, also known as the Ferguson Effect (Madhani, 2017; Matter, 2016; Roorda, 2016). As culturally and linguistically diverse students, oftentimes with the support of White allies, accomplices, and leaders for racial justice (Jaschik, 2016), demand university administrators make more concerted efforts to curb racism on campus, largely White detractors cite limitations on free speech and political correctness run amok in order to delegitimize the protests and feelings of the marginalized (Burleigh, 2016; Deresiewicz, 2017; Fingerhut, 2016). However, we cannot forget nor minimize the fact that millions of White allies, accomplices, and leaders for racial social justice are part of the struggle. Many White folks see and feel the immorality and inhumanity of systemic and institutionally racist practices, and many are also in the process of learning how this system of racism works, a frustrating set of lessons. Regardless of that frustration, for both historically marginalized and White students, it is something we must face in the name of social justice, if our intention is actually toward social justice and not retribution.

My first priority is to my students, and if part of my responsibility is to help students understand race and racism *from where they are*, then it is incumbent upon me to rethink and conceptualize strategies, constructs, and ideas that help *unstick and further* them in their learning and development. I have been guilty of approaching my White students through a deficit model, centering on what I think they don't know. I have even been so bold to proclaim, when I was younger, that all my White students are racists and my course would explain why! That is a terrible way to start a conversation, without doubt. But again, as a teacher, I have the responsibility of assessing what my students' needs are in their struggles to understand this complex phenomenon. I also have the responsibility to critically reflect on my practices and pedagogy in the effort of creating more inclusive and liberating engagement for all my students.

This book is not a "how to" manual. Rather, it is a philosophical and pedagogical exploration of an idea, White fatigue. Curriculum theorist Bill Schubert (1991) calls this a speculative essay, "a kind of meta-analysis or research synthesis that uses the informed and insightful scholar (rather than a set of statistical rules) as the instrument for synthesis and illumination" (p. 64). In the coming pages I will consider our current social and racial context and situate the phenomenon of White fatigue as fundamental to the working of classrooms and the challenge many White folks have in gaining an understanding of race and racism. This book is an attempt to rethink how we construct students in classrooms, not in the effort of justifying the skirting of these issues and letting students, particularly White students, off the proverbial hook, but in the effort of creating more progressive and empowering approaches for building bridges across borders and boundaries.

The following chapters will further define and elucidate the idea of White fatigue. Chapter 1 begins with an exploration of our current racial context. Specifically, the chapter will begin to define White fatigue with examples of how it can manifest, highlighting examples from popular music and a wayward conversation over Facebook. Furthermore the chapter situates multicultural and teacher education in the struggle for anti-racism and other forms of anti-oppression. The chapter will also consider a range of challenges in learning and teaching about racism.

Chapter 2 will operationalize the notion of White fatigue. Drawing distinctions among other privilege-based constructs like White resistance, White guilt, and White fragility, White fatigue is positioned as a pedagogical consideration for engaging White students. As discussed previously, the binary construction of White students as either allies or resisters does not allow for a more complex reading of students' experiences, reactions, and struggles to learn. Furthermore, the aforementioned privilege-based constructs fail to fully consider the range of experiences White students bring into classrooms that often manifest as struggle, frustration, resignation, and even silence. Apart from our students representing varying stages of White Racial Identity Development (Fasching-Varner, 2014; Helms, 1993; Wijeyesinghe & Jackson, 2012), they must also navigate the stereotype threat (Steele, 2011) of being seen as a racist due to a question of misunderstanding or a poorly phrased statement. In other words, although one's heart may be in the right place, displaying a lack of knowing—or struggling to know, for that matter—can be interpreted as the person being ignorant at best, and racist at worst. Such simplistic responses fail to recognize both the humanity in White students and the challenges in understanding race and racism generally. But, as discussed above, ignorance about the reality of the experiences of racially minoritized groups for many White folks is a logical and manifestly real and ongoing byproduct of a racially oppressive system.

Chapter 3 further considers our current racial context, specifically the impact of Presidents Barack Obama and Donald Trump. The chapter begins by considering the challenges in furthering conversations about race expressed in President (then Senator) Barack Obama's Philadelphia speech on race in American in 2008. Despite the enthusiastic good will expressed by Senator Obama, after his inauguration the message of good will gave way to mischaracterization and racist caricature. This chapter also considers and the rise of the #BlackLivesMatter movement and culminates with a discussion of the backlash to President Obama and #BlackLivesMatter via the sharply divisive campaign of President Donald Trump.

What is central to this chapter is the simple fact that there was always a diversity of opinion from the White community about these events and others. Simply put, we cannot paint the White community in monochrome and then be surprised when White folks respond with frustrations. Allies and accomplices understand why that monochromatic painting happens, but those in the process of understanding may find frustration that obstructs progression toward allies and accomplices. Again, this is not to give White folks a pass on learning about and addressing race but to point out the complexity of ameliorating racism and further arguing for more progressive language that recognizes the reality of *their* struggles *along with* the struggles of historically marginalized *others*.

Chapter 4 considers multicultural education. There has been an incessant series of misinformation and half-truths about race and oppression. Traditionally we think about this phenomenon as a "miseducation" of so-called minorities, but the reality is that White students are miseducated too. Those White students eventually bring those ideas into our courses and find that their education has been built on a shaky foundation and they wonder, "Why didn't they tell us all this in middle school and high school?" This adds to their fatigue. Additionally, to be blunt, our nation's students are not taught the crucial history of racial oppression and how systems and institutions are fundamental to the development of racial oppression, as human relations approaches to multicultural education that focus on heroes and holidays and surface culture characteristics are privileged in schools (Sleeter & Grant, 2009).

The rise of multicultural education has been an important movement in curriculum and pedagogy (Pinar, Reynolds, Slattery, & Taubman, 2006) and it has encouraged teachers to be more mindful of not only the identities and cultures of student but also their own identities, assumptions, and proclivities. However, many students and citizens in general continue to possess minimal racial literacy (Epstein & Gist, 2015; Skerrett, 2011; Stevenson, 2014; Twine, 2004). Despite decades of teacher professional development, there seems to be a lack of critical and complex understanding of how racism (and other forms of oppression for that matter) functions and shapes our society. The chapter considers what students learn about race in K-12 education and the ways in which historical narratives have been hijacked and manipulated to repeat lullabies that bolster White privilege and the myth of the rugged individual.

Chapter 5 takes a deeper examination on the question of why it is challenging to learn, and by extension teach, about race and racism for White students. The chapter explores ideas developed by the French sociologist Pierre Bourdieu (1977; Bourdieu & Passeron, 1990), specifically his concept of habitus. Bourdieu's notion of cultural capital has attained a sacred space in the sociology of education and has been quite useful in helping explain the nature of cultural and racial disparities in schools (MacLeod, 2008). However, the notion of habitus affords us the ability to talk about group trends and individual experiences simultaneously (Hillier & Rooksby, 2005). Talking about groups is necessary when considering macro-level phenomena and systems that dictate trends in experiences for large groups. However, the curse is that talking about structures can obfuscate the diversity of experiences that brims within those groups at all times. Bourdieu's notion of habitus allows for that complexity to be productively explored, and can encourage us educators to see a fuller picture of how race and racism shape the lives and receptivity of our students.

Finally, Chapter 6 offers three overarching ideas about negotiating White fatigue: encouraging racial literacy at all levels of K-12 education; rethinking curriculum and standards; and shifting our language about White folks. The idea of race is an inconvenience for many and understanding race and racism is not viewed as a necessary part of being a fully realized democratic citizen. For anyone to present themselves as an advocate of social justice, peace, and/or inclusion then one can not like the notion of White fatigue, but must nonetheless consider it as a part of a conceptual constellation we use to talk about how race emerges in daily life. Resistance … Fragility … Fatigue. … If fragility and resistance or allyship are the only options we allow in the dialogue then we are creating the conditions for self-fulfilling prophesies of resignation and resentment, which is wholly against the intentions of multiculturalists and social justice educators and advocates. It is essential as we move further into the twenty-first century that educators and policymakers think more critically about the tools youth and other citizens will need to carry us even further into the future. After all, the ally does not begin at blind acquiescence but at constructive inquisition.

Through this chapter I have offered a narrativized positioning of myself as a way of helping you understand some of my values, motives, experiences and purposes that informed my creation of this idea White fatigue. In the following chapter I will begin to explore this idea. Through the next chapter I will begin to offer a clearer definition and contextualize its roots in American society, teacher education, and education generally.

Note

1. I recognize the danger of using dictionary definitions, as the meanings of words are laden with social and political factors. However, dictionaries are the primary way in which laypersons gain their understanding of how words are used. In this spirit I felt it was important to use reputable dictionary definitions of ally, accomplice, and leader to make a direct connection to popular sensibilities.

Bibliography

Alexander, M. (2012). *The new Jim Crow: Mass incarceration in the age of colorblindness*. New York, NY: The New Press.

Aud, S., Fox, M. A., & Kewal Ramani, A. (2010). *Status and trends in the education of racial and ethnic groups*. Washington, DC: National Center for Education Statistics. Retrieved from https://nces.ed.gov/pubs2010/2010015.pdf

Bourdieu, P. (1977). *Outline of a theory of practice*. Cambridge: Cambridge University Press.

Bourdieu, P., & Passeron, J. (1990). *Reproduction in education, society, and culture* (Reprint ed.). Thousand Oaks, CA: Sage Publications.

Burleigh, N. (2016, May 26). The battle against "hate speech" on college campuses give rise to a generation that hates speech. *Newsweek*. Retrieved from http://www.newsweek.com/2016/06/03/college-campus-free-speech-thought police-463536.html

Carmichael, S., & Hamilton, C. V. (1967/1992). *Black power: The politics of liberation in America* (Vintage ed.). New York, NY: Vintage Books.

Carmichael, S., & Hamilton, C. V. (2008). The myths of coalitions from *Black power: The politics of liberation in America. Race/Ethnicity: Multidisciplinary Global Contexts, 1*(2), 171–188.

Conference on English Education Commission on Social Justice. (2009, December). *Beliefs about social justice in English education* [CEE position statement]. Retrieved from http://www.ncte.org/cee/positions/socialjustice

Deresiewicz, W. (2017, March 6). On political correctness: Power, class, and the new campus religion. *The American Scholar*. Retrieved from https://theamericanscholar.org/on-political-correctness/#

DiAngelo, R. (2011). White fragility. *International Journal of Critical Pedagogy, 3*(3), 54–70.

Epstein, T., & Gist, C. (2015, January 1). Teaching racial literacy in secondary humanities classrooms: Challenging adolescents' of color concepts of race and racism. *Race, Ethnicity and Education, 18*(1), 40–60.

Fasching-Varner, K. J. (2014). *Working through Whiteness: Examining white racial identity and profession with pre-service teachers.* Lanham, MD: Lexington Books.

Fingerhut, H. (2016, July 20). In "political correctness" debate, most Americans think too many people are easily offended. *Pew Research Center.* Retrieved from http://www.pewresearch.org/fact-tank/2016/07/20/in-political-correctness-debate most-americans-think-too-many-people-are-easily-offended/

Flynn, J. (2015). White fatigue: Naming the challenge in moving from and individual to a systemic understanding of racism. *Multicultural Perspectives, 17*(3), 115–124.

Freire, P. (1970/1997). *Pedagogy of the oppressed* (New Revised 20th anniversary ed.). New York, NY: Continuum.

Glaser, B. G., & Strauss, A. L. (1967). *The discovery of grounded theory: Strategies for qualitative research.* London: Wiedenfeld and Nicholson.

Goodman, D. J. (2011). *Promoting diversity and social justice: Educating people from privileged groups* (2nd ed.). New York, NY: Routledge.

Helms, J. E. (1993). *Black and White racial identity: Theory, research, and practice.* Westport, CT: Praeger.

Hillier, J., & Rooksby, E. (2005). *Habitus: A sense of place.* Farnham: Ashgate.

Howard, G. R. (2006). *We can't teach what we don't know: White teachers, multiracial schools* (2nd ed.). New York, NY: Teachers College Press.

Hussar, W. J., & Bailey, T. M. (2014). *Projection of education statistics to 2022.* Washington, DC: National Center for Education Statistics. Retrieved from https://nces.ed.gov/pubs2014/2014051.pdf

King, J. (1991). Dysconscious racism: Ideology, identity, and the miseducation of teachers. *The Journal of Negro Education, 60*(2), 133–146.

Irving, D. (2014). *Waking up White and finding myself in the story of race.* Cambridge, MA: Elephant Room Press.

Jaschik, S. (2016, September 26). Epidemic of racist incidents. *Inside Higher Ed.* Retrieved from https://www.insidehighered.com/news/2016/09/26/campuses-see-lurry-racist-incidents-and-protests-against-racism

Jensen, R. (2005). *The heart of Whiteness: Confronting race, racism, and White privilege.* San Francisco, CA: City Lights.

King, J. E. (1991). Dysconscious racism: Ideology, identity, and the miseducation of teachers. The Journal of Negro Education, 60(2), 133–146.

Leonardo, Z. (2004). The color of supremacy: Beyond the discourse of "white privilege." *Educational Philosophy and Theory, 36*(2), 137–152.

MacLeod, J. (2008). *Ain't no makin' it: Aspirations and attainment in a low-income neighborhood* (3rd ed.). Denver, CO: Westview Press.

Madhani, A. (2017, January 11). "Ferguson effect": 72% of U.S. cops reluctant to make stops. *USA Today.* Retrieved from https://www.usatoday.com/story/news/2017/01/11/ferguson-effect-study-72-uscops-reluctant-make-stops/96446504/

Matter, G. (2016, September 30). Is there a "Ferguson effect"? *New York Times.* Retrieved from https://www.nytimes.com/2016/10/02/opinion/sunday/is-there-a ferguson-effect. html?_r=0

McIntosh, P. (1988). White privilege and male privilege: A personal account of coming to see correspondences through work in women's studies. In M. L. Anderson & P. Hill-Collins (Eds.), *Race, class, and gender: An anthology* (pp. 70–81). Wellesley, MA: Wellesley College Center for Research on Women.

National Center for Education Statistics. (2011a). Public elementary and secondary enrollment, student race/ethnicity, schools, school size, and pupil/teacher ratios, by type of locale: 2008–09 and 2009–10. *Digest of Education Statistics.* Retrieved from http://nces.ed.gov/ programs/digest/d11/tables/dt11_094.asp

National Center for Education Statistics. (2011b). Teacher trends. *Fast Facts.* Retrieved from http://nces.ed.gov/fastfacts/display.asp?id=28

Oxford English Dictionary Online. Retrieved from http://www.ulib.niu.edu:2250/view/ Entry/5541?rskey=HslQOh&result=1#eid

Pinar, W. F., Reynolds, W. M., Slattery, P., & Taubman, P. M. (2006). *Understanding curriculum: An introduction to the study of historical and contemporary curriculum discourses* (5th ed.). New York, NY: Peter Lang.

Roorda, J. (2016). *The war on police: How the Ferguson effect is making America unsafe.* New York, NY: WND Books.

Schubert, W. (1991). Philosophical inquiry: The speculative essay. In E. Short (Ed.), *Forms of curriculum inquiry* (pp. 61–76). Albany, NY: State University of New York Press.

Sensoy, O., & DiAngelo, R. (2012a). *Is everyone really equal?: An introduction to key concepts in social justice education.* New York, NY: Teachers College Press.

Sensoy, O., & DiAngelo, R. (2012b). *Is everyone really equal? An introduction to key concepts in social justice education* (Kindle ed.). New York, NY: Teachers College Press.

Skerrett, A. (2011, June 1). English teachers' racial literacy knowledge and practice. *Race Ethnicity and Education, 14* (3), 313–330.

Sleeter, C. E., & Grant, C. A. (2009). *Making choices for multicultural education: Five approaches to race, class, and gender.* Hoboken, NJ: John Wiley & Sons.

Smedley, A. & Smedley, B. D. (2012). *Race in North America: Origin and evolution of a worldview.* Boulder, CO: Westview Press.

Steele, C. M. (2011). *Whistling Vivaldi: How stereotypes affect us and what we can do* (Reprint ed.). New York, NY: W. W. Norton.

Stevenson, H. (2014). *Promoting racial literacy in schools.* New York, NY: Teachers College Press.

Tatum, B. D. (1994). Teaching White students about racism: The search for White allies and the restoration of hope. *Teachers College Record, 95*(4), 462–467.

Tatum, B. D. (2003). *Why are all the Black kids sitting together in the cafeteria: And other conversations about race* (5th Anniversary revised ed.). New York, NY: Basic Books.

Twine, F. W. (2004, January 1). A white side of black Britain: The concept of racial literacy. *Ethnic and Racial Studies, 27*(6), 878–907.

Wellman, D. (1993). *Portraits of White racism.* New York, NY: Cambridge University Press.

Wijeyesinghe, C. L., & Jackson, B. W. (Eds.). (2012). *New perspectives on racial identity development: Integrating emerging frameworks* (2nd ed.). New York, NY: New York University Press.

Wildman, S., & Davis, A. (2005. Making systems of privilege visible. In P. Rothenberg (Ed.), *White privilege: Essential readings on the other side of racism (3rd Ed.)*, pp. 109–116. New York, NY: Worth Publishers.

CHAPTER ONE

On Talking and Learning About Race and Racism in the Obama Era and After

"Long is the way, and hard, that out of Hell leads up to Light."
—MILTON *PARADISE LOST* BOOK II LINE 432–433

In Debby Irving's wonderful memoir (2014), *Waking Up White*, she openly discusses her process of moving from unconscious reproducer of racist practices to committed leader against racial oppression and social justice. Each chapter explores a key theme in her process and she writes about her privilege (economic and racial) with an unflinching honesty throughout the text. Although she does not name it specifically, she writes about her struggles with learning to understand racism and White privilege. As she says:

> Learning about how racism works didn't challenge me just because it was new information. It was *completely contradictory* information, a 180-degree paradigm reversal, flying in the face of everything I'd been taught as a child and had believed up to this moment. America's use of racial categories seemed fraught with unfairness, cruelty, and dishonesty. Yet my parents', grandparents', and entire extended family's life philosophy, as I understood it, had revolved around fairness, compassion, and honor. This was my legacy, to one I took the most pride in passing on to my children. Discovering I'd been complicit in perpetuating a system that was so very terribly bad flew in the face of all I'd understood about myself. (p. 95)

Her point is simple, yet profoundly important to consider for educators of all stripes when teaching about race and racism. It is a personal struggle, and simply because one understands that racism is wrong, advancing the understanding of the complexities of systemic and institutional racism is wrought with personal, emotional, and spiritual challenges. Those moments of challenge may be displayed as withdrawal, confusion, or frustration. This phenomenon is the focus of this book and I refer to it as *White fatigue*.

White fatigue is a temporary state in which individuals who are understanding of the moral imperative of antiracism disengage from or assume they no longer need to continue learning about how racism functions due to a simplistic understanding of racism as primarily an individual's problem (i.e., prejudice and discrimination). White fatigue is not meant to serve as a magic bullet to explain away resistance. Rather, it is another kind of resistance, a sort of quasi-resistance if you will, that recognizes there are in fact millions of White Americans who fundamentally believe racism is wrong, but nonetheless struggle through learning how racism functions.

These students are on the path, so to speak, but ferreting out that complexity and understanding the range of theories and ideas used to explain racism is a long, challenging process—intellectually, emotionally, and spiritually. Recognition of White fatigue is crucial in today's context. Racism cannot be ameliorated without White allies, accomplices, or leaders. If we label students as simply resistant we are creating a situation in which White students (White people in general for that matter) may feel alienation, and that alienation can reproduce an unwillingness to do the heavy lifting of unlearning and relearning key concepts and ideas to move one from an understanding of racism as an individual problem to a systemic and institutional phenomenon. After all, a fundamental aspect of White privilege is the freedom to not engage if one chooses (Delpit, 1988; Hitchcock, 2002; McIntosh, 1988). To introduce White fatigue, let's look at an example in the larger arena of popular culture, specifically popular country music.

Accidental Racist: Accidentally Displaying White Fatigue

In the spring of 2013, country music artist Brad Paisley and hip hop icon LL Cool J recorded a song. The song, "Accidental Racist," (Paisley, Smith, & Miller, 2013) was the artists' attempt to express how each feels about the struggle to understand race and move forward. (Right now I encourage you to go online and listen to the song while also reading the lyrics. That is the best way to get a feeling for the song.)

The song begins with Brad speaking to an African American barista at Starbucks, and Brad tries to reassure him that the Confederate battle flag emblazoned on his shirt is not about the hate associated with the symbol but is a part of the iconography of the Southern rock band Lynard Skynard. Later, LL, declares that he will not judge the Confederate flag if White folks do not judge common African American headwear, most notably do-rags. The song goes on to briefly explore the failure of Reconstruction, and that fact that despite well over a century later we are still caught in a state of misunderstanding and resentment. And, the song further promotes liberal notions of equality. LL's verse is constructed as a letter addressed to White folks. In his lyrical letter, LL attempts to undo stereotypes and tries to encourage the White listener to not automatically construct the images connected to Black culture and fashion as negative signifiers worthy of stoking fear. LL also goes on to reinforce the dread and prejudgement African Americans have for clothing with the Confederate battle flag and White cowboy hats, essentially arguing that both White and Black folks are responsible for furthering racially based misgivings. In the end, LL reinforces Brad's message and encourages the listener to move past racism, or at the least stereotyping.

The song is a complicated work with many implications. In a sense, this kind of activity is the kind of action social justice and anti-racist educators encourage! Pleas for more open and critical discussions about race relations and racism is essential in developing a new national discourse, and we have to give Brad Paisley his due credit. It is not often that a popular country artist takes on a challenging topic like racism. Unfortunately, the song is highly flawed and projects an important trend in our collective "conversation" about race.

The discourse furthered through the song reinforces the notion that racism is an antiquated idea and should no longer be engaged; we must move on. Furthermore, the song promotes the idea that if we all just, like Rodney King encouraged, got along and stopped assuming negative dispositions about the other because of stereotypes then racism will naturally subside. On the other hand, the song fails to engage some fundamentally key concepts in understanding race and racism, troubling the call to just move past race.

The text of the song focuses on individual notions of racism at the expense of systemic and institutional racism. Brad and LL throughout the text consistently reference the misgivings and misunderstandings of individuals. What is lacking is an introduction, let alone exploration, of how and why racism persists despite the many gains made across the history of the United States. The song wholly disregards the impact of structural, political, economic, and social marginalization and dehumanization. Furthermore, the song avoids introducing the notion that stereotypes and misgivings have historic structural and institutional roots that persist to this day. Therein lies the heart of the matter.

The urge to move to a post-racial society on the surface may be noble goal, but begs an essential question: If we begin to disregard or *move past* race, does it mean racism is ameliorated? In order to ameliorate racism, our society must first understand not only its history but also it's functioning and persistence. Songs like "Accidental Racist" are brave and important attempts to further a discussion but the vision of the song (to move past race and stereotypes) is a rush to action and keeps the focus of the discussion on the moral failings of individuals rather than systemic and institutional obstacles.

Given that racist incidents happen everyday, perpetrated consciously, unconsciously, and dysconsciouly by White folks, there are nonetheless a sizeable portion of the White American community that recognizes these actions are morally bankrupt and antithetical to a socially just society. At the same time, it seems that race relations in the United States constantly oscillate between pastoral declarations of humanistic commonality and misinformed or manipulated racial resentment. There remains a great divide in the American consciousness that reifies the intractability of racism. This begs an important question for education and teacher education. How do we better prepare students—and citizens—to effectively participate in a multicultural society and commit to missions of social justice, including racial justice?

Before moving on, one may be questioning the role of LL Cool J and whether or not he, or any non-White person for that matter can exhibit White fatigue. White fatigue is squarely focused on the struggles of White folks in learning about race and racism. As will be discussed later, the process of learning about these realities is a different trajectory for White folks compared to non-White folks (Helms, 1993; Tatum, 1994). Because of this point and the need to develop more White allies, accomplices, and leaders, I am choosing to focus on the struggles of White students and citizens. I will speak to this more in the following chapters, but at this point I want to consider trends in how White students respond to learning about race.

The Resistant, the Believers, and the Quiet: Considering Our Students in the Process of Learning About Race in Classrooms

One of the most persistently challenging sets of concepts we teach is race and racism in the United States (Fox, 2009; Singleton, 2014). No matter who you are, race (a socially constructed concept predicated primarily on skin color and embodied through cultural and social practices) (Fine, et al., 1997) and racism (a system of advantage based on race) (Sensoy & DiAngelo, 2012; Tatum, 2003; Wellman,

1993) touch each of us, but *depending* on who you are it touches us in divergent ways. By the same token, since race and racism touch each of us in different ways, there is contention about the role of race in our lives generally and the recurrent realities of racism daily.

For well over a decade, I have encountered a broad spectrum of students, people in general, in regards to their understanding of race and racism. I have had the opportunity to meet students who came into my classes hungry—starving—for literature and theories that help explain the phenomena related to race and racism. I have had students who were indifferent, and clearly participated in class activities and discussions in order to get a good grade and credit fulfillment. I have encountered students who flatly rejected long-standing theories and perspectives gleaned from experts, researchers, and scholars. I engaged with students who actively struggled with these ideas and regularly approached me after class to ask questions, offer cases for complication, or beam at reporting "something" they noticed in media and popular culture. I have had students speak with both passionate pride and guilty frustration about their families' and friends' ideas about racism. I have had students who seethed in denial about the reality of White privilege and the perceived lack of personal responsibility and grit of racial groups other than their own. I have seen crisis, resistance, struggle, acceptance, and activism. I know I am not unique in these observations. I cannot count the number of conversations I've had with colleagues about lessons, activities, insights, frustrations, and invigorations.

Like many of us, the students in my classes have been overwhelmingly White, and their Whiteness matters with regard to how those students are positioned to learn and become teachers themselves in a diverse society. Although there is a range of exposure and understanding in terms of how race and racism impact our daily lives, for many of those White students, their collective understanding of race is frequently limited for multiple and complex reasons which will be discussed later. For the moment though, I can generally classify my students into three groups: *resisters, true believers,* and the *quiet.*

The Resisters

I have the "loud" *resister,* the student that decries any notion of White privilege, systemic and/or institutional hurdles for non-Whites, or lack of opportunity for non-Whites. By "loud" I mean they openly share their resistance in not only class discussions and activities but also in assignments. They also champion personal responsibility (as though personal responsibility is both devoid of context and immune to sociocultural politics), anti-affirmative action arguments, and other negative or oppositional responses.

The True Believers

True believers display an understanding of the depth and intransigent nature of racism. Those are the students who regularly participate in class. They are the ones quick to offer examples and discuss the ideas. They nod in agreement with critical literature that uncovers the complexities of institutional and systemic oppression. They bring news of racism in society and popular culture to class. They stay after class to ask more questions for understanding of theories and ideas that help them more firmly grasp how racism impacted and continues to impact society and individuals. They ask for additional readings and documentaries. They make connections to ideas learned in other courses. However, they can also show dismay, impatience, and frustration with the resisters. I have seen the demarcations of the true believers and the resisters play out in classrooms time and again, despite best intentions, detailed explorations of theories, cooperative learning activities, reflections, open debates, group projects, experiential activities, and other tried and true strategies.

The Quiet and the Challenge in Their Presence

I also regularly notice a much larger group of students in my classes: the quiet. By quiet I do not mean they do not participate in class. Rather, they show neither excitement nor resistance toward the literature and ideas explored. Members of this group can be tricky to figure out and engage. Since class participation is a graded activity in my courses (as is true for many of us who teach) I have no problem prompting quiet students to be active in class discussions. Oftentimes I see the frustrations of struggle on their faces when trying to grasp the range of theories we study and trying to decipher the advanced-level reading containing those theories. I see the look of painful awe when they learn about the myriad ways in which federal policies directly curtailed the possibilities of non-White groups during the 19th and 20th centuries, or the extreme reactions of White protesters during school desegregation efforts of early 1970s Boston. I have seen their quizzical looks when I tell them White women benefitted from affirmative action far more than any other group (Baunach, 2002; Patterson, 1998; Wise, 1998). When these students ask questions they are typically seeking clarification. They have a need for further explanation of theories and ideas as opposed to attempts to dismiss what is causing their cognitive dissonance. They are quiet, and they may be uncomfortable, but they are not necessarily disengaged. Diane Goodman (2011) points out that students in the midst of struggle, who critically question material are not resistant. However, when those students get quiet, disengage, or shut down altogether they can be seen as resistant. They are often facing complex ideas that challenge their understanding of the world. Shutting down is a sensible response, an extension of the fight-or-flight reflex. We have to remember they are learners, and often beginners, coming into our classes with limited knowledge curated from popular culture and personal experiences with family and friends, but little from their kindergarten through high school curricular experiences.

It is clear, to varying degrees, this group of White students show struggle, and yes, some of them display guilt about their new knowledge and what it may mean in relation to their prior experiences and the multitude of social interactions often governed by those phenomena. Some of them resign themselves to resistance and feel attacked and besieged, dismissing the subject matter and discussions as a liberal conspiracy. Some of them progress with a new sense of intellectual empowerment. Some of them seek to lie in a limbo of neither resistance nor full-blown true belief. They fear being wrong or saying the wrong thing, lest they are indicted as racist. Oftentimes, White students in this group also talk openly about their intercultural friendships and relationships and how that must mean something, some progress has been made.

What is most emblematic of this group is a persistent but premature question: How can we fix this or what do we do now? Although this question is often premature, the sentiment may express recognition of the moral bankruptcy of racism and a desire among those learners—beginners—to do better, individually and societally. Yet and still, despite this range of experiences and reactions, educators continue to use language that perpetuates the binary oppositions of resister/accepter, racist/ally.

Understanding race and racism is a complex and challenging enterprise that takes years, and the process of *unlearning* the misinformation about race and racism from k-12 education, media and popular culture, and personal experience is challenging—intellectually, conceptually, and spiritually—no matter what racial backgrounds or racialized experiences they may bring into the classroom. Furthermore, it takes much more than a single class to accomplish this for any person. This book proposes a different way of thinking about how we construct White students (and White people generally) and their responses to learning about race and racism.

Introducing White Fatigue: A Guiding Set of Assumptions

White fatigue is a pedagogical consideration predicated on three important assumptions. First, many White folks may not be understanding of how race and racism function in society, but that does not necessarily mean they do not understand the immorality of racism. Knowing that racism is wrong (or bad) does not equate with developing and using a critical lens to see and critique how mass incarceration, for example, is a racist enterprise in U.S. society that some members consciously profit from, or why #BlackLivesMatter is not a declaration that other racial lives do *not* matter, or why anti-immigration policies rooted in Latinx xenophobia is just as racist as assuming anyone from Middle Eastern or Persian countries intends harm to the United States.

Second, individuals' life experiences are never invalid; those experiences are impossible to curb when learning about race and racism, and in fact are probably essential for us all to explore if we hope to attain true understanding and agency in operating as educators and professionals who teach and work for social justice. In other words, learning new terminology and theories in a college course or two does not and cannot counteract a life's worth of stereotyping representations, misrepresented or erased histories, uncritical lessons and curricula, unacknowledged hidden curricula, recollections of negative experiences with family members and peers, and other factors unique to every individual's personal experiences and perceptions. It is a beginning, to be sure, but only a beginning nonetheless. This is especially challenging for White folks when the majority of the information in our social world systematically privileges Whiteness and White people and perpetuates the White racial framing (Feagin, 2013, 2014) of the United States. Prior experiences in relation to race are a challenge for any given individual to square. This is true for anyone, and French sociologist Pierre Bourdieu's theory of habitus (Bourdieu, 1977) is helpful in explaining why this is the case.

Finally, ignorance does not dismiss requirements for social justice educators to focus their work on benefiting humanity or taking responsibility for educating children to both navigate and overcome race and racism as one requirement of justice and equity in schools. Anytime people have an expertise, they may tend to forget that even some of the most basic ideas could be complex for others who are novices, or others who may not even be remotely aware of them due to a simple lack of opportunity for explicit introduction. There is enough research and scholarship on race and racism to fill libraries, and much of it is challenging to our national status quo (Alexander, 2012; Bonilla-Silva, 2013; Coates, 2015; Katznelson, 2006; Kendi, 2016). Although many of us use emotive and experiential strategies or examples from media and popular culture, we sometimes forget that all of our students are entering these discussions from different places, intellectually *and* spiritually. Many of our students may be having critical discussions like this for the first time and it may be difficult for them to challenge long-held messages from back home. Additionally, since we are seeing the first generation of students educated under *No Child Left Behind*, whom are used to a standardized testing and rubrics regime, "very bright students now come to college and even law school ill-prepared for critical thinking, rigourous reading, high-level writing, and working independently" (Goodwin, 2013, para. 3).

That does not diminish the responsibility of the student—in this case the White student—to understand how race and racism function, but it is another hurdle for us educators of all stripes to reckon with. Consideration of the theories, ideas, and activities we employ to teach these often-complex issues related to oppression generally and racial oppression specifically is tantamount to consideration of the language we employ to construct our students.

The Relationship Between Anti-Oppression and Teacher Education

Moving into a new era of race relations requires cross-racial cooperation. Freire pointed out in *Pedagogy of the Oppressed* (1970/1997) that oppression dehumanizes both the oppressed *and* the oppressor. If we are invested in promoting social justice, then we must also be invested in promoting the humanity of *all*. Essentially, seeing White students as sometimes guilty, sometimes fragile, sometimes resistant, *and sometimes fatigued* are all steps toward progress in embracing and humanizing the often-demonized White other. That is social justice, if social justice is in fact a project of actual inclusion and justice for all.

These observations are especially crucial for teacher education. New teachers will be entering classrooms that are more diverse than they were twenty years ago. In 2014, the U.S. student population became a majority of minorities for the first time in history (Maxwell, 2014). Because of that reality, it is crucial to consider the challenges and opportunities for teaching White students about anti-racism and social justice, to develop new ways of engaging them, and to engender new ways of seeing humanity. This must be balanced with an ever-vigilant, relentless pursuit in continuing the work of anti-racism and social justice such that *everyone* involved is responsible and responsive, especially those who come from unexamined backgrounds of privilege and when those people express resistance, fragility, or fatigue. These are not excuses. They are pedagogical issues we can and must understand and overcome, professionally and ethically, in our roles as teachers and scholars for social justice.

☺ or ☹ Considerations From Our Current Sociopolitical Context

Since the election of President Barack Obama, there has been a consistent debate emoticons about a post-racial America (Capehart, 2014; Ledwidge, Verney, & Parmar,

2013; Speri, 2014; Wise, 2010). Concurrently, the country has seen a steady stream of examples in media and popular culture that shows the nation is far from post-racial. Just consider for a moment: The detaining of Dr. Henry Louis Gates by a Boston police officer who attempted to charge him with breaking and entering his own home; consistent disparaging comments and racist iconography depicting President Obama, First Lady Michelle Obama, and Supreme Court Justice Sonya Sotomayor; accusations that President Obama was born in Kenya and challenges to his academic career at Harvard; the deaths of Trayvon Martin, Michael Brown, Eric Garner, Tamir Rice, Sandra Bland, and many others with little to no accountability; a xenophobic immigration debate; the revealing of mass incarceration and the school-to-prison pipeline; a fraternity secretly filmed singing a racist song; the annual parade of college students that decide dressing in blackface is funny and merely politically incorrect; the shift from "nigger" to "thug" in describing Black males; Serena Williams and the challenge of the beauty myth of women— Black women, specifically—in sports and culture; and on and on. The racial strife ultimately culminated in the election of the 45th president of the United States, Donald J. Trump.

President Trump ran a campaign described as racist and xenophobic by many political observers and journalists (Beauchamp, 2016; Goodman, 2016; Haney-Lopez, 2016). He lodged chilling and offensive remarks at many historically marginalized groups and others: Mexicans; women; African Americans; the poor; the lesbian, gay, bisexual, and transgender community; Jews; Gold Star families and veterans; Asians; the disabled; and, Muslims (Cohn, 2016; Fausset, Blinder, & Eligon, 2016; Kopan, 2015; Ornitz, 2016). All of these slights and offenses were chronicled across both traditional news media and social media.

The reality is, in the era of social media, we are seeing an explosion of stories filed by the alternative press and citizen journalists that shed light on intractable problems of race and racism in our culture. The current environment is ripe—once again—for a national conversation about race and racism in the United States, and we are having that conversation on television, on radio, at dinner tables, in classrooms, and on Facebook, Twitter, and Instagram.

I say "once again" because as a nation we regularly extol the need and opportunity for a conversation about race. There is nothing new about this discussion or our stated hopes to resolve the problems. As a matter of fact, these conversations have been part of public (and educational) discourses for the entire history of this nation (Aptheker, 1993; Battalora, 2013; Smedley & Smedley, 2012). Both race and racism are concepts that were built over centuries through a number of laws and social practices (Battalora, 2013) framed by those laws, and all along the way dialogues occurred. Communities had conversations about race during the eras of colonization, abolition, Reconstruction, Jim Crow, desegregation, and integration.

Circumstances demanded us once again to have conversations after the wave of racial uprisings and protests following the assassinations of Dr. Martin Luther King, Jr. and Robert Kennedy. We were pushed to talk about race once again in the early 1990s after the beating of Rodney King and the subsequent acquittal of the four officers charged with his beating and the racial politics of the O. J. Simpson murder trial. In the middle 1990s, President Bill Clinton called for a national conversation on race. Twenty years later, after the first African American president, the nation is urged once again to have a conversation about race. Ironically, that urge alone starkly answers the question of whether or not we have moved to post-racial, colorblind era. Considering the recurrent prompting to have such a national conversation, such movement is clearly a challenge for the body politic of the United States.[1]

In order to have effective, productive conversations about racism—a system of advantage based on race (Alexander, 2012; Sensoy & DiAngelo, 2012 Wellman, 1993)—it becomes necessary to examine how race functions through institutions and not merely individual beliefs and action, for those beliefs and actions are *always* bound within contexts. This is by no means a simple discussion, especially since there is so much assumed personal knowledge about race and an American penchant for opinion over facts, theory, and research (Campbell & Friesen, 2015). The so-called national conversation is less of a discussion and more of a predictable passion play where everyone shouts tribalized derisions at opposing camps (in ALL CAPS); anonymously post unconstructive screeds to message boards; boos, mockings and outright dismissals of others for principled disagreement; or, deciding to not watch or listen to countervailing perspectives anywhere, anytime. People have a tendency to disregard facts that contradict or problematize their opinions which causes them to defend their positions more doggedly (Friesen, Campbell, & Kay, 2015; Gal & Rucker, 2010; Nyhan & Reifler, 2010). This is especially true for issues that aid in defining a person's identity or community memberships, like religious beliefs, political values, and racial attitudes (Gal & Rucker, 2010; Gee, 2007).

It is easy to slip into cynicism about our racial horizon, but as we move further into the 21st century, the problem of race and racism is becoming increasingly difficult to avoid. This can be attributed to, in part, the last forty-plus years of multicultural education (and its progeny social justice education and anti-racist education) that has had a strong presence in schools in the United States, at all levels.

Multicultural Education: Intensions of Teaching More Than Tolerance

Multicultural education began in the late 1960s and early 1970s with the creation of ethnic studies programs at colleges and universities across the country (Banks,

2004; Boyle-Baise, 1999). Across the subsequent decades the presence of multi-cultural education moved from the Ivory Tower to K-12 schools as debates ensued about curricular and canonical representations of historically marginalized groups, and calls for tolerance of minoritized others took root. In a strange twist, as poli-cymakers began to shift educational policy strategy in the wake of *A Nation at Risk* (National Commission on Excellence in Education, 1983), which lamented a "ris-ing tide of mediocrity" (p. 5), there were increasing calls to reconsider and develop more effective strategies for bridging what became known as the "achievement gap" between White students and historically marginalized students.

Despite the expansion of the pedagogical and curricular landscape, it can be argued that the intentions of these efforts ultimately have not matched the results. James Banks, one of the leading voices in multicultural education, pointed out at the turn of the 21st century the theory of multicultural education continues to outpace its actual practice (Banks, 2004), despite nearly three decades worth of professional development for educators, revisions to teacher preparation curricula across the nation, and the institutionalization of professional and curriculum stan-dards "enforcing" attention to diversity.

Pedagogical and curricular reforms have been effective at promoting tolerance for others, but the reforms have not been as efficacious in helping students—citizens—develop either a more critical consciousness or an understanding of how oppression functions, specifically racism in this case. In other words, collective *tolerance* of others has become a norm in our national culture, but tolerance and understanding are not necessarily equivalent, nor do they always operate in healthy concert. Until recently, the spirit of curricular and pedagogical changes has been less about critical examinations of Whiteness and White people but more about the inclusion of historically marginalized "others" (i.e. African Americans, Asian Americans, Indigenous cultures, Latinxs, women, and most recently the LGBT+ community). This leaves our nation mired in discussions that are based on the idea that as long as we "treat each other nicely" then racism does not exist and any com-plaints about systemic or institutional manifestations of racism are ill-conceived, destructive, and flat out wrong.

A Dangerous Intersection: Facebook, Wine, and Social Justice

I am going to admit something that may shock some readers. I'm tired of getting mad at White people, but I'm more tired of White denials of racism. The cycle never fails. Something happens in the world that gets deemed racist. White folks often misunderstand or resist labeling it racist. Then it spills over into popular culture, and finally the news and commentary about it blows up my social media feeds. Then someone posts a comment on Facebook or sends an ill-considered Tweet that shows a certain level of insensitivity. Here is a prototypical example.

When my son was in preschool, we became friendly with a few of his playmates' families. The kids went to school together. They went on play dates together. They played tee ball together. We went on family outings for movies and pizza together. The moms went to spas and shopping together. The dads watched sports and had a few pints of beer together. We got together for birthday parties—not just the kids' birthdays but the adults' too. We were becoming a nice little community of friends. The families included[2] Scott and Myra Underhill who had one son, Paul and Patricia O'Bryan who had two boys, Joel and Tina Warren who had a girl and a younger boy, and of course us. Everyone but my family was White.

We adults had great conversations about life, work, parenting, popular culture, and of course politics. Occasionally we could get a little excited. After all, we were adults sharing a few libations that loosened tongues. The Warrens tended to be more conservative in their political leanings, but they also openly criticized extreme positions like the Tea Party and the Birther movement.[3] We all seemed to feel comfortable with one another and truly enjoyed each other's company (which was great since our children were so close). Being the only Black family was noticed, of course, but we never felt marginalized and always felt respected.

One evening Tina invited the moms over for wine and "girl time." Joel was out of town for work. Since we lived within ten minutes of each other, I offered to be the designated driver. At the end of the evening as I was leaving to pick up my wife, I received a text message from her, "OMG, Tina is crying about not wanting to be racist. NEVER TALK ABOUT RACE ON WINE NIGHT!" All I could think of for a response was the technical phrase, "Well, duh!" When I arrived, the ladies were listening to Tina divulge her family's secret history of racism, lamenting the old racist slurs and stereotypes that were common fodder in her parents' home and rampant throughout the small Midwestern city where she grew up. The other ladies consoled her and reassured her that her struggles were normal and she should talk about her questions and experiences. The evening ended with smiles and laughter.

The families had gotten together again a few days later for another gathering, and Tina's initial reaction to seeing us was mortification. I offered words of reassurance and intoned that it was far more important that she saw the problems of those past practices and actively resisted them. She, my wife, and I went on to talk about things further, in a side conversation, before too much wine was poured, and we had a nice discussion. My wife had suggested to her that if she had any questions we were always open to talking about them.

It was clear that Tina was struggling with many difficult questions about race and racism, questions that are difficult for millions of people. She was confused about Affirmative Action. She did not understand what people meant by White Privilege. She knew that racism was wrong, but she also did not understand the links among race, racism, equity, equality, and fairness. She did not see why being suspicious of young Black men wearing low-hanging pants was racist. In the words of Rodney King, she wondered why everyone couldn't "just get along." On the other hand, she would comment on how happy she was that our children were friends, and by extension we adults being friends too. She was a genial and gregarious person, always quick with a joke and a warm hug. Unfortunately, the Warrens had to move away to a new state but we all kept in touch through Facebook. This is where things began to ... change.

Occasionally, Gena would show me a posting from Tina that questioned something about race, but to me the questions seemed to be reflective of an inquisitive nature, not necessarily firm manifestos of racial resentment. Then I saw a post about a school desegregation issue in Tina's suburban community. She lamented her children's schooling being interrupted because the state was requiring the local school district to develop a desegregation plan that included low-income, mostly Black students from a neighboring community. Then, November 24, 2014 came: The day a grand jury decided not to indict Officer Darren Wilson for shooting unarmed Michael Brown dead in Ferguson, Missouri. What follows is the transcript from the Facebook exchange with Tina that ensued (it has since been deleted entirely from my page to protect Tina's anonymity):

Joseph:	No probable cause to indict Officer Wilson ... (the initial post)
Tina:	Wilson was defending himself clearly against a thug!
Tina:	Crap. Live in fear in St. Louis because of this crap and schools being cancelled. He was robbing a market and tried to attack an officer. Wilson was protecting himself. This is why we have law enforcement. I am really disappointed.
Tina:	Whatever! Lets burn police vehicles.
Joseph:	@Tina ... He was robbing a market, actually he stole a handful of cigarillos while walking out of a store.[4] So we go from that to it is alright for the police office to shoot him, multiple times? No pepper spray? No tazer? I can tell you this. ... You know what? No. I am not. If you (or anyone) is interested in a dialogue or learning more about why folks would riot or the history of the relationship between African Americans and law enforcement I am more than happy to help.
Tina:	Are you serious? Did you not listen to McCullough (the prosecutor)? Clearly you are not listening to the facts and are not here in St Louis. Now protesters are looting and burning businesses. Who does this?
Tina:	I am not interested in your dialogue.
Joseph:	If you are not interested then why are you posting to the wall of someone that clearly advocated for anti-racism and anti-oppression? Trust

> me, I probably know more about this than you. And honestly, if you
> are not interest in my dialogue please unfriend me. (Joseph Flynn's
> Facebook page, November 24, 2014)

I admit this "dialogue" was doomed from the start, a bad alchemy of emotions in the wake of a culturally and politically charged moment. Rather than promoting dialogue by asking Tina questions to understand the source of her frustration, I began by denying her feelings and perceived reality. I forgot that I once had a revealing conversation with her about these very issues in which she expressed a desire to understand. I forgot about her humanity and I saw her, for a moment, as another talking head on FOX News or any other anti-anti-racist outlet. I forgot that our children played together. I forgot.

To put it simply, sometimes I (and many of my colleagues) get tired of fighting, debating, and trying to *prove* the reality of racism, again and again ad nauseum. We are teachers, yeah, but we are human too, and being engaged with these issues and White resistance takes a toll on many of us. The recurrent struggles, especially if you are not White, can produce what bell hooks (1996) calls a "killing rage" and can be crushing to the spirit. I used to get invigorated at the opportunity to engage, seamlessly moving back and forth between "Joseph Flynn: Concerned Citizen of the World" and "Joseph Flynn: Concerned Black Social Justice Teacher Educator." Over the past decade of Facebook and social media generally, having posted hundreds of messages and exchanges about race and racism, I have seen much more futility than progress. But I am not hopeless, not at all.

As I reflected on this exchange with Tina I realized something. Tina's personal analysis of the Michael Brown incident was missing a great deal of information, but that information meant nothing in the face of what she perceived as a threat and disruption to her family and personal identity based on a lifetime of a particular experience that was in fact racially limited. I knew that she was not taking a college course on the sociology or psychology of racism, or mounting her own independent study of race relations in the United States. I knew that she did not have a significant number of non-White friends she engaged with regularly. I knew that she lived in a predominantly White suburban community in which racial diversity was mostly visible by its absence. I knew that her life experiences did not afford her a different lens to see the reality of Michael Brown, Sr. and Lesley McSpadden (Michael Brown's parents) and their Black neighbors in the community of Ferguson.[5] Her life experiences—nor presumably her education— did not provide the critical tools to critique race and racism.

Yet and still, she did not want to *be* a racist and she *wanted* to understand. Was she merely resistant at her core? Or, was the reality of understanding how race and racism function as a complex intellectual, emotional, and spiritual endeavor that takes years to master more challenging than she and many others anticipate? Does our lexicon of race and racism further a cycle of dehumanization that literally dissuades some people, primarily White folks in this case, from wanting to engage? After all, if someone is positioned as "the bad guy" or resistant from the start how does that shape the ways in which that person continues in the dialogue? This is not just a matter of how to talk about race on Facebook and out in our common social spaces. It is an essential question for all educators.

Hurdles to Learning About Racism: Constructs, Attitudes, and Language

Often, mainstream discussions about racism seem to focus on the moral failings of individuals, rarely moving to the more substantive systemic and institutional levels. Especially for those new to a deliberate and critical exploration of the topic, making that conceptual leap takes time to fully grasp. Yet, those explorations are often relegated to the one or two "diversity courses" in a college student's course of study. After all, not everyone chooses to pursue degrees in sociology, anthropology, or cultural studies.

As will be further discussed later, in order to investigate these issues properly, one is exposed to ideas from a broad range of disciplines, which adds to the academic complexity of understanding race and racism. Unfortunately this comes at the cost of some students growing impatient with the dialogue and looking for short cuts to the utopian idea of a post-racial United States. Those White students are then positioned as resistant and the actual problem, rather than potential agents of healthy change and essential to solutions who are in the midst of intellectual, psychological, and spiritual struggle. Like Zeus Leonardo (2004) points out, "they become over concerned with whether or not they 'look racist' and forsake the more central project of understanding the contours of structural racism" (p. 140).

How many times can any person be required to study a problem and be told in the same breath that they can never understand it because they *are* the problem? How many times can they be told to achieve the impossible before they grow tired and frustrated? Without excusing such responses, we can and must at least understand them for pedagogical purposes. We must, if we mean what we say when we proclaim that we teach for social justice and not retribution.

Due to changes in our social mores, many White folks in the post-Baby Boomer generations feel as though they "get it" when it comes to racial issues due to the increase of cross-racial friendships and relationships and exposure to other cultures via hip hop, suburbanization, diverse college campuses (specifically residence halls), and media (Flynn, 2013; Smitherman, 2006). However, as scholars like Picca and Feagin (2007), Pollock (2005), and Leonardo (2004) point out, there remain significant numbers of White folks who either continue to avoid or deny dialogues about race in public spaces or who continue to use racist language and stereotypes when talking about non-White people in the backstage. For instance, consider movements like *hipster racism* (West, 2012).

The term first appeared in the 2007 online essay "The 10 Biggest Race and Pop Culture Trends of 2006" by Carmen Van Kerkhove. The term was ill-defined in the essay and the writer only used examples to explore the term. Years later in the Spring of 2012, writer and activist Lindy West posted an essay about hipster racism for the online magazine *Jezebel*. Since then, the essay has gained over 1.3 million views, an impressive number for the academic community. In defining hipster racism West stated:

> There's been a lot of talk these last couple of weeks about "hipster racism" or "ironic racism"—or, as I like to call it, racism. It's, you know, introducing your black friend as "my black friend"—as a joke!!!—to show everybody how totally not preoccupied you are with your black friend's blackness. It's the gentler, more clueless, and more insidious cousin of a hick in a hood; the domain for educated, middle-class white people (like me—to be clear, I am one of those) who believe that not *wanting* to be racist make it okay for them to be totally racist. (West, para. 1)

In addition to calling out your Black friend, the essay includes many more examples of hipster racism, like: "suburban white girls flashing gang signs" (para. 7); " … white kids whining that it's 'unfair' that black people 'get to use "it"' (the n-word, that is)" (para. 9); or claiming any degrading or insensitive statement is just a joke. White youth may try to be ironic about race and racism as a way of displaying a cosmopolitan and generational understanding that race and racism are silly concepts that are well past their sell-by-date and race doesn't matter, a noble yet terribly flawed position. The idea of hipster racism is predicated on the notions that "racism is dead" and a general malaise about sustaining the discussion. In effect, within the community of Whiteness there is a *fatigue* toward racial dialogues and the desire to just "move on" has emerged. This is a dangerous position since it leaves a significant number of loose ends, and the suspension of dialogue and learning about how race and racism function and impact each of us limits our collective possibility for positive growth toward a beloved, empowered, egalitarian community.

It seems as though we are always at DEFCON 1 with racism in America, restlessly waiting for the next nuclear moment that will serve as the new meme announcing the dawn of a new day. As we see events spreading across social media at the speed of a hyper-virus, each one is pregnant with the anticipation that it will turn into the seed of the next movement. Are we fooling ourselves? Has there ever truly been that "watershed moment" that changed everything? Is it the ascent and election of Donald Trump such a moment? Without doubt, there have been moments that galvanized communities and pushed us toward action, toward protest, toward revolution. But *no singular event* has pushed White folks en masse to commit themselves to a critical investigation of how racism functions through our institutions and impacts our personal lives in sometimes covert and sometimes overt ways. After all, despite impassioned, logical, and gut-wrenching polemics for reparations (Coates, 2014) the country remains sharply divided on even entertaining a national discussion about reparations, a point that has not changed much over time (Moore, 2014; Washburn & Garrett, 2001).

That is not to say there is an insignificant number of White folks understanding of the ways in which racism (and other forms of oppression) damage communities. It is also not to say that there is not a long history of White folks whom chose the difficult path and resisted the establishment of a racial hierarchy that would become dominant in the United States (Earp, Jhally & Morris, 2013; Wise, 2012). Early exposure to these "alternative" lessons from racial history could have a profound impact on how we engage and talk about race. Noted anti-racist educator Tim Wise (2012) challenges:

> Imagine how different the racial dialogue might feel for us if we knew and had been taught from a young age of the history of white allyship and antiracist resistance? If as children we had been introduced not only to the black and brown heroes and sheroes of the antiracist struggle—Like Frederick Douglass, Sojourner Truth, Rosa Parks, Fannie Lou Hamer, Ella Baker and of course Dr. King—but also to those white freedom fighters who stood beside them? What if we learned of the alternative tradition in our history, the one in which members of our community said no to racism and white domination, said no to racial hegemony and yes to justice? (p. 149)

Countless numbers of White folks fought and protested alongside the oppressed as equals, yet the textbooks in our nation's schools have rendered those White folk nearly invisible (apart from John Brown of course). Perhaps not having any significant exposure to that history traps White folks in a false consciousness that is the creation of their forbearers, and this reinforces the need for more exposure to the history of the interracial struggle for racial justice to offer all students examples of the ways in which White folks also struggled against racial oppression (Tatum, 1994).

Simply stated, White folks are caught in the same cycle of misinformation and historical erasures as so-called minorities, and that fact has had a profound impact on the ways in which we talk about and engage race and racism. It makes me wonder, if we as a nation are truly dedicated to racial justice, then why are examples of interracial activisim for racial justice all but absent in our nation's schools, teacher education programs, and professional development initiatives? To punctuate the point, Tatum (1999) encourages educators to seek out possible tools that represent and promote White anti-racist activism:

> While it is necessary to be honest about the racism of our past and present, it is also necessary to provide children (and adults) with a vision that change is possible. Where can we find this vision? We can look for it in our history, we can create it with our colleagues, and we can demonstrate it in our classrooms. ... All whites were not bad, and some black resisters found white allies. ... Let students see themselves as agents of change and healing. (p. 29)

The Vanguard of Footsoldiers: White Fatigue and the Preparation of Teachers in the Age of Obama ... but Definitely Not the Post-Racial Age

We must ask ourselves a challenging question, continuously: Are we doing an effective job of teaching our students about race and racism? After all, if we do not teach about race and racism, how will younger generations have the opportunity to grow from the mistakes of previous generations? Our society has made truly significant advances over the past fifty years. However, Dr. Martin Luther King's dream of a beloved community has yet to be fully realized. We do know there have been some significant changes in tolerance and understanding. After all, saying anything even remotely racist is no longer socially accepted or tolerated in popular culture. Just ask Paula Deen, Cliven Bundy, Julianne Hough, Kendall Jenner, Hulk Hogan, Mel Gibson, Dog the Bounty Hunter, Alec Baldwin, Gweneth Paltrow, Daniel Snyder, owner of the National Football League team from Washington, D.C., or Donald Trump. There are a number of significant hurdles and lingering questions about what racism is, how it functions, why some seem to continue to "complain" about it, how White folks (and others) can be complicit in the reification of White racism, and how (and why) they can be unaware of their complicity?

Great concern and dismay is displayed in colleges of education—and universities in general—regarding the numbers, presence, and persistence of racial and ethnic minorities. Due to the lack of institutional action and dubious commitment to changing environments, we are seeing a rise in student activism on college campuses that have resulted in the resignations of university presidents and other officials across the country, most notably at the University of Missouri (Eligon & Pérez-Peña, 2015), after heated protests by students regarding the treatment and lack of action to create safer environments. The University of Missouri was not the only campus embroiled in protests. Yale, the University of California at Los Angeles, the University of Michigan, the University of Oklahoma, Arizona State

University and many others have all seen protests to campus conditions and other racially charged concerns (Hartocollis & Bidgood, 2015). Colleges and universities across the country are creating and hiring chief diversity officers or directors of inclusion at an unprecedented rate (Gose, 2006). Sometimes this is a proactive step in order to develop and coordinate a vision for diversity and inclusion for institutions. Other times it is a reactionary measure, like at the University of Oklahoma in the wake of the Sigma Alpha Epsilon members being caught singing a racist song in a viral video (New, 2015). The drive to diversify teacher education is filled with great ideas and promise (Sleeter, Neal, & Kumishiro, 2015). This is not only a benefit for so-called minorities; it is also of great benefit for White students as well.

There are decades' worth of research and scholarship that shows the academic and social importance of a diverse educational environment at all levels of education (Banks, 2015; DeVillar, 1994; Nieto, 2009). This belief is not solely the belief of progressive, multicultural, anti-racist, or social justice educators. The United States Supreme Court in the *Gratz v. Bollinger* (2003) and *Grutter v. Bollinger* (2003) decisions regarding the University of Michigan's affirmative action and admission policies is an important point of reference. Although the Court ultimately found the University's undergraduate admission process unconstitutional, the Court upheld the law school's holistic review procedures.[6] The Court went on to opine that diversity is a compelling interest and that a diverse environment allows students of all backgrounds to be exposed to a broad range of ideas, perspectives, and experiences—enriching the educational experience for all students. Simply put, diversity is important.

As we rapidly move forward into the 21st century, one fact about education remains true. Although non-White students are rapidly becoming the majority of students (although many areas around the country remain racially isolated and overwhelmingly White), only 17% of teachers are non-White, and projections show the teaching force will remain predominantly White for years to come (NCES, 2011). These facts and projections not only tell us that the role and presence of White folks in the classroom is indispensible, as well as principals, superintendents, school board members, curriculum developers, test designers, policymakers, advocates, journalists, and pundits. Each of these stakeholders is just as crucial to public education as teachers. It is essential that teacher educators—in fact all professors dedicated to the field of education— be mindful of this reality and advance curricular, practical, and pedagogical discussions around two key question: First, what is the role of White educators in the negotiation and reshaping of educational practices that promote not only student achievement for all but also social justice? Second, what are the challenges for teacher education in helping White students develop greater understanding of how systems of oppression function—particularly racism—in the hopes of developing a teaching force that sees diversity, inclusion, and social justice as fundamental to successful teaching and a high-quality education for all students?

In my own travels as a teacher educator, I have met hundreds of students that openly shared how there were few racial or ethnic minorities in their schools and neighborhoods, or that they did not have substantive relationships or friendships with non-White people. This is not necessarily because of any overtly racist inclinations but rather simply because of lack of exposure or opportunities. After all, if one lives in the rural regions of Nebraska, Illinois, or the Dakotas, where there are very low numbers of non-White citizens, one has severely limited opportunities to create meaningful relationships with racial others. This happens while experiencing a deluge of negative or misrepresented images and stereotypes of minorities that consistently circulate throughout media and popular culture. Residential segregation, gentrification, media and popular culture, curricula, and other systemic and institutional challenges also frame their opportunities and understanding, leaving them with their own questions, suspicions, misgivings and revelations. In all these contexts, access and opportunity matter, but so do the pedagogies and language we use to help learners acquire, engage, and use new knowledge about race and racism in order to truly teach for social justice. As Sobel and Taylor (2005) pointed out, "Though promoting acceptance, tolerance, and respect for diversity are commendable goals, multicultural coursework in general can stop short of affirming one's own and others' diversity" (p. 84).

What follows is based on a key assumption that has been repeated in the literature on race and racism for quite some time. The generally accepted operationalized definition of racism is a system of advantage based on race (Sensoy & DiAngelo, 2012; Tatum, 1999; Wellman, 1993). Race is not the operative word of that definition. The operative word is: *system*. Racism is a *system*. Racism is not just a matter of taste or preference of individuals. It is an all-encompassing reality or worldview (Smedley & Smedley, 2012), and it is a system for thinking and acting that continuously operates with and without the willful awareness of individuals. In other words, as I have told my students over the years, just because we all start treating each other nicer, or better, or with more respect that does not necessarily mean racism is eradicated. Essential to the functioning of racism are our social institutions. As such, racism is reliant upon a number of moving parts *and* actors. We can see these moving parts across our social landscape: media, government, law enforcement, commerce, education, and other social institutions.

Johnathan Turner (1997) offers a comprehensive definition of social institutions. He states that a social institution is a:

... complex of positions, roles, norms, and values lodged in particular types of social structures and organizing relatively stable patterns of human activity with respect to fundamental problems in producing life-sustaining resources, in reproducing individuals, and in sustaining viable societal structures within a given environment. (p. 6)

Understanding race and racism is about recognizing how an entire society—a network of systems and institutions—functions, and how individual lives are shaped and manipulated by often-obscured machinations. Considering the complexity of how systems and social institutions function is essential in understanding racism and those lessons are challenging. As such, we educators ought to consider how our language assuages and aggravates how White students see themselves in this process. Seeing students as fatigued—rather than simply resistant, guilty, or fragile—acknowledges their personal, intellectual, and spiritual struggles.

And the actors? We all are actors, and our roles have been carved out by the nature and functioning of a system of advantage based on race that has a 400-year history and built, from its impetus, by people who went on to call themselves White. And those people spent hundreds of years advancing laws, policies, and social practices that manufactured and reified their position of privilege at the expense of other groups. That fact brings us to today. For White folks that fact of racism is your progeny, and regardless of never having owned slaves, or stopped someone from eating at a lunch counter, or never being involved in committing genocide, those actions created a context that constructed all our realities. If we expect change then we must give credence to the notion of racism as a system and further examine how each of us are positioned within that system, as both individuals and members of groups.

Now, let's explore the notion of White fatigue.

Notes

1. This book focuses on the United States. There is a great deal of scholarship on the dynamics of race and racism in other countries and global regions (Bhattacharyya, Gabriel, & Small, 2008; Hollinsworth, 2006; Lentin, 2004; MacMaster, 2001; Pettigrew, 1998). Although theoretical underpinnings that can explain racism can be generalized across global contexts, each context has its own unique factors, histories, and challenges. Therefore, this text will keep its lens on the experience of race and racism in the United States.

2. All the names, except for my family, have been changed to protect anonymity.

3. The Birthers were a once fringe group that gained popularity. Fueled by suppositions and accusations by Donald Trump, they argued that President Barack Obama was in fact born in Kenya (President Obama's father was in fact Kenyan born, but he was born in Ha'waii), rendering his election to the presidency unconstitutional and void. The President, in an unprecedented move, had his birth certificate released, but the move did not assuage the

detractors and the "rumor" followed President Obama throughout his presidency to the extent that Republican Congressional leaders and others continued to further the aspersion with little to no repercussions.

4. As of the late drafting stages.

5. In the following months, the Department of Justice conducted an investigation for civil rights violations against the Ferguson, MO police department. The report was a scathing indictment and found widespread discrimination against African Americans, including: local law enforcement was dictated by revenue needs rather than public safety; African Americans comprised 67% of the city but 93% of arrests between 2012 and 2014; a disproportionate number of arrests, tickets, and uses of force were from unlawful bias rather than African Americans committing crimes; rude treatment of Black citizens; and a culture of racial intolerance within the department, among other equally appalling findings (Andrews, Desantis, & Kellar, 2015; Berman & Lowrey, 2015; United States Department of Justice Civil Rights Division, 2015).

6. In the *Gratz v. Bollinger* case, the University of Michigan's (U of M) undergraduate admissions review and acceptance process was in question. U of M used a point system. For various aspects of applicants' profiles a certain number of points were assigned, and if an applicant achieved 100 points the applicant earned entry to the university. For example, applicants could receive points for being a racial minority; from out of state; from the upper peninsula of Michigan; an athlete on scholarship; high school grade point average; standardized test scores; among other factors. Underrepresented racial and ethnic groups were awarded an automatic twenty points, and that awarding served to admit nearly all underrepresented minority applicants. The Court determined the process unconstitutional, violating the Equal Protection Clause, since the automatic points for underrepresented minorities disallowed individual consideration of each applicant, especially non-racial factors. The procedure was not narrowly defined and ultimately violated previous jurisprudence (Gratz v. Bollinger, 2003). On the other hand, the *Grutter v. Bollinger* case held the University of Michigan's Law School's admission's review process under scrutiny. Since the Law School took a holistic approach to their review, using race among a myriad of factors for each applicant, there was more narrow use of race and not a near automatic admittance determinant, unlike the Gratz case (*Grutter v. Bollinger*, 2003).

Bibliography

Alexander, M. (2012). *The new Jim Crow: Mass incarceration in the age of colorblindness.* New York, NY: The New Press.

Andrews, W., Desantis, A., & Keller, J. (March 4, 2015). Justice Department's report on the Ferguson Police Department. *New York Times.* Retrieved from https://www.nytimes.com/interactive/2015/03/04/us/ferguson-police-racial-discrimination.html

Aptheker, H. (1993). *A documentary history of the Negro people in the United States.* New York, NY: Carol Publishing.

Banks, J. (2004). Multicultural education: Historical development, dimensions, and practice. In J. A. Banks & C. McGee Banks (Eds.), *Handbook of research on multicultural education* (pp. 3–29). San Francisco, CA: Jossey Bass.

Banks, J. A. (2015). *Cultural diversity and education* (6th ed.). New York, NY: Routledge.

Battalora, J. (2013). *Birth of a White nation: The invention of White people and its relevance today.* Houston, TX: Strategic Book Publishing and Rights.

Baunach, D. M. (2002, January 1). Progress, opportunity, and backlash: Explaining attitudes toward gender-based affirmative action. *Sociological Focus, 35*(4), 345.

Beauchamp, Z. (2016, November 9). Donald Trump's victory is part of a global White backlash. *Vox.* Retrieved from http://www.vox.com/world/2016/11/9/13572174/president-elect-donald-trump-2016-victory-racism-xenophobia

Berman, M., & Lowery, W. (March 4, 2015). The 12 key highlights from the DOJ's scathing Ferguson report. *The Washington Post.* Retrieve from https://www.washingtonpost.com/news/post-nation/wp/2015/03/04/the-12-key-highlights-from-the-dojs-scathing-ferguson-report/?utm_term=.4b34256215ec

Bhattacharyya, G., Gabriel, J., & Small, S. (2008). *Race and power: Global racism in the twenty-first century.* London, UK: Routledge.

Bonilla-Silva, E. (2013). *Racism without racists: Color-blind racism and the persistence of racial inequality in America* (4th ed.). Lanham, MD: Rowan and Littlefield.

Bourdieu, P. (1977). *Outline of a theory of practice.* Cambridge: Cambridge University Press.

Boyle-Baise, M. (1999, January 1). Bleeding boundaries or uncertain center? A historical exploration of multicultural education. *Journal of Curriculum and Supervision, 14*(3), 191–215.

Campbell, T., & Friesen, J. (2015, March 3). Why people "fly from facts." *Scientific American.* Retrieved from https://www.scientificamerican.com/article/why-people-fly-from-facts/

Capehart, J. (2014, December 30). The fallacy of a post-racial America. *The Washington Post.* Retrieved from http://www.chicagotribune.com/news/opinion/commentary/sns-wp-washpost-bc-race-comment29-20141229-story.html

Coates, T. (2014, June). The case for reparations. *The Atlantic.* Retrieved from https://www.theatlantic.com/magazine/archive/2014/06/the-case-for-reparations/361631/

Coates, T. (2015). *Between the world and me.* New York, NY: Spiegel & Grau.

Cohn, J. (2016, June 9). The comprehensive guide to Trump's most outrageous statements. *The Huffington Post.* Retrieved from http://www.huffingtonpost.com/entry/worst-trump-quotes_us_5756e8e6e4b07823f9514fb1

Delpit, L. D. (1988). The silenced dialogue: Power and pedagogy in educating other people's children. *Harvard Educational Review, 58*(3), 280–298.

DeVillar, R. A. (Ed.). (1994). *Cultural diversity in schools: From rhetoric to practice.* Albany, NY: State University of New York Press.

Earp, J., Jhally, S., & Morris, S. (2013). *White like me: Race, racism, and White privilege in America.* Northampton, MA: Media Education Foundation.

Eligon, J., & Pérez-Peña, R. (2015, November 9). University of Missouri protests spur a day of change. *The New York Times.* Retrieved from https://www.nytimes.com/2015/11/10/us/university-of-missouri-system-president-resigns.html

Fausset, R., Blinder, A., & Eligon, J. (2016, August 24). Donald Trump's description of Black America is offending those living in it. *The New York Times.* Retrieved from https://www.nytimes.com/2016/08/25/us/politics/donald-trump-black-voters.html

Feagin, J. (2013). *The White racial frame: Centuries of racial framing and counter framing* (2nd ed.). New York, NY: Routledge.

Feagin, J. (2014). *Racist America: Roots, current realities, and future reparations* (3rd ed.). New York, NY: Routledge.

Fine, M. E., Wong, L. M. E., Powell, L. C. E., & Weis, L. E. (1997). *Off White: Readings on Race, Power, and Society*. New York, NY: Routledge.

Flynn, J. (2013). Say what's the word? An exploration of the controversy around the "n-words." *Illinois Committee on Black Concerns in Higher Education Journal, 27*(1), 50–70.

Flynn, J. (2014, November 24). Facebook page posting.

Fox, H. (2009). *"When race breaks out": Conversations about race and racism in college classrooms*. New York, NY: Peter Lang.

Freire, P. (1970/1997). *Pedagogy of the oppressed* (New Revised 20th Anniversary ed.). New York, NY: Continuum.

Friesen, J. P., Campbell, T. H., & Kay, A. C. (2015, January 1). The psychological advantage of unfalsifiability: The appeal of untestable religious and political ideologies. *Journal of Personality and Social Psychology, 108*(3), 515–529.

Gal, D., & Rucker, D. D. (2010). When in doubt, shout! paradoxical influences of doubt on proselytizing. *Psychological Science, 21*(11), 1701–1707.

Gee, J. P. (2007). *Social linguistics and literacies: Ideology in discourses*. London: Routledge.

Goodman, A. (2016, February 10). After running xenophobic and racist campaign Donald Trump wins easily in New Hampshire. *Democracy Now*. Retrieved from https://www.democracynow.org/2016/2/10/after_running_xenophobic_racist_capaign_donald

Goodman, D. J. (2011). *Promoting diversity and social justice: Educating people from privileged groups*. London: Routledge.

Goodwin, M. (2013, March 12). Law professors see the damage done by "No Child Left Behind." *The Chronicle of Higher Education*. Retrieved from http://www.chronicle.com/blogs/conversation/2013/03/12/law-professors-see-the-damage-done-by-no-child-left-behind/

Gose, B. (2006, September 29). The rise of the chief diversity officer. *The Chronicle of Higher Education*. Retrieved from http://www.chronicle.com/article/The-Rise-of-the-Chief/7327

Gratz v. Bollinger. (2003). (02–516) 539 U.S. 244. Retrieved from https://www.law.cornell.edu/supct/html/02-516.ZO.html

Grutter v. Bollinger. (2003). (02–241). 539 U.S. 306. Retrieved from https://www.law.cornell.edu/supct/html/02-241.ZO.html

Haney-Lopez, I. (2016, August 2). This is how Trump convinces his supporters they're not racist. *The Nation*. Retrieved from https://www.thenation.com/article/this-is-how-trump-supporters-convince-themselves-theyre-not-racist/

Hartocollis, A., & Bidgood, J. (2015, November 11). Racial discrimination protests ignite at colleges across the U.S. *The New York Times*. Retrieved fromhttps://www.nytimes.com/2015/11/12/us/racial-discrimination-protests-ignite-at-colleges-across-the-us.html

Helms, J. E. (1993). *Black and White racial identity: Theory, research, and practice*. Westport, CT: Praeger.

Hitchcock, J. (2002). *Lifting the White veil: An exploration of White American culture in a multiracial context*. Roselle, NJ: Crandall, Dostie & Douglass Books.

Hollinsworth, D. (2006). *Race and racism in Australia*. South Melbourne, AU: Thomson/Social Science Press.

hooks, b., & Henry Holt and Company. (2006). *Killing rage: Ending racism*. New York, NY: Henry Holt.

Irving, D. (2014). *Waking up White, and finding myself in the story of race*. Cambridge, MA: Elephant Room Press.

Katznelson, I. (2006). *When affirmative action was White: An untold history of racial inequality in twentieth-century America* (Reprint ed.). New York, NY: W. W. Norton.

Kendi, I. X. (2016). *Stamped from the beginning: The definitive history of racist ideas in America*. New York, NY: Nation Books.

Kopan, T. (2015, November 29). 10 groups Donald Trump offended since launching his campaign. *CNN Politics*. Retrieved from http://www.cnn.com/2015/11/27/politics/donald-trump-insults-groups-list/

Ledwidge, M., Verney, K., & Parmar, I. (2013). *Barack Obama and the myth of a post racial America*. New York, NY: Routledge.

Lentin, A. (2004). *Racism and anti-racism in Europe*. London, UK: Pluto Press.

Leonardo, Z. (2004, January 1). The color of supremacy: Beyond the discourse of "white privilege." *Educational Philosophy and Theory, 36*(2), 137–152.

MacMaster, N. (2013). *Racism in Europe 1870–2000*. Hampshire, UK: Palgrave.

Maxwell, L. (2014, August 19). U.S. school enrollment hits majority-minority milestone. *Education Week*. Retrieved from http://www.edweek.org/ew/articles/2014/08/20/01demographics.h34.html

McIntosh, P. (1988). White privilege and male privilege: A personal account of coming to see correspondences through work in women's studies. In M. L. Anderson & P. Hill-Collins (Eds.), *Race, class, and gender: An anthology* (pp. 70–81). Wellesley, MA: Wellesley College Center for Research on Women.

Moore, A. (2014, June 20). Slavery's shadow: Reparations and the cost to build a nation. *Huffpost: The Blog*. Retrieved from http://www.huffingtonpost.com/antoni-omoore/slaverys-shadow-how-forbe_b_5505319.html

National Center for Education Statistics. (2011). Teacher trends. *Fast Facts*. Retrieved from http://nces.ed.gov/fastfacts/display.asp?id=28

National Commission on Excellence in Education. (1983). *A nation at risk: The imperative for educational reform. An open letter to the American people. A report to the Nation and the Secretary of Education*. Washington, DC: Government Printing Office.

Nieto, S. (2009). *The light in their eyes: Creating multicultural learning communities* (10th anniversary ed.). New York, NY: Teachers College Press.

Nyhan, B., & Reifler, J. (2010, January 1). When corrections fail: The persistence of political misperceptions. *Political Behavior, 32*(2), 303–330.

Ornitz, J. (2016, August 31). Veterans group chastises Trump for attacks on fallen soldier's parents. *Los Angeles Times*. Retrieved from http://www.latimes.com/nation/politics/trailguide/

la-na-trailguide-updates-veterans-group-chastises-trump-for-1470072947-htmlstory. html

Paisley, B., Smith, T., & Miller, T. (2013). Accidental racist [Recorded by Brad Paisley with LL Cool J]. On *Wheelhouse* [CD]. Nashville, TN: Nashville Arista.

Patterson, O. (1998). *The ordeal of integration: Progress and resentment in America's "racial" crisis.* Washington, DC: Civitas/Counterpoint.

Pettigrew, T. F. (1998). Reactions toward the new minorities of western Europe. *Annual Review of Sociology, 24*(1), 77–104.

Picca, L. H., & Feagin, J. R. (2007). *Two-faced racism: Whites in the backstage and frontstage.* New York, NY: Routledge.

Pollock, M. (2005). *Colormute: Race talk dilemmas in an American school.* Princeton, NJ: Princeton University Press.

Sensoy, O., & DiAngelo, R. (2012). *Is everyone really equal? An introduction to key concepts in social justice education.* New York, NY: Teachers College Press.

Singleton, G. E. (2014). *Courageous conversations about race: A field guide for achieving equity in schools* (2nd ed.). Thousand Oaks, CA: Corwin Press.

Sleeter, C. E., Neal, L. I., & Kumishiro, K. K. (eds.) (2015). *Diversifying the teacher workforce: Preparing and retaining highly effective teachers.* New York, NY: Routledge.

Smedley, A., & Smedley, B. D. (2012). *Race in North America: Origin and evolution of a worldview.* Boulder, CO: Westview Press.

Smitherman, G. (2006). *Word from the mother.* Hoboken, NJ: Taylor & Francis.

Sobel, M., & Taylor, S. (2005). Diversity preparedness in teacher education. *Kappa Delta Pi Record, 41*, 83–86.

Speri, A. (2014, December 9). Half of America thinks we live in a post-racial society—the other half, not so much. *Vice News.* Retrieved from https://news.vice.com/article/ half-of-america-thinks-we-live-in-a-post-racial-society-the-other-half-not-so-much

Tatum, B. D. (1994). Teaching White students about racism: The search for White allies and the restoration of hope. *Teachers College Record, 95*(4), 462–467.

Tatum, B. D. (1999). *"Why are all the Black kids sitting together in the cafeteria?": And other conversations about race.* New York, NY: Basic Books.

Tatum, B. D. (2003). *Why are all the Black kids sitting together in the cafeteria: And other conversations about race* (5th anniversary revised ed.). New York, NY: Basic Books.

Turner, J. (1997). *The institutional order.* New York, NY: Longman.

United States Department of Justice Civil Rights Division. (2015). *Investigation of the Ferguson Police Department.* Washington, DC: United States Department of Justice.

Washburn, G., & Garrett, C. (2001, May 20). Races differ on reparations: Very few Whites, most Blacks want slavery redress. *The Chicago Tribune.* Retrieved from http://articles.chicagotribune.com/2001-05-20/news/0105200360_1_reparations-whites-slavery

Wellman, D. (1993). *Portraits of White racism.* New York, NY: Cambridge University Press.

West, L. (2012, April 26). A complete guide to "hipster racism." *Jezebel.* Retrieved from http:// jezebel.com/5905291/a-complete-guide-to-hipster-racism

Wise, T. (1998, September 23). Is sisterhood conditional?: White women and the rollback of affirmative action. *National Women's Studies Association Journal, 10*(3), 1–26.

Wise, T. (2010). *Colorblind: The rise of post-racial politics and the retreat from racial equity*. San Francisco, CA: City Lights Books.

Wise, T. (2012). *Dear White America: Letter to a new minority*. San Francisco, CA: City Lights Books.

CHAPTER TWO

White Fatigue

Naming the Challenge in Moving From an Individual to a Systemic Understanding of Racism

Multicultural educators (MCEs) regularly encounter students who are on a broad spectrum in their willingness or preparedness to engage in discussions about racism and other forms of oppression. For example, MCEs may encounter resistance that looks like provocative argument, or quiet discomfort. On the other end of the spectrum, MCEs may encounter students that are excited about the exchange of ideas and may voice validation of their own experiences or the new ability to apply a term or theory to something they have "always" noticed. This range is common. As such, it is necessary for us to be aware of concepts that can more appropriately describe students and their experience in learning about racism.

In this chapter I describe a phenomenon I call *White fatigue*.[1] Simply, White fatigue attempts to identify and name the dynamic of White students who intuitively understand or recognize the moral imperative of antiracism, primarily individual racism. However, they are not yet fully understanding of the complexity of racism and how it functions as an institutional and systemic phenomenon—significantly more complex ideas. Due to the complexity engaged by critical explorations of racism compared to the simplistic notions of racism furthered through media, popular culture, the general K-12 curriculum, and personal experiences, those who are fatigued claim to be tired of talking about racism, despite the intuitive understanding that racism is morally wrong. This phenomenon is further aggravated by students' desire to not be judged as racist.

White fatigue should not be conflated with *racial battle fatigue* (Smith, 2004; Smith, Hung, & Franklin, 2011; Smith, Yosso, & Solorzano, 2006) or *White people fatigue syndrome* (hooks, 1992). These are defined as fatigue experienced by racially minoritized peoples in the United States (particularly African Americans) that arise from constantly addressing or *teaching* White people how and why actions and microaggressions are racist. In contrast, White fatigue focuses on the set of White Americas that understands attitudes and actions reflect certain forms of racism (i.e. individual racism) due to the arguably successful promotion of racial tolerance and respect via media, popular culture, and schooling, but they do not yet fully grasp the underpinnings of systemic and institutional racism, and how those forms of racism directly impact the ways in which people are socialized into racist worldviews (Smedley & Smedley, 2012).

White fatigue is related to, but distinct from other concepts such as *White guilt* (Leonardo, 2004; Tatum, 1994), *or White fragility* (DiAngelo, 2011). Although a quasi form of White resistance, White fatigue is brought about by the challenges and complexities of learning about racism. I construct White fatigue as a quasi form of resistance. On one hand fatigue can appear as resistance, but on the other hand the fatigued do not reject the reality of racism. The conflicting stream of messages from anti-racist and multicultural educators, media and popular culture, and personal experiences is a conceptual challenge for White students in moving from focusing on individual racism (i.e. prejudice and discrimination) toward an understanding of institutional and systemic racism.

The common reaction is to label these students as simply resistant. However, reflexively labeling this group of students as resistant disregards their basic understanding of antiracism and, perhaps, the reality of multiculturalism within their own lives. Oftentimes, students will promote the notion of colorblindness (Bonilla-Silva, 2013; Bonilla-Silva & Dietrich, 2011; Wise, 2010) as the best approach for dealing with racism, especially now in the Obama era. Although for us multicultural and antiracist educators the claim of colorblindness is indicative of not understanding racism, the spirit behind the claim of colorblindness for some is well intentioned, especially considering the messages of tolerance and respect that consistently circulate throughout society.

Flatly labeling those students as resistant draws a conceptual line in the sand that challenges their sense of morality and forces them into a conceptual and rhetorical corner. Rather than being an empowering discourse, antiracism and multiculturalism becomes a marginalizing discourse for these students. That conceptual dissonance can foster frustration and resignation, making antiracist work that much more complicated. This is not necessarily a "free pass" to exempt White students from continuing the difficult work of excavating how racism functions.

Rather, it is a way of recognizing both the intellectual challenges of learning about racism in the face of the popular focus on individual behaviors and the human desire to not be singularly or flatly defined in negative terms.

In what follows, I will begin with a short vignette that frames White fatigue. Then, I will explicate its relationship with White resistance, White guilt, and White fragility. Next, I will situate White fatigue within the White Racial Identity Development framework and further comment on how stereotype threat, embedded in the idea of "Whites equal oppressors," further complicates and hinders positive White racial identity development, resulting in fatigue.

A Slap to the Face? Or a Sentiment of Frustration? A Vignette of White Fatigue

"For no person I've ever known has ever done more to make me feel more sure, more insecure, more important, and less significant."

—SUMMER OF '42 (1971)

I began my career as a teacher educator at Michigan State University in the fall of 2000. The first class I taught, *Human Diversity, Power, and Opportunity in Social Institutions*, was dubbed the "diversity course." The course focused on social and cultural foundations of education and curriculum with an eye toward critical issues related to social justice and diversity. The first time I taught the class I was introduced to a persistent phenomenon many of my colleagues and I have seen across contexts over the sixteen years since that inaugural class.

During a session in which we explored White privilege, centering the discussion around Lisa Delpit's "The Silenced Dialogue" (Delpit, 1988) and Peggy McIntosh's "Unpacking the Invisible Knapsack" (McIntosh, 1988), I noticed a young White female student who seemed rather despondent and displaying a detached gaze. I asked her what was the matter and she replied, "You don't want to know." I delicately pressed, voicing that my classroom was an open and safe space and that all ideas were welcomed. She retorted, "Well, race wouldn't be a problem if it weren't for people like you and the NAACP. I am so sick of talking about this stuff!"

After class, the student and I spoke at length. She apologized for the sharp recrimination and went on to explain how life was back at home and her struggles with developing a new racial consciousness. She was raised in a small town that had little racial diversity and many folks in her world displayed negative dispositions toward non-White folks in which she quietly resisted participation. Both of her parents routinely used racial epithets, even at the dinner table, which always made her uncomfortable. She did not use racial epithets herself and understood the notion that racism was "wrong." She was at a point in her life where she routinely encountered a wide spectrum of non-White peers in substantive ways; now attending a large university with a diverse student community, she was making interracial friendships and learning a great deal socially. She grew to feel more comfortable around non-White folks and recognized the commonalities behind our differences. In her words, she "got it." But, she also felt that since she "got it" there was no need to keep "hammering away" at how *bad* White people are. Despite her growth in tolerance, respect, and appreciation for racial differences (i.e. her intuitive understanding of individual racism), she had yet to fully grasp the full nature of racism, specifically the critical and more intractable forms of systemic and institutional racism. Had she understood the complexity of racism as institutional and systemic phenomena beyond simple prejudice and discrimination, she could have seen the conceptual flaw of her pointed recrimination.

As I have reflected upon this event over the years I focused less on the recrimination and more on the aftermath. She stayed in the course. She continued to engage, question, and challenge. I am fully aware of the idea that she could have just been putting on a show for the instructor, but as the semester went on she displayed greater understanding of systemic and institutional racism. This is not to imply that her work on these issues was complete by the semester's end, but to point out that she *chose* to stay the course.

For me an essential point emerged: although she began the class with the recognition that prejudice and discrimination were "wrong," the introduction of more complex realities and theories of institutional and systemic racism posed a new set of challenges, and simple edicts like "you don't choose your friends like you choose your socks" or "we are all human" were wholly insufficient for a fuller understanding of how racism functions. Furthermore, the insertion of the idea of privilege, as a personal phenomenon, served as a pothole for her and many other students, as the totality of the ideas left her questioning "what can I do about any of this?"

A Struggle of the Mind and Spirit: Defining and Differentiating White Fatigue, White Guilt, White Fragility, and Resistance

"In spite of everything, I still believe people are good at heart."
—ANNE FRANK (1952)

As introduced above, I define White fatigue as a temporary state in which individuals that are understanding of the moral imperative of antiracism disengage from or assume one no longer needs to continue learning about how racism and/or White privilege function in light of the basic understanding of individual racism (i.e. prejudice and discrimination). Characterized by responses like impatience, flippancy, sarcasm, frustration, or resignation, White fatigue arises from the suspension of critical thinking about the complex nature of systemic and institutional racism. However, White fatigue is the antithesis of White guilt because it occurs with individuals who do not necessarily feel guilty about their Whiteness or the role White people have played in shaping historic institutionally and systemically racist practices.

To differentiate fatigue from guilt, resistance, and fragility it must be pointed out that White guilt is associated with the negative or uncomfortable feelings that arise from White folks' initial exposure to the ill actions of previous generations and the unearned assets accumulated through racial privilege (Hitchcock, 2002). White guilt emerges from the feelings that arise when trying to come to grips with the weight and repercussions of historic events, and the crippling feeling that one has no idea of what to do to *make it all better*.

On the other hand, White resistance is a flat-out rejection of the principles of anti-racism altogether. Goodman (2011) writes that:

> When people are **resistant**, they are unable to seriously engage with the material. They *refuse* to consider alternative perspectives that challenge the dominant ideology that maintains the status quo. They resist information or experiences that may cause them to question their worldview. *They may dismiss the idea that oppression or systemic inequalities are real.* ... It is *irrational, an automatic reaction rather than a considered choice* (emphasis added). (p. 51)

What is essential to understand about White resistance, as Goodman shows, is that there is a lack of critical engagement with the ideas en masse. The resistant do not yet see the reality of systemic and institutional racism and the default response wholly disallows critically engaging with a set of ideas that expose how racism functions and how White privilege is all but guaranteed through daily systemic and institutional practices. Moreover, the resistant do not see their own complicity in perpetuating systems of oppression. White fatigue is a quasi form of White resistance because there is a suspension of the critical thinking necessary to fundamentally understand how race and racism function, but the recognition of larger systemic and institutional manifestations of racism is real and complex. This is quite different from White fragility.

Robin DiAngelo's (2011) idea of White fragility is more closely related to White fatigue than the concept of White guilt. DiAngelo defines White fragility as

A state in which even a minimum amount of racial stress becomes intolerable, triggering a range of defensive moves. These moves include the outward display of emotions such as anger, fear, and guilt, and behaviors such as argumentation, silence, and leaving the stress-inducing situation. These behaviors, in turn, function to reinstate white racial equilibrium. (p. 54)

Throughout her article, DiAngelo offers examples of moments in which she has witnessed White Fragility. DiAngelo situates fragility as a direct result of the racial insulation of White folks that functions to support their own privilege, and the negative reactions about even broaching the subject of race or being made to sit through a workshop on race in the workplace can incite a range of negative and extreme reactions. In effect, White Fragility also may be seen as an automatic, uncritical response to the introduction of critical conversations about race and racism. If we can think of these responses as a continuum of understanding or willingness to engage, White fragility is on the weaker end. Then moving on to guilt. Then on to fatigue.

In contrast to White fragility and White guilt, White fatigue is a response to the intricacies of a social phenomenon that has many constituent parts. Again, the issue is not that a White person does not see the value in understanding racism, but that learning about systemic and institutional racism (which is essential for ameliorating racism and promoting social justice) is very complex and oftentimes learning is truncated at the level of individual racism. This is a sensible problem since there remains a large gap between the theory and practice of multicultural education in U.S. schools at all levels of education (Banks, 2004; Gay, 2010), and schools at all levels have a tendency to privilege less critical forms of multicultural education and curriculum (Flynn, Kemp, & Page, 2013; Gorski, 2009; Sleeter & Grant, 2007; Villegas & Lucas, 2002).

Illustrating this point, Gorski (2009) conducted a study of syllabi from multicultural teacher education courses across the country. Through his analysis of what is taught in these courses, he concluded that multicultural education courses largely focus on pragmatic, hands-on approaches and personal awareness. He states, "most of these syllabi appeared crafted to prepare teachers with cultural sensitivity, tolerance, and multicultural competence. Most of the courses were not designed to prepare teachers to identify or eliminate educational inequities or to create equitable learning environments" (p. 316). In effect, learning about diversity, race, privilege, and social justice is often reduced to an examination of one's soul, and embracing these ideas is not necessarily sound pedagogy and practice but is often experienced as an indictment of students' moral inferiority.

White Fatigue, Racial Battle Fatigue, White People Fatigue Syndrome: Divergent Trajectories

It is key that White fatigue not be confused with concepts like Racial Battle Fatigue or White People Fatigue Syndrome. Racial Battle Fatigue (Smith, 2004; Smith, Hung, & Franklin, 2011; Smith, Yosso, & Solorzano, 2006) is defined as:

> ... An interdisciplinary theoretical framework that considers the increased levels of psychosocial stressors and subsequent psychological (e.g., frustration, shock, anger, disappointment, resentment, hopelessness), physiological (e.g., headache, backache, "butterflies," teeth grinding, high blood pressure, insomnia) and behavioral responses (e.g. stereotype threat, John Henryism, social withdrawal, self-doubt, and a dramatic change in diet) of fighting racial microaggressions in MEES (mundane, extreme, environmental stress). (Smith, Hung, & Franklin, 2011, p. 67)

Racial Battle Fatigue is a concept used to define the manifestation of stress African Americans exhibit in the face of dealing with daily microaggressions enacted by White people. According to Smith's research these challenges and their effects are tangible. He further comments that "African American men, as well as all People of Color, must have competent theoretical understanding of racism, racial microaggressions, and racial battle fatigue in order to dilute their crippling effects on the individual, family, and in the work place" (p. 78). Thus, Racial Battle Fatigue is defined as a phenomenon experienced by all Peoples of Color and is a response to White racism.

Similarly, bell hooks (1992) intoned the notion of White people fatigue syndrome, which predating Smith, encapsulates a likeminded ethic. hooks never actually defined or applied White People Fatigue Syndrome as a theoretical construct. Rather, she reported the use of the term by a colleague at a conference. hooks stated:

> At this same conference, I bonded with a progressive black woman and her companion, a white man. Like me, they were troubled by the extent to which folks chose to ignore the way white supremacy was informing the structure of the conference. Talking with, the black woman, I asked her: "What do you do, when you are tired of confronting white racism, tired of the day-to-day incidental acts of racial terrorism? I mean, how do you deal with coming home to a white person?" Laughing she said, "Oh, you mean when I am suffering from White People Fatigue Syndrome? He gets that more than I do." (p. 177)

Racially minoritized people get tired of explaining to White people (including self-defined White allies) the challenges of racism. In *The Feminist Griote* blog (2013), the blogger personalizes the nature of White People Fatigue Syndrome by stating "I am tired of always having to prove to whites that racism exists. ... I am tired of whites trying to prove to me that they aren't racist, but as soon as it is time for them to interrupt oppression on my behalf, I am on my own" (para. 1).

The frustrations of minoritized groups dealing with racism in its covert and overt forms is a long, storied history, and the ideas of White people fatigue syndrome and Racial Battle Fatigue are important concepts for further understanding the social, psychological, spiritual, and physical effects of dealing with that burden. Simultaneously, as White students are engaged in discourses and discussions about the intricacies of racism and the role of White people in this particular system of oppression, they too begin to feel the weight of the challenge, oftentimes in spite of their own personal attempts to cross borders and boundaries in their personal and professional lives.

White fatigue is a framing of the struggle *White folks* have in both coming to grips with and fully understanding the depth and complexity of systemic and institutional racism. If the experience of race is different for White folks and non-White folks, then we must be willing to recognize the conceptual and spiritual struggle each group uniquely experiences. White fatigue is an attempt to consider the humanity and struggle of White folks that are in the process of gaining a more nuanced understanding of how racism functions, which is not an easy process by any means.

In the United States we have made significant advances in encouraging more egalitarian social practices that reduce prejudice and discrimination, but that does not necessarily translate into a societal understanding of institutional and systemic racism, nor does it translate into a commitment to enact policies, pedagogies, and practices designed to ameliorate racial oppression (all forms of oppression for that matter). Hence, many White students who recognize individual racism feel as though they *get it* and try to encourage, at best, anti-bias and intercultural communication, or, at worst, colorblindness and post-racialism. After all, there is a stream of television shows, movies, magazine articles, and public service announcements that encourage understanding, intercultural communication, and tolerance. However, when the question turns to issues that are reflective of ongoing institutional or systemic racism (i.e. police brutality, voter suppression, un/der-employment, housing segregation, the achievement gap, the school-to-prison pipeline, mass incarceration, etc.) the debates in media and popular culture obfuscate the issues and foster confusion and frustration.

The fatigued are understanding of individual racial bias—which essentially reduces to behaviors of prejudice and discrimination—but have yet to fully grasp the more nuanced and critical ideas of systemic and institutional racism. Although the fatigued may show support for ameliorating systemic and institutional racism, they also struggle with the complexity of the ideas. This is a sharp contrast to White resistance (a rejection of these ideas), and both can be identified at different stages in the process of White Racial Identity Development (Helms, 1993).

Mapping the Location of White Fatigue: White Racial Identity Development and Recasting Stereotype Threat

The framework of White Racial Identity Development (WRID) (Helms, 1993) is an important schema for understanding race and racism, but it must be approached cautiously. The central complicating factor of WRID is that the process of identity development is often presented as a process in which an individual progresses linearly. The reality is that WRID is not always linear and can be messy. Howard (2006) points out that "Helm's description of stages in the development of White racial identity, like any theoretical construct, is merely an approximation of actual experience" (p. 98). An individual's unique experiences and circumstances can throw progression to the final stage, Autonomy, into a tailspin, and the individual can find herself back into the Disintegration or Reintegration stages. Or, it is equally plausible that a stage could be skipped. Regardless, the framework can help us consider the struggles of a person(s) because WRID allows us to locate, and thus differentiate, resistance and fatigue. As Leonardo (2013) posits, Helms

> ... Builds in the dimension of nonlinearity through stages, wherein Whites do not simply travel from point A to B of Whiteness and may revert to previous stages. ... The model ends with a White subject who accepts his or her racial difference as part of a constellation of differences rather than assuming a superior place among them. (p. 104)

Understanding that acceptance of "his or her racial difference as part of a constellation of differences rather than assuming a superior place among them" is the best example of a positive racial identity.

There are six stages of WRID as explicated by Helms. Since WRID has been extensively explored previously (Helms, 1993; McIntyre, 1997; Tatum, 2003; Wijeyesinghe & Jackson, 2012), here I will list the stages, offer a brief definition of each stage, and provide a typical statement reflective of the stage:

1. **Contact**: unexamined racial identity ("We are all the same").
2. **Disintegration**: acknowledges racial differences but does not fully understand racial hierarchies and their implications ("It's too bad that bad stuff happened to them but that was hundreds of years ago; why don't they just get over it already")?

3. **Reintegration:** sustained subconscious or dysconcious (King, 1991) beliefs of White superiority ("I am fine with any race as long as they act right [i.e. act White]").
4. **Pseudo-independence:** recognizes racial oppression and privilege but not fully understanding of systemic and institutional manifestations of racism ("I am not racist, I have friends of all racial backgrounds").
5. **Immersion-Emersion:** understands White complicity in racial oppression and privilege and begins to seek allies ("Oppression is a problem we all can be a part of dealing with").
6. **Autonomy:** fully embraces humanistic ideals of equity and social justice individually, institutionally, and systemically ("Racism persists, here's why, and this is how *we* can work together to eradicate it").

What is most germane about WRID for understanding White fatigue is that as an individual moves through these stages s/he first begins to see oneself as a racialized being, just like the *others*. As one continues to learn about how racism functions one can begin to locate Whiteness as part of a system and the ways in which racial hierarchies have a history and persistence that shapes reality differently for all racial groups and individuals.

White resistance is highly evident in the *Contact, Disintegration, and Reintegration* stages in which there is little to no recognition of race or criticality about racism. White fatigue on the other hand settles in during the Pseudo-independence stage and/or the Immersion-Emersion stage. It is during these stages when an individual makes the shift from a focus on individual manifestations of racism—the individual has become understanding of the idea that actions reflect dispositions—toward the critical examination of how systems and institutions function to shape the contexts in which individuals operate.

As WRID displays, the first three stages are characterized by an immersion into one's own identity, while the latter stages reflect the individual's reengagement as a more socially conscious person. As alluded to earlier, many students begin this process through media, popular culture, personal interactions, and K-12 education long before entering a "diversity course." Unfortunately, the focus on individual manifestations of race and racism is wholly insufficient for understanding and ameliorating racism.

During the latter stages, students may begin to consider their own positionality in the racial hierarchy. They may begin to seriously grapple with the ways in which curricula in U.S. schools privilege White, Eurocentric canons and marginalize minoritized others. During these stages, students may be fascinated with the idea of microaggressions in social spaces. They may begin to understand the

White racial framing of our social contexts (Feagin, 2014). However, oftentimes this is where students also begin to think they *got it.* They have learned and begun to appreciate important perspectives and theories about racism, but their learning has only just begun. Again, they recognize the reality of racism and acknowledge racism as a complex, societal problem, but they have not come to fully understand the depth of the problem, the complicated theories that explain the problem, and the need for sustained interracial healing and cooperation in order to one day eradicate the problem. These shifts beg the question of why is their learning truncated?

Racism: A Complex Phenomenon to Learn

Understanding racism is a transdisciplinary endeavor. In any given course addressing race, diversity, or multiculturalism, educators bring to bear a wide array of terminology, frameworks, and theories from across the academic spectrum: anthropology (Baker, 2010; Geertz, 1977); cultural studies (Bourdieu, 1993; Hall, 1997; Johnson, 2003; San Juan, 2002); psychology (Helms, 1993; Steele, 2003; Tatum, 2003); history (Blackmon, 2009; Ignatiev, 2008; Loewen, 2007; Zinn, 2005); law (Alexander, 2012; Crenshaw, 1991, 1995; Kennedy, 1998); economics (Massey & Denton, 1998; Shapiro, 2005; Wilson, 2012); philosophy (Cesaire, 2000; Fanon, 2005; Sullivan, 2014); public health (Barr, 2008; Farmer, 2004); and sociology (Allen, 2012; MacLeod, 2008). Additionally, particularly in the case of higher education, students are exposed to these ideas in the confines of classes that are typically ten or sixteen weeks in duration. It is rare that these discussions are engaged throughout their academic studies, and students are engaged in these issues only when they have an educator who actively encourages the interrogation of racism (and White privilege) as essential subject matter. Even when academic programs have professional accrediting standards that promote diversity, it is not a guarantee that those lessons will promote a critical lens that moves students beyond a basic understanding of human diversity.

Aggravating this problem is that college classrooms are not the only spaces where conversations about race happen. They are on television, in film, in letters to the editor, in books, on internet message boards, in popular music, on talk shows, in residence hall rooms, on billboards, in comedy clubs, in churches, in bars, around dinner tables. We often spend a great deal of time engaged in teaching our students, particularly White students, what to unlearn. The conversation about race and racism has been ongoing and many students have ideas about race already formed—some of which are well-informed, ill-informed, critical, and resistant. Drawing a distinction between one who is fatigued and one who is resistant allows for the possibility of a more complex representation of students' experiences and self-identification that does not immediately cast them in the negative light of resistant.

White students are often constructed negatively when discussing racism: as oppressors; unconscious receivers of privilege; ignorant to how the world works; and a host of other negative labels. They are told by "experts" to step up and own their privilege and oppressor status. To wit, there is a growing body of literature that challenges the wisdom of the primacy of the White privilege pedagogy (Jupp & Slattery, 2010; Lensmire et al., 2013; Leonardo, 2004). For example, Lensmire et al. (2013), in a recent study that critiques the challenges of using Peggy McIntosh's (1988) watershed essay on White and male privilege, point out that:

> McIntosh's characterization of White privilege tends to simplify and flatten how we think of the racial identities of our White students and ourselves. That is, within White privilege pedagogy, White people are "addressed" as little more than the smooth embodiment of privilege, leaving little room for exploring what is meant that Jessie (one of the study's participants), for example, both feared the Black man approaching her car and rejected that fear in herself and wanted to overcome it. (p. 429)

Although the concept of White privilege is important to our work it can nonetheless produce stifling results for students, even though some students have the understanding that racism is wrong.

This barrage of negative signifiers coalesces into stereotypes for White students that are hard to escape and result in an obvious question: If I am a beneficiary of White privilege and by extension an oppressor or racist, then what is the point? Gary Howard (2006) cautioned against talking about the connection between White people and racism in flatly negative terms, lest it becomes much more difficult for White students to develop a positive racial identity. The consistent construction of White students as oppressors reduces to a stereotype that White students must confront in their learning, and this confrontation develops a host of problems for both students and educators.

Stereotyped Into Silence: Stereotype Threat and White Fatigue

Stereotype threat (Aronson et al., 1999; Steele, 2011; Steele & Aronson, 1995) has become an indispensible construct for explaining why individuals who may otherwise perform a particular task well can perform poorly. Simply, stereotype threat is a contextual phenomenon in which a person feels as though their actions may confirm an existing stereotype about a group to which one belongs, which ultimately hampers performance (Steele & Aronson, 1995). Explaining stereotype threat, Claude Steele (2003) writes:

> This term stressed that the cause of (negative) effects was contextual, the situationally aroused predicament of having a negative stereotype about one's group be relevant to an important performance or behavior. No particular susceptibility of the person seemed necessary to experience this pressure. It could be felt by anyone who cared about a performance and yet knew that any faltering at it could cause them to be reduced to a negative group stereotype. (p. 316)

Stereotype threat is popularly discussed in relation to the performance of minoritized groups, primarily people of color and women (Beasley & Fischer, 2012; Davis, Aronson, & Salinas, 2006; Deemer, Thoman, & Chase, 2014; Fischer, 2010; Mello, Mallett, Andretta, & Worrell, 2012; Tomasetto & Apploni, 2013). However, as Steele points out, stereotype threat appears in *any* context in which *anyone* must deal with a stereotype.

I argue that this phenomenon can also happen to those who are White and/or male—who are typically situated at the zenith of racial and gender privilege. Aronson, Lustina, Good, Keough, Steele, and Brown (1999) support this assertion as evidenced through their study in which White males were told Asian students performed better on a math tests. In this case, the stereotyped White males did in fact perform less well on the math test than did the non-stereotype-threatened control group of White males. Aronson et al. summarize the study's findings by stating:

> It is sufficient to be identified enough with a domain to be threatened by the possibility of limited prospects there and unlucky enough to be on the wrong end of a stereotype about an intellectual ability. And, clearly, if stereotype threat can be aroused in highly able, nonstereotyped students merely by making them aware of a stereotype that predicts lower performance for their group relative to another, then it is not some exotic phenomenon felt only by the members of historically stigmatized groups. (pp. 43–44)

In effect, this research on stereotype threat shows that the threat is not a phenomenon unique to racial or gender minoritized groups. Rather, it is a phenomenon that can occur to any groups (or individuals) who feel that their performance is related to a stereotype.

In my experience, very few want to be associated with the term racist, and the public pillories of Cliven Bundy, Paula Deen, Mel Gibson, Michael Richards, Don Imus, George Zimmerman, and many others is testament to that notion. This is important to understand when considering anti-racist education because, as pointed out above, when the label of racist hangs over the head of a student trying to understand racism they can become hobbled by the association and display a range of negative responses—including resistance, guilt, *and* fatigue. This is not necessarily meant to give White people and White students a "free pass," but to acknowledge *their* struggle in the process of anti-racism and racial identity development.

Expanding on Steele's notion of stereotype threat, Cohen and Garcia (2005) posit the idea of "collective threat." They operationalize collective threats in circumstances wherein:

> Individuals are concerned about the potentially stereotyping confirming acts of other members of their group. We call this concern *collective threat*, as it issues from the collectively shared nature of social identities. We further suggest that in situations where one's group is negatively stereotyped, an "I am us" mindset may arise out of the awareness that the way one is viewed and defined depends, in part, on the way that other group members are viewed and defined. (p. 566)

For White students in the process of transitioning through latter stages of identity development, the notion of collective threat can wedge them into a proverbial conceptual corner and leave them fatigued from the attempt to differentiate themselves from their less thoughtful White counterparts.

The notion of stereotype threat, and by extension collective threat, is not necessarily about *race*, it is about any stereotype and how the realities of stereotypes have tangible effects. This holds true for African Americans, women, and yes, White folks too. Just because White students may be constructed as benefiting from White racism via White privilege, that does not make them any more or less human than minoritized others. Recognizing the primacy of humanity that resides in all is a necessary step in dismantling oppressive systemic and institutional practices that ultimately frame all our lives.

Systems, Humanity, and Love: Choosing a Different Path

Once at a conference on race, a colleague asked a group of us a question that undergirds this essay. He asked, "I wonder how it feels to be White? I mean how would it feel to go through your life believing a bunch of myths and misrepresentations that make you think there is something special about you?" We all looked around at each other and one colleague replied, "It doesn't matter who you are; it always sucks to find out you've been lied too."

And there it is. The discourse around race has been framed as an "us versus them" binary for so long, it has become useless and even distracting. Racism, as a *system* of advantage based on race (Sensoy & DiAngelo, 2012; Tatum, 2003; Wellman, 1993), has been perpetrating physical, emotional, psychological, and spiritual violence on each and every one of us for over 400 years, albeit in drastically differ-ent ways. I say racism has perpetrated violence upon *each* of us because as a system we all occupy roles, dictated by the nature of the system. Have White folks been privileged in this particular system of oppression? Absolutely. Along with that position of privilege, however, White people also have to carry a history of geno-cide, manipulation, force, theft, lying, and dehumanization, all of which they are systematically and institutionally encouraged to disregard. Again, it always "sucks" to be lied too. Racism is and has been painful for all of us; just because one does not necessarily recognize that history and reality does not necessarily mean it is not functioning nor causing further damage. We always use the racism-as-cancer metaphor. Well, many people have cancer festering in their bodies for quite some time before becoming aware of its destruction.

The White racial framing of the United States literally robbed the group that became known as White people a host of *other* possibilities that could have led to a more inclusive and beloved society. And for every crack of the whip on the back of an African, for every Indigenous person forced to abandon her culture in a board-ing school, for every Asian killed under a railroad tie, or every Latina denigrated for speaking her first language, a piece of humanity is stripped from the oppressor. Again, Freire (1970/1997) reminds us that under regimes of oppression both the oppressed *and* the oppressor are dehumanized. In turn, through the process of liberation both the oppressed *and* the oppressor must be humanized, and if the oppressed continues to perpetuate the practices of the oppressor, *no one* is truly liberated.

Now, some may misconstrue these ideas and suggest that I am appeasing White folks, but I reject that notion. As expressed above, the notion of White fatigue is not meant to absolve White folks from any responsibility they have—as a group and individuals—in understanding the realities and complexities of racism in order to help ameliorate racism. We anti-racist, multicultural, and social justice educators must be on the vanguard of helping our communities consider new ways of engaging students while honoring the significant changes over the past fifty years in social relations across borders and boundaries.

As we move forward with further reconceptualizing and honing our anti-rac-ist pedagogies, practices, and research, White fatigue is a way of acknowledging the reality that many White students come into our classes bringing to bear inter-racial experiences, relationships, and understanding. They are bringing into our classes a level of savvy culled from growing up in diverse schools, communities, organizations, and workplaces. They embrace a broad spectrum of media and pop-ular culture, especially hip-hop. And, some students enroll in our classes *knowing* that they need to know more. In order to honor those students, it is essential to inject more nuance about their reactions and struggles that is beyond vulgar resistance or guilt to include those who are understanding of the moral imperative of anti-racism but also wrestling with the challenges of learning that complexity— the fatigued.

Segue: Introducing the Man Who Couldn't Walk on Water, the Man Who Uncovered Our Derision, and the Most Misrepresented Movement

As the Obama era closes and the Trump era begins, we can better reflect on how the current context, which is arguably re-inscribing deeply racist, oppressive, and violent ways reminiscent of not just Detroit or Watts of the 1960s, or Los Angeles of the 1980s and 1990s, but also Reconstruction of post-Civil War America. As 2008 presidential candidate Barack Obama opined in his historic Philadelphia address on race in America during his Democratic nomination campaign, the history of race is a contested history and our current reality is rooted to that history (Obama, 2008).

Since his historic first oath of office in January of 2009 many cities have seen the full force of angered, frustrated protest and activism: New York City; Chicago; Cleveland; Baltimore; Milwaukee; Ferguson, Missouri—places that have burned from the scorch of long-standing systemic and institutional racism. Many more cities and college campuses have all had to flinchingly, cringingly learn some troubling lessons about institutional and systemic racism yet again. Travyon Martin, Eric Garner, Tamir Rice, Sandra Bland, Walter Scott, Tanisha Anderson, and hundreds of other African Americans have been summarily killed, oftentimes unarmed, by our nation's police officers. Movements like #BlackLivesMatter (#BLM) have drawn increased attention to dubious institutional and systemic practices that continue the marginalization of African Americans, specifically, along with other racial and ethnic minorities, like Michael Cho, Adrian Simental, Alfred Rials-Torres, Hector Morejon, Luis Ramirez, Rexdale Henry, Paul Castaway, and more.

What is essential to know about the #BlackLivesMatter movement is that although this is a movement launched by African American, there is a significant interracial support base that includes White folks. Even though conservative leaning news and infotainment outlets like talk radio and FOX News routinely attempts to delegitimize and demonize #BLM and the larger discussion about White racism and White privilege (Cherry, 2015; Reilly, 2016), there is a growing segment of White America calling out these institutional practices and trends as foul. In other words, there are a growing number of White allies, accomplices, and leaders, perhaps slowly growing but growing nonetheless.

This trend illustrates the fact that the pedagogical consideration advocated here is important and necessary if we really want to affect change and grow together as/in a pluralistic society. At the same time, the counter-current of White resistance is strong and the election of Donald Trump in 2016, in part, is reflective of that backlash. However, that backlash was not inclusive of all White folks. Even though there continues to be a great divide in the ways in which White and non-White Americans (particularly African Americans) view race relations, significant numbers of White folks know racism when they see it and care about it, as will be detailed in the following chapter by considering the racial rhetoric of President Barack Obama, the embrace of the #BlackLivesMatter movement, and the counter-rhetoric of newly elected President Donald Trump.

Note

1. This chapter is reprinted with permission from Taylor and Francis. Although reprinted, there have been some revision from the original article. Specifically, the original article attempted to draw sharp distinction between White fatigue and White resistance. In this version, White fatigue has been reconceptualized to be a quasi form of White resistance that begs further investigation and consideration in teaching contexts.

Bibliography

Allen, T. W. (2012). *The invention of the White race* (2nd ed.). New York, NY: Verso.

Alexander, M. (2012). *The new Jim Crow: Mass incarceration in the age of colorblindness.* New York, NY: The New Press.

Aptheker, H. (1993). *Anti-racism in U.S. history: The first two hundred years.* Westport, CT: Praeger.

Aronson, J., Lustina, M. J., Good, C., Keough, K., Steele, C. M., & Brown, J. (1999). When white men can't do math: Necessary and sufficient factors in stereotype threat. *Journal of Experimental Psychology, 35*, 29–46.

Baker, L. D. (2010). *Anthropology and the racial politics of culture.* Durham, NC: Duke University Press.

Banks, J. (2004). Multicultural education: Historical development, dimensions, and practice. In J. A. Banks & C. McGee Banks (Eds.), *Handbook of research on multicultural education* (pp. 3–29). San Francisco, CA: Jossey Bass.

Barr, D. A. (2008). *Health disparities in the United States: Social class, race, ethnicity, and health.* Baltimore, MD: Johns Hopkins University Press.

Battalora, J. (2013). *Birth of a White nation: The invention of White people and its relevance today.* Houston, TX: Strategic Book Publishing and Rights.

Baunach, D. M. (2002). Progress, opportunity, and backlash: Explaining attitudes toward gender-based affirmative action. *Sociological Focus, 35*(4), 345–362.

Beasley, M. A., & Fischer, M. J. (2012). Why they leave: The impact of stereotype threat on the attrition of women and minorities from science, math and engineering majors. *Social Psychology of Education: An International Journal, 15*(4), 427–448.

Bhattacharyya, G., Gabriel, J., & Small, S. (2002). *Race and power: Global racism in the twenty-first century.* New York, NY: Routledge.

Blackmon, D. A. (2009). *Slavery by another name: The re-enslavement of Black Americans from the Civil War to World War II* (Reprint ed.). Rockland, MA: Anchor Press.

Bonilla-Silva, E. (2013). *Racism without racists: Color-blind racism and the persistence of racial inequality in America.* Lanham, MD: Rowman & Littlefield.

Bonilla-Silva, E., & Dietrich, D. (2011, January 1). The sweet enchantment of color blind racism in Obamerica. *The Annals of the American Academy of Political and Social Science, 634*, 190–206.

Bourdieu, P. (1993). *The field of cultural production.* New York, NY: Columbia University Press.

Boyle-Baise, M. (1999). Bleeding boundaries or uncertain center? An historical exploration of the field of multicultural education. *Journal of Curriculum and Supervision, 14*(3), 191–215.

Brinker, L. (2014, October 1). 7 disgustingly racist anti-Obama cartoons. *Slate.com.* Retrieved from http://www.salon.com/2014/10/01/7_disgustingly_racist_anti_obama_cartons_2/

Capehart, J. (2014, December 29). The fallacy of a "post-racial" society. *The Washington Post.* Retrieved from https://www.washingtonpost.com/blogs/post-partisan/wp/2014/12/29/the-fallacy-of-a-post-racial-society/

Cesaire, A. (2000). *Discourse on colonialism.* New York, NY: Monthly Review Press.

Cherry, T. (2015, December 29). How Fox News' primetime lineup demonized Black Lives Mater in 2015. *Media Matters for America.* Retrieved from https://mediamatters.org/blog/2015/12/29/how-fox-news-primetime-lineup-demonized-black-l/207637

Coates, T. (2014, June). The case for reparations. *The Atlantic.* Retrieved from http://www.theatlantic.com/magazine/archive/2014/06/the-case-for-reparations/361631/

Cohen, G. L., & Garcia, J. (2005). "I am us": Negative stereotypes as collective threats. *Journal of Personality and Social Psychology, 98*(4), 566–582.

Crenshaw, K. (1991). Mapping the margins: Intersectionality, identity politics, and violence against women of color. *Stanford Law Review, 43*(6), 1241–1299.

Crenshaw, K. (1995). Mapping the margins: Intersectionality, identity politics, and violence against women of color. In K. Crenshaw, N. Gotanda, G. Peller, & K. Thomas (Eds.), *Critical race theory: The key writings that formed the movement* (pp. 357–383). New York, NY: New Press.

Davis, C., III, Aronson, J., & Salinas, M. (2006). Shades of threat: Racial identity as a moderator of stereotype threat. *Journal of Black Psychology, 32*(4), 399–417.

Deemer, E. D., Thoman, D. B., & Chase, J. P. (2014). Feeling the threat: Stereotype threat as a contextual barrier to women's science career choice intentions. *Journal of Career Development, 41*(2), 141–158.

Delpit, L. D. (1988). The silenced dialogue: Power and pedagogy in educating other people's children. *Harvard Educational Review, 58*(3), 280–298.

DiAngelo, R. (2011). White fragility. *International Journal of Critical Pedagogy, 3*(3), 54–70.

Fanon, F. (2005). *The wretched of the earth* (Reprint ed.). New York, NY: Grove Press.

Farmer, P. (2004). *Pathologies of power: Health, human rights, and the new war on the poor.* Berkley, CA: University of California Press.

Feagin, J. (2013). *The White racial frame: Centuries of racial framing and counter framing* (2nd ed.). New York, NY: Routledge.

Feagin, J. (2014). *Racist America: Roots, current realities, and future reparations* (3rd ed.). New York, NY: Routledge.

The Feminist Griote. (2013, April 23). White people fatigue syndrome [Web log comment]. Retrieved from http://thefeministgriote.com/white-people-fatigue-syndrome/

Flynn, J. E., Kemp, A. T., & Page, C. S. (2013). Promoting philosophical diversity: Exploring racial differences in beliefs about the purposes of education. *Journal of the Texas Alliance for Black School Educators, 5,* 53–71.

Fischer, M. J. (2010). A longitudinal examination of the role of stereotype threat and racial climate on college outcomes for minorities at elite institutions. *Social Psychology of Education: An International Journal, 13*(1), 19–40.

Frank, A. (1952/1993). Anne Frank: The diary of a young girl. New York, NY: Bantam Books.

Fredrickson, G. (2002). *Racism: A short history.* Princeton, NJ: Princeton University Press.

Freire, P. (1970/1997). *Pedagogy of the oppressed* (New revised 20th anniversary ed.). New York, NY: Continuum.

Gay, G. (2010). *Culturally responsive teaching: Theory, research, and practice* (2nd ed.). New York, NY: Teachers College Press.

Geertz, C. (1977). *The interpretation of cultures.* New York, NY: Basic Books.

Goodman, D. J. (2011). *Promoting diversity and social justice: Educating people from privileged groups* (2nd ed.). New York, NY: Routledge.

Gorski, P. (2009). What we're teaching teachers: An analysis of multicultural teacher education coursework syllabi. *Teaching and Teacher Education, 25*(2009), 309–318.

Hall, S. (1997). *Representation: Cultural representations and signifying practices.* Thousand Oaks, CA: Sage Publications.

Helms, J. E. (1993). *Black and White racial identity: Theory, research, and practice.* Westport, CT: Praeger.

Hitchcock, J. (2002). *Lifting the White veil: An exploration of White American culture in a multiracial context.* Roselle, NJ: Crandall, Dostie & Douglass Books.

hooks, b. (1992). *Black looks: Race and representation.* Boston, MA: South End Press.

hooks, b. (1996). *Killing rage: Ending racism.* New York, NY: Holt Paperbacks.

Howard, G. R. (2006). *We can't teach what we don't know: White teachers, multiracial schools* (2nd ed.). New York, NY: Teachers College Press.

Ignatiev, N. (2008). *How the Irish became White.* New York, NY: Routledge.

Johnson, E. P. (2003). *Appropriating blackness: Performance and the politics of authenticity.* Durham, NC: Duke University Press.

Kennedy, R. (1998). *Race, crime, and the law.* New York, NY: Vintage Press.

King, J. E. (1991). Dysconscious racism: Ideology, identity, and the miseducation of teachers. *The Journal of Negro Education, 60*(2), 133–146.

Kranze, D., & Roth, R. (Producers), & Mulligan, R. (Director). (1971). *Summer of '42* [Motion picture]. United States: Warner Bros.

Ledwidge, M., & Verney, K. (2013). *Barack Obama and the myth of a post-racial America*. New York, NY: Routledge.

Lensmire, T. J., McManimon, S. K., Tierney, J. D., Lee-Nichols, M. E., Casey, Z. A., Lensmire, A., & Davis, B. M. (2013). McIntosh as synecdoche: How teachereducation's focus on White privilege undermines antiracism. *Harvard Educational Review, 83*, 410–431. http://dx.doi.org/10.17763/haer.83.3.35054h1418230574

Leonardo, Z. (2013). *Race frameworks: A multidimensional theory of racism and education*. New York, NY: Teachers College Press.

Lentin, A. (2004). *Race and anti-racism in Europe*. London: Pluto Press.

Leonardo, Z. (2004). The color of supremacy: Beyond the discourse of "white privilege." *Educational Philosophy and Theory, 36*(2), 137–152.

Lewis, P. (2008, July 14). New Yorker's "terrorist" Obama cover under fire. *Theguardian.com*. Retrieved from http://www.theguardian.com/world/deadlineusa/2008/jul/14/newyorkercovr

Loewen, J. W. (2007). *Lies my teacher told me: Everything your American history textbook got wrong* (Revised ed.). New York, NY: Touchstone Books.

MacLeod, J. (2008). *Ain't no makin' it: Aspirations and attainment in a low income neighborhood* (3rd ed.). Boulder, CO: Westview Press.

MacMaster, N. (2001). *Racism in Europe: 1870–2000*. Basingstoke, UK: Palgrave.

Massey, D. S., & Denton, N. A. (1998). *American apartheid: Segregation and the making of the underclass*. Cambridge, MA: Harvard University Press.

McIntosh, P. (1988). White privilege and male privilege: A personal account of coming to see correspondences through work in women's studies. In M. L. Anderson & P. Hill-Collins (Eds.), *Race, class, and gender: An anthology* (pp. 70–81). Wellesley, MA: Wellesley College Center for Research on Women.

McIntyre, A. (1997). *Making meaning of whiteness: Exploring racial identity with white teachers*. Albany, NY: State University of New York Press.

Mello, Z. R., Mallett, R. K., Andretta, J. R., & Worrell, F. C. (2012). Stereotype threat and school belonging in adolescents from diverse racial/ethnic backgrounds. *Journal of At-Risk Issues, 17*(1), 9–14.

Moore, P. (2014, June 2). *Overwhelming opposition to reparations for slavery and Jim Crow*. Retrieved from https://today.yougov.com/news/2014/06/02/reparations/

National Commission on Excellence in Education. (1983). *A nation at risk: The imperative for educational reform*. Washington, DC: United States Department of Education.

New, J. (2015, March 25). About time? *Inside Higher Education*. Retrieved from https://www.insidehighered.com/news/2015/03/25/after-racist-video-u-oklahoma-hire-chief-diversity-officer

Obama, B. (2008). *A more perfect union* [speech]. Retrieved from http://www.npr.org/templates/story/story.php?storyId=88478467

The Opinion Pages: Room for Debate [Editorial]. (2011, September 21). Under Obama, is America "post-racial"? *The New York Times.* Retrieved from http://www.nytimes.com/roomfordebate/2011/09/21/under-obama-is-america-post-racial

Patterson, O. (1997). *The ordeal of integration: Progress and resentment in America's "racial" crisis.* Washington, DC: Civitas Counterpoint.

Pettigrew, T. F. (1998). Reactions toward the new minorities of western Europe. *Annual Review of Sociology, 24,* 77–103.

Reilly, M. (2016, July 8). Rush Limbaugh: Black lives matter is a "terrorist group." *The Huffington Post.* Retrieved from http://www.huffingtonpost.com/entry/rush-limbaugh-black-lives-matter_us_577fd49de4b0344d514f0c95

San Juan, E., Jr. (2002). *Racism and cultural studies: Critiques of multiculturalist ideology and the politics of difference.* Durham, NC: Duke University Press.

Sensoy, O., & DiAngelo, R. (2012). *Is everyone really equal? An introduction to key concepts in social justice education.* New York, NY: Teachers College Press.

Shapiro, T. M. (2005). *The hidden cost of being African American: How wealth perpetuates inequality.* New York, NY: Oxford University Press.

Sleeter, C., & Grant, C. (2007). Making choices for multicultural education: Five approaches to race, class, and gender (6th ed.). Hoboken, NJ: John Wiley & Sons Publishing.

Smedley, A., & Smedley, B. D. (2012). *Race in North America: Origin and evolution of a worldview.* Boulder, CO: Westview Press.

Smith, W. A. (2004). Black faculty coping with racial battle fatigue: The campus racial climate in a post-civil rights era. In D. Cleveland (Ed.), *A long way to go: Conversations about race by African American faculty and graduate students* (pp. 171–190). Thousand Oaks, CA: Sage.

Smith, W. A., Hung, M., & Franklin, J. D. (2011). Racial battle fatigue and the miseducation of Black men: Racial microaggressions, societal problems, and environmental stress. *The Journal of Negro Education, 80*(1), 63–82.

Smith, W. A., Yosso, T. J., & Solorzano, D. G. (2006). Challenging racial battle fatigue on historically White campuses: A critical race examination of race-related stress. In C. A. Stanley (Ed.), *Faculty of color teaching in predominantly White colleges and universities* (pp. 299–327). Bolton, MA: Anker.

Speri, A. (2014, December 9). Half of America thinks we live in a post-racial society—the other half, not so much. *Vice News.* Retrieved from https://news.vice.com/article/half-of-america-thinks-we-live-in-a-postracial-society-the-other-half-not-so-much

Steele, C. M. (2003). Through the back door to theory. *Psychological Inquiry, 14*(3/4), 314–317.

Steele, C. M. (2011). *Whistling Vivaldi: How stereotypes affect us and what we can do* (Reprint ed.). New York, NY: W. W. Norton.

Steele, C. M., & Aronson, J. (1995). Stereotype threat and the intellectual test performance of African Americans. *Journal of Personality and Social Psychology, 69,* 797–811.

Sullivan, S. (2014). *Good White people: The problem with middle-class White anti-racism.* Albany, NY: State University of New York Press.

Tatum, B. D. (1994). Teaching White students about racism: The search for White allies and the restoration of hope. *Teachers College Record, 95*(4), 462–467.

Tatum, B. D. (2003). *Why are all the Black kids sitting together in the cafeteria: And other conversations about race* (5th anniversary revised ed.). New York, NY: Basic Books.

Tomasetto, C., & Apploni, S. (2013). A lesson not to be learned? Understanding stereotype threat does not protect women from stereotype threat. *Social Psychology of Education: An International Journal, 16*(2), 199–213.

Urbanski, D. (2013, December 3). The "ape-like" Obama depiction that landed a cartoonist in hot water. … But it's not about what you think. *The Blaze.com.* Retrieved from http://www.theblaze.com/stories/2013/12/03/the-ape-like-obama-depiction that-landed-a-cartoonist-in-hot-water-but-its-not-about-what-you-think/

Villegas, A., & Lucas, T. (2002). *Educating culturally responsive teachers: A cohesive approach.* Albany, NY: State University of New York Press.

Washburn, G., & Garrett, C. (2001, May 20). Races differ on reparations: Very few whites, most blacks want slavery redress. *Chicago Tribune.* Retrieved from http://articles.chicagotribune.com/2001-0520/news/0105200360_1_reparationswhites-slavery

Wellman, D. (1993). *Portraits of White racism.* New York, NY: Cambridge University Press.

Welsh, D. (2010). *The rise and fall of apartheid.* Charlottesville, VA: University of Virginia Press.

Wijeyesinghe, C. L., & Jackson, B. W. (Eds.). (2012). *New perspectives on racial identity development: Integrating emerging frameworks* (2nd ed.). New York, NY: New York University Press.

Wilson, W. J. (2012). *The truly disadvantaged: The inner city, the underclass, and public policy* (2nd ed.). Chicago, IL: University of Chicago Press.

Wise, T. (1998, September 23). Is sisterhood conditional?: White women and the rollback of affirmative action. *National Women's Studies Association Journal, 10*(3), 1–26.

Wise, T. (2010). *Colorblind: The rise of post-racial politics and the retreat from racial equity.* San Francisco, CA: City Lights Books.

Zinn, H. (2005). *A people's history of the United States.* New York, NY: Harper Perennial Modern Classics.

CHAPTER THREE

From Obama to Trump

Tripping Over Post-Racial America's Intentions

(My story) is a story that has seared into my genetic makeup the idea that this nation is more than the sum of its parts—that out of many, we are truly one.

—BARACK OBAMA (2008)

We are committed to collectively, lovingly, and courageously working vigorously for freedom and justice for Black people and by extension all people. As we forge our path we intentionally build and nurture a beloved community that is bonded together through a beautiful struggle that is restorative, not depleting.

—A #BLACKLIVESMATTER GUIDING PRINCIPLE (N.D.)

I will build a great wall—and nobody builds walls better than me, believe me ...

—DONALD J. TRUMP (KOPAN, 2016)

It is essential that educators of all stripes pay close attention to popular culture and engage in the stories outside education lest we continuously stay behind the issues and ideas that pervade our students' realities, and we must use these instances as tools to encourage conversations and transdisciplinary learning opportunities. Over the past decade there has been an incessant stream of opportunities to popularly, personally, and pedagogically examine racism's dynamics and realities. From the Seattle Seahawk's, Stanford University educated cornerback Richard Sherman described as a thug after celebrating an amazing win leading to the Super Bowl, to increased attention to the mass incarceration of Black and Brown citizens, to protests over the lack of representation of minorities at the Oscars (a trend that has begun to turn, albeit like an aircraft carrier) to the revelation of Rachel Dolezal—arguably the first White person on record attempting to pass as Black (and John Howard Griffin, the writer of *Black Like Me* (1962/2010), doesn't count since that was an experiment)—to Colin Kaepernick kneeling during the national anthem in silent protest over the maintenance of systemic and institutional racism in its various forms, to the rise in the visibility of the shootings of unarmed citizens (particularly African Americans) by law enforcement, the conversation about race and racism has been front and center, as it always has been.

That list is by no means exhaustive, but it is reflective of the breadth of racial issues that arose in popular culture and featured in the public discourse on race on morning and late night talk shows, pundit programs, and the news itself. The unfortunate thing is that oftentimes these moments of national education on race and racial literacy devolved into arguments about legitimacy. I find it funny that the nation can largely admit that race has been and continues to be a problem (Race relations; Hartig, Lapinski, & Psyllos, 2016) but many are remiss to admit racism when victims of racism point it out. This phenomenon is far more prevalent among White folks than any other racial group (Race relations) and that trend has persisted for decades. However, there are other ways to look at the current racial climate. Jim Norman (2016) of Gallup summarized the findings of a poll on race relations taken in early 2016 as follows:

> Race relations may not worry as many Americans as do issues such as the economy, affordable health care or crime, but Gallup's polling clearly shows that racial tensions over the past few years have significantly affected public opinion.
>
> Not only are far more Americans—no matter their race or political beliefs—worried about race relations, Americans have also become less satisfied with the way Blacks are treated and more likely to list race relations as the most important problem the nation faces. (paras. 5 and 6)

Arguably though, despite the incessant stream of race related stories, the most substantial development and factor on race relations in the United States is the 2008 election of Barack Hussein Obama, the first African American president (well, the first non-White American, at least).

In the immediate wake of the election of President Obama, the nation was abuzz with the hope that his ascendency signaled the ushering in of a new racial age—the age of post-racial America (McWhorter, 2008; Nagourney, 2008). Unfortunately, that buzz wore off quickly. The Southern Poverty Law Center found a spike in hate crimes almost immediately after that historic election (Bigg, 2008). Political unrest and disagreement is a norm in the United States; all presidents suffer their fair share of slings and arrows from citizens. All presidents are also lampooned. However, criticisms against President Obama often had a tinge of—and sometimes full on—racial insensitivity. Signs and placards at rallies, political cartoons, magazine covers, off the cuff statements on news programs, and a host of other incidents emerged, even before he actually won the election!

This is a strange context for those struggling to understand race and racism. On one hand we witnessed an historic event in race relations, or should I say interracial relations. After all, President Obama won a majority of the White vote (twice, by the way). By the same token, polls showed some Whites voted for him for economic reasons but continued to harbor negative feelings toward African Americans in general (Wise, 2009). So, albeit a simple question for some of us, how can a Black man win the presidency but there still be racism is a complex question for some, and understanding those dynamics, even if you are inclined to be supportive of anti-racism, can be challenging. I have had many conversations with students and others in which the beginning phrase of a stream of questions is, "But what about … But what about … But what about … But what about … ?" It is not necessarily the case that these "but what about" queries are asked out of resistance but because the explanations we offer tend to counter what they have always been told or surmised on their own.

The election of Barack Obama most definitely ushered in a new age in race relations, but much to the chagrin of millions of citizens our current era is not marked by post-racialism. To the contrary, this new racial age is much more critical and engaged for some, and recalcitrant and uncritical for others. In the following chapter I will consider three important aspects of race, racism, and our national engagement/discussion: President Obama's racial message; the influence of the #BlackLivesMatter movement; and the rise of Donald Trump as a backlash against Obama. What is key to always remember is that despite what can oftentimes seem like frustrating polling numbers, the numbers also show a growing number of concerned and committed White folks that understand the moral imperative of racial social justice. It is necessary to stay attentive to this fact in order to continue to recruit and educate those who can be allies, accomplices, and leaders in the struggle against racial oppression, and the language we use can serve as either a hindrance or an encouragement in this intellectual and spiritual struggle.

Damned If You Do; Damned If You Don't: The Challenge of Being the First Black President Talking About Race

March 18, 2008 was a watershed moment in both the general history of the United States and the history of our national race relations. In the wake of allegedly controversial statements by the Reverend Jeremiah Wright, leader of Trinity United Church of Christ in Chicago, Illinois and the minister of the political wunderkind Barack Obama, then Senator Obama delivered arguably one of the most profound and substantial statements on race in America by any politician in quite some time. A clip of Reverend Wright repeatedly shouting "God damn America" was leaked to the media and, of course, caused an uproar, to say the least.[1] In the forty-five minute-long speech, entitled *A More Perfect Union*, Senator Obama offered the public a reasoned location and explanation of the current state of race relations. In simple and direct statements, he reminds (or reveals depending on who you are) a history of institutional and systemic racism—White racism specifically—that has hampered progress in Black and Latinx communities, adding much needed texture to Reverend Wright's allegedly inflammatory rhetoric. A longer clip of the sermon was later distributed that gave much-needed context to Reverend Wright's powerful declarations. However, the damage had already been done, and a significant portion of White America had questioned how could anyone sit and listen to such assumed vitriol. Senator Obama did not exhibit support for Reverend Wright's more so-called radical views, but Obama helped explain to the electorate how and why Rev. Wright's views were shaped.

Senator Obama's speech did not stop there. He used this platform not merely as a bully pulpit to ward off criticism from conservative media and political rivals but as a rallying cry to encourage all Americans to actively engage in order to heal our racial divide. In the speech he stated:

> The fact is that the comments that have been made and the issues that have surfaced over the last few weeks reflect the complexities of race in this country that we've never really worked through—a part of our union that we have not yet made perfect. And if we walk away now, if we simply retreat into our respective corners, we will never be able to come together and solve challenges like health care or education or the need to find good jobs for every American. (Obama, 2008, para. 25)

He went on to explore how systemic and institutional racism created a bevy of hurdles that ultimately degraded opportunities for Black Americans, and he went on to offer credence to the frustrations of White Americans, specifically middle and working class White Americans, and the collective vexation about ideas like White privilege. After all, how can one be privileged when one struggles just like everyone else? Obama validates their perspective by saying:

> Most working- and middle-class white Americans don't feel that they have been particularly privileged by their race. Their experience is the immigrant experience—as far as they're concerned, no one handed them anything. They built it from scratch. They've worked hard all their lives, many times only to see their jobs shipped overseas

or their pensions dumped after a lifetime of labor. They are anxious about their futures, and they feel their dreams slipping away. And in an era of stagnant wages and global competition, opportunity comes to be seen as a zero sum game, in which your dreams come at my expense. (Obama, 2008, para. 33)

It is clear that Senator Obama was laying a foundation through this speech and he does so like a cat on a high fence. On one side of the fence he could possibly alienate non-White Americans by substantiating White anger and resentment. On the other side of the fence he could possibly alienate White Americans by encouraging them to truly consider the damage of institutional and systemic racism on non-White communities and the lasting reverberations of generations of inequitable, unfair, and inhumane treatment at the hand of White folks. He goes on to clarify to White Americans the kind of work that needs to be done to move our society forward racially:

> In the white community, the path to a more perfect union means acknowledging that what ails the African-American community does not just exist in the minds of black people; that the legacy of discrimination—and current incidents of discrimination, *while less overt* than in the past—are real and must be addressed, not just with words, but with deeds, by investing in our schools and our communities; by enforcing our civil rights laws and ensuring fairness in our criminal justice system; by providing this generation with ladders of opportunity that were unavailable for previous generations. *It requires all Americans to realize that your dreams do not have to come at the expense of my dreams; that investing in the health, welfare and education of black and brown and white children will ultimately help all of America prosper.* (Obama, 2008, para. 41) (Emphasis added)

Future President Obama reminded (or informed) the nation that racism has a long history that has had lasting and current effects on the targets of marginalization. Furthermore, he issued challenges to both the non-White and White communities to be more mindful in tending to the matters over which they have control and to educate one another about how the past aggravates the present and hinders future progress. What is most essential to take away from President Obama's statement on race is that he makes an important move. He explains the importance of history for historically marginalized Americans, rationalizes the frustrations of White Americans, issues challenges for all communities, and ultimately ties us all together. (On a personal note, it's a damn good speech)! Mr. Obama recognizes that race relations will not move forward without the understanding and engagement of *a critical mass* of Americans. After all, as we say, "E pluribus unum."

Pardon Me Mr. President, But Please Allow Me to Be Critical ...

Despite the power and scope of the 2008 speech, Mr. Obama pulled some truly important punches. Although he situated many White Americans as seeing the world through the lens of an immigrant's experience and earning what one has through the sweat of the brow, Mr. Obama ought to have used a few minutes to offer concrete examples of how institutional and systemic racism advanced the status of European immigrants and White citizens at the expense of non-Whites, and how those actions and policies have a lasting, reverberating impact on non-White *and* White communities.

He did not talk about housing discrimination, redlining, block busting, and inequitable distribution of Federal Housing Authority loans from the 1930s into the 1970s (Massey & Denton, 1993; Mehlhorn, 1998). He did not talk about the legions of African Americans and Latinxs systematically denied admission into higher education across the 20th century, let alone fair and equitable K-12 educational opportunities. He did not talk about the gerrymandering of predominantly historically marginalized communities to the extent their collective votes mean little in elections. He did not talk about *historic* attempts to disenfranchise Black and Brown voters, despite the Voting Rights Act of 1965. He did not talk about the consistent fear mongering of young Black and Latino males. He did not talk about the damaging impact of the Violent Crime Control and Law Enforcement Act of 1994, the War-on-Drugs, nor the privatization of prisons and mass incarceration of Black and Latinx communities.

In retrospect, his speech laid a foundation for a critical conversation, but he ultimately left a number of dots unconnected. If Senator Obama's speech was intended to open a dialog for understanding race and racism he would have done those things, as those issues are not necessarily taught through your typical K-12 school curriculum and are vital to understanding racism as a system of advantage. For example, recently after teaching a graduate class about the practice of redlining, a student commented that even though she is just over fifty years old, a graduate students, *and* a teacher, she had never heard of the practice. When she told her husband, he refused to believe redlining was true, until he randomly saw it discussed on a TV show a couple of weeks later!

Opening a dialogue was only part of Senator Obama's purpose. The other part was damage control—to placate White voters and make them more comfortable with him as a candidate, given the rancorous reaction many had to Reverend Wright's decontextualized comments. Therefore he did not engage the more critical perspectives about the role of White folks, historically and currently, in the maintenance of our historic racial hierarchy and racism. He pulled his moral and educational punches in favor of political points.

Notwithstanding my own enthusiasm at a politician who could stand flat-footed and racially critique the nation, it was popularly argued that he was the only politician that could pull off such a statement, despite its flaws. After all—as regularly reminded in this speech, his book *Dreams From My Father* (Obama, 2004), and throughout the campaign trail—Mr. Obama is the child of a White mother and Black (Kenyan) father, and reared by White grandparents in the wake of his mother's untimely and tragic death from cancer during his adolescence. Many felt that his biracial identity could make him a safe and reliable conduit for engaging a national conversation about race. Unfortunately, too much hope and promise was laid at his feet, and his meteoric rise in national politics, culminating with winning the presidency, became the assumed proof that the nation has moved past race; we are now post-racial America. But of course, the proleptic post-racial America was a complete overestimation and flew in the face of what has happened in the country since the 2009 inauguration.

The Myth of a Post-Racial America and the Sting of the Backlash

In the months leading up to the historic election in November of 2008, a recurrent question bandied about in media was, "Are we ready for a Black president?" (To be fair, during the Democratic nomination campaign, the nation also asked "Are we ready for a woman as president?) Asking the question alone is dubious and begs an answer of no (otherwise why would we even have to ask the question)! As he won the election and began his first term in office, President Obama was met with the realities of the entrenched racism that rages just below the surface of our national consciousness. From claims that President Obama was not born in this country to false claims that he was secretly a Muslim, President Obama has been the object of intense racially based ridicule that seemed to stick for significant numbers of White conservatives.

Placards and signs held up by protesters and political cartoons have depicted President Obama (and First Lady Michelle Obama) as classic racist caricatures. A Google search of "Racist images Obama" yields troubling and startling (depending on who you are) results. On the Def Shepard blog, posted October 19, 2012, images and messages about President Obama include: the Obama buck (a $10.00 food stamp depicting President Obama dressed as a donkey with Mr. Kool-Aid, a watermelon, a rack of ribs, and a bucket of chicken); "Obama is my slave;" "Put the white back in the White House;" "Don't re-nig in 2012;" "Hang in there Obama" (printed next to a picture of a noose); and President Obama pictured in Black-face with an unkempt afro, a bucket of fried chicken and a watermelon with the caption, "Lawdy I sho love campainnin" (Sheppard, 2012.) There are many more littered across the Internet. President Obama, at least publicly, writes off this racist vitriol, and rarely talks about the personal feelings of the First Family, short of intoning that politics is risky business and one must have a "thick skin," or "When they go low, we go high."

Public officials do need a thick skin, but President Obama's often needed to be three-ply and steel reinforced. In addition to racist messages at Tea Party rallies, consider a few of the unprecedented actions against the first African American president:

- Congressman Joe Wilson of South Carolina shouted "You lie!" at the President during a speech on healthcare before a joint session of Congress.
- Arizona governor, Jan Brewer, shoved a finger in President Obama's face on the tarmac and shouted her frustrations over the immigration debate. She later went on to claim she "felt a little bit threatened" by the first Black president despite having described him as cordial and positive (Coard, 2012).
- Former Speaker of the House of Representatives, Newt Gingrich, referred to President Obama as "the most successful food stamp president in American history."
- Repeated attempts to define President Obama as "foreign" or "alien" (Burke, 2012). These claims were initially started by a staffer for Secretary Hillary Clinton, Mr. Obama's opponent for the Democratic nomination, but Secretary Clinton found the accusation beyond the pale. But then, Sarah Palin, former governor of Alaska and Republican vice-presidential nominee in the 2008 election, took the ball and the claims proliferated throughout Republican circles and right-wing media, fueling the fire of Donald Trump's birther claims.
- The July 21, 2008 cover of the *New Yorker* depicted the Obamas as terrorists (with a portrait of Osama Bin Laden and the U.S. flag burning in the fire place of the Oval Office) giving each other dap (also known as a "fist bump"). Then candidate Obama is drawn dressed in traditional Muslim attire while Mrs. Obama is depicted sporting an afro, combat boots, and a machine gun over her shoulder. David Remnick, longtime editor of the *New Yorker* defended the cover art, pointing out its sarcasm. He told CNN's "The Situation Room," "The idea is to attack lies and misconceptions and distortions about the Obamas and their background and their politics" (Mooney, 2008). Despite *The New Yorker's* sophisticated attempt at satire, many just found the cover funny, dismissing the satirical implications.

Many, especially African Americans, were not under any illusions about the potential backlash that could happen with the election of the first African American president (Blake, 2008). To this point, former President Jimmy Carter highlighted the racial animus at the heart of the backlash and criticism of President Obama. He said, "I think an overwhelming portion of the intensely demonstrated animosity toward President Barack Obama is based on the fact that he is a Black man, that he's African American" (MacAskill, 2009, para. 3). President Carter went further, saying:

> I live in the South, and I've seen the South come a long way, and I've seen the rest of the country that shared the South's attitude toward minority groups at that time, particularly African Americans. And that racism inclination still exists. And I think it's bubbled up to the surface because of the belief among many White people, not just in the South but around the country, that African Americans are not qualified to lead this great country. (paras. 6–7)

Given the fact that so many White folks chose to believe xenophobic and racially charged rumors about President Obama, based purely on speculation and misinformation, seeing the overt racist implications is not a stretch. What is necessary for all of us to recognize though, is that not all members of the White American community supported such ludicrous aspersions and actions. Many White folks stood in protest against the racist vitriol directed at the First Family, and many are on the front lines of fighting for racial understanding and growth.

Noted anti-racist educator and activist Tim Wise (2009) offered the White American community a bold and necessary challenge. He stated:

> Just as Obama has issued a challenge to Black folks to be more responsible for the problems in their communities—in part a message he sincerely believes, of course, but also one intended to make Whites more comfortable with his candidacy—so too must Whites take personal responsibility for ongoing racism, racial injustice, and the unearned privileges we continue to reap as a result. In other words, while it is certainly advisable for persons of color to take responsibility for their lives, no matter the presence of racism, it is just as important for Whites to take responsibility for our mess, including the mess of racism and privilege, irrespective of how we believe (often incorrectly) Black and Brown folks are behaving. Personal responsibility is a two-way street, in other words. (p. 12)

Tim Wise is on point here. An inconvenient truth White folks must grapple with is the historic fact that these ideas—race, racism, White people, Whiteness—were created by their forbearers and regularly perpetuated systemically and institutionally until they distilled into individuals' actions and self-concept across time. In other words, White people created the group called *White people* themselves and then created policies and social practices that secured themselves at the top of a manufactured racial hierarchy for centuries. By the same token it is essential for all of us to recognize that White folks today are *also* products of that history and occupy a particular space in this system of racism. Just as systemic and institutional racism has marginalized non-White folks, White folks have been inundated with messages that reinscribe privilege and particular discourses that mask systemic and institutional racism—like the myth of meritocracy, the primacy of western Europe in world history, the White beauty myth, or the myth of rugged individualism. As will be discussed later, the American curriculum has historically miseducated us about the histories and realities of non-White groups (Lowen, 2007; Woodson, 1933; Zinn, 2015), creating a false reality and inherent misunderstanding about how race and racism function. I do not mean to say that White folks today are simply victims of a system that has been functioning for a long time; rather, a more accurate way of representing White folks is en masse they are literally trained to think about their history and positionality by key institutions that perpetuate those myths, including media and education via curriculum and pedagogy.

We cannot dismiss the notions of both personal responsibility and racial unification as mutual, transracial responsibilities—missions to which all individuals and groups are accountable. As alluded to earlier, social and racial justice is not solely about ameliorating marginalization. Social justice is about seeing and constructing the world differently. It is about consistently acknowledging the humanity in all people, even when you do not agree politically, socially, religiously, philosophically, or otherwise. Consider the backlash from some in the African American community against statements made by hip-hop artist and activist Common.

A Different Sort of Backlash

On the heels of winning an Oscar for best song for the film *Selma*, on March 17, 2015 Common was interviewed on *The Daily Show with Jon Stewart*. In regards to how we can move forward with race relations in the United States the two shared this exchange:

> Stewart: What I always find interesting is there's the movement now to take the injuries and the bitterness of racism and return them to White people, the majority culture, the dominant culture. There's a real anger, a real vein of anger that's (like), "Hey, man. I didn't have slaves!" "No no no …" But they (black folks) are not talking about that. They're talking about a power structure.

Common: Yeah. Well my thing is, now its like, "Hey, we all know there's been some bad history in our country. We know that the racism exists." I, I'm like, "Hey ya'll. I'm extending a hand," and I'm hoping a lot of, I'm thinking a lot of generations and different cultures are saying, "Hey, we want to get past this." If we been bullied; we been beat down. We don't want it anymore, and we're not extending a fist. We're not saying you did us wrong. It's more like, "Hey. I'm extending my hand in love. Let's forget about the past as much as we can and let's move from where we are now." Now how can we help each other? Can you try to help us because we are gonna help ourselves too. That's really where we are right now. (Stewart, 2015)

Stewart, to his credit, tipped his hand toward the reality that oftentimes when protests against racism are sparked, the issue may emanate from a particular event but is actually more reflective of the ways in which systemic and institutional power functions to silence the expressed challenges of marginalized communities. Common, to his credit, answered the question to highlight the importance of privileging love, for without love we cannot embrace humanity and co-construct strategies for deep, lasting change.

Immediately after that interview, social networking sites exploded and pilloried Common's declaration. On one Facebook page I saw a post that said, "Ha ha ha now this is what I call a coon" (Teaching Black Historical Facts America Doesn't Want You to Know 99%, March 17, 2015). Many other responses to the post were equally critical of Common's declaration (comments are posted as is from the page but I decided to redact names to keep participants anonymous):

This clown coon thing can't be taken serious just like the clown Common. I don't know if or how racism will end but I will most definitely not be listening to or seeking out these fools' opinions about anything.

We been holding out a hand of peace to these demons for thousands of years, they seem to always put our hands in chains.

He inhaled too much dust off of his Oscar, Brother please, snap out of it.

There is no mathematical or science to it. Nigga sold out. Period. Accept it let's move on. More will follow. I'm bombin. On Common. Sense … Chicago is mine. Nigga hit the fence. Intense. Bing bing. Nigga world wide. Lol

Martin Luther King Jr. Extended his hand in Love and got a bullet. The loving blacks in Selma, got beat bloody.

I honestly don't have the answer to your questions if i did I would have been fixed it a long time ago. But I do know that we are hated by lots of whites and trying to embrace these demons are not going to stop the killings of our people. Why apologize for not loving our abusers?

These posts, to a certain degree, were disappointing to read. Given the fact that Common was on *The Daily Show* for winning an Oscar for a song featured in a film about Dr. Martin Luther King and the historic Selma marches of 1965, I found the posted comments to be counterintuitive of not only Common's expressed idealism but also the social justice envisioned, written, and sermonized by Dr. King.

On the other hand, I understand the frustration and dissatisfaction expressed by the commenters and many other non-White women and men. I used to get *really* angry when White students and White people generally would make declarations like, "I didn't own slaves, etc." But, there is some validity to those declarations. No they didn't, but what many White folks today miss is how that history created a context in which they are at the zenith of a racial hierarchy and it takes a willingness to listen and engage to understand the reality of that hierarchy as lived by those not deemed White. Understanding these phenomena is crucial in ameliorating racism and advancing social justice. This is essential to consider for White fatigue, for as those who understand that racism is morally bankrupt, navigating the "flaws" of a statement like "I didn't own slaves" may be challenging.

For many, and by a bevy of statistical and researched measures it does not seem as though "things" have gotten better in terms of race relations in the United States, systemically or institutionally. (As a little side research challenge, look up any statistic used to describe life in our society and the lion's share will show White folks in privileged positions). In addition to the treatment of the first African American presidential family, headlines over the past years display example after example of systemic and institutional racism, most notably: mass incarceration; the growth of the school-to-prison pipeline; the educational achievement gap; the resegregation of schools; divestment in low income non-White communities; devastation from the housing market crash; struggles for representation in popular cultural spaces; racial profiling; and legitimate complaints on college campuses. This has left many of us to wonder, "Will this ever end," and some, even though they define these phenomena as wrong can grow fatigued from trying to figure them out, as each of the above are highly complex. The answer to that question is popularly left at the doorsteps of individuals' correcting behaviors and morality rather than a reconsideration of our national approach to proactive policies that promote interracial systemic and institutional reform.

Selective Chastisement and the President's Limited Privilege

Although the African American community (and many others) was ecstatic about the election of the first Black president, and recorded a higher turnout rate than White voters for the first time (Merca, 2013; Weiner, 2013), as his tenure progressed there were a number of instances that did not resonate well with the larger Black community. It was not uncommon for President Obama to chastise Black men and women for behaviors seen as negative or destructive to African Americans, including the absence of Black fathers, struggling educational achievement, and even legitimate protesting (Alexander, 2012; Coates, 2013; Craven, 2017; Senior, 2015). For example, in a 2013 commencement address at Morehouse College—a preeminent institution of higher learning and historically Black college—President Obama told the graduates:

> We know that too many young men in our community continue to make bad choices. Growing up, I made a few myself. And I have to confess, sometimes I wrote off my own failings as just another example of the world trying to keep a black man down. But one of the things you've learned over the last four years is that there's no longer any room for excuses. I understand that there's a common fraternity creed here at Morehouse: "excuses are tools of the incompetent, used to build bridges to nowhere and monuments of nothingness." We've got no time for excuses—not because the bitter legacies of slavery and segregation have vanished entirely; they haven't. Not because racism and discrimination no longer exist; that's still out there. It's just that in today's hyperconnected, hypercompetitive world, with a billion young people from China and India and Brazil entering the global workforce alongside you, nobody is going to give you anything you haven't earned. And whatever hardships you may experience because of your race, they pale in comparison to the hardships previous generations endured—and overcame. (Peralta, 2013)

The chastisement was not necessarily problematic in and of itself, but across his tenure President Obama did little (and said even less) to either assuage the challenges of systemic and institutional racism faced by non-Whites nor to educate the public on these issues and their root causes.

I do not dismiss the notion of personal responsibility and hard work, but like one of my mentors back at Michigan State University, Dr. Chris Wheeler, used to say, "Hard work is necessary but insufficient for explaining success," alluding to the host of extrinsic factors that frame an individual's and family's reality and aspirations formation (McLeod, 2008). Although many studies show that children reared in single-parent homes are at greater risk for a host of negative outcomes, the proposition that intact families are the solution to generations of institutional and systemic oppression is touted as sacrosanct and championed at the expense of minimizing those single parent homes that thrive. Moreover, along with disrespecting single parent homes, a host of factors mediating success are left by the wayside. Columnist Michael Denzel Smith (2017) pointed out:

> What these studies often don't take into account is the impact of depressed wages, chronic unemployment, discriminatory hiring practices, the history of mass incarceration, housing segregation and inequality in educational opportunity, not just on family structure but on the resources available to black families to produce results similar to their white counterparts. (para. 8)

President Obama's personal history growing up in a single-parent household and being Black offered him a license to engage such issues, and his recurrent theme of individual responsibility in the Black community was unrelenting, but he took a different approach in his statements toward the White community.

During his historic campaign, President Obama went to great lengths to remind White voters that he is also half-White, raised by a White single-mother and two White grandparents. Unfortunately, those characteristics did not offer him the license to chastise the White community as candidly after the Philadelphia speech. There were no reports of President Obama standing in front of White families and voters declaring personal responsibility for dealing with the growing opioid epidemic or lower academic achievement in rural, low-income communities. Literally, President Obama had dual guises: as the President of the United States of America and the President of Black America, and he took decidedly different rhetorical approaches to both constituencies. This was the catch-22 of the Obama presidency. If he had championed policies designed specifically to bolster struggling African American families he would have been accused of being the President of Black America, but since he was offering *advice* and criticism that promoted middle class, and to a certain degree White sensibilities, the general public did not find his statements to large Black audiences troubling.

Much like his Philadelphia speech, President Obama often extolled the virtues of Americans in speeches and interviews, and in his farewell letter to the nation he described Americans as "the source of goodness, resilience, and hope from which I've pulled strength" (McCaskill, 2017). Unfortunately, President Obama rarely offered critical critiques to the White American community. An historic opportunity was missed. President Obama was a Constitutional law scholar steeped in the theory and practice of Critical Race Theory (Crenshaw, 1991; Crenshaw, Gotanda, Peller, & Thomas, 1995; Oremus, n.d.), and he ran his historic campaign on the slogan of "hope and change." He could have reset the ways in which our elected leaders communicate with the public, beyond Tweeting. Although his Saturday radio addresses were interesting they could have been used as teaching tools to explain to the nation the *hows and whys* of our public institutions, lawmaking, or social and cultural relations. The White House could have posted PowerPoint or Prezi presentations to explain complex issues and processes. The nation could have used clearer explanations about the impact of changes to the Voting Rights Act after the *Shelby County v. Holder* (2012) decision that deemed key provisions of the Act now unconstitutional. The White House could have offered tutorials that helped explain why citizens protest and riot and offered the nation a clear-eyed explanation of why we would say, "Black lives matter." With so many other ways in which the Obama White House changed things, it is frustrating that the administration could not figure out how to re-engage our national dialogue on race and racism. However, considering the divisive racial politics of our nation and the dog-eat-dog nature of presidential politics it is sensible that President Obama pulled punches—more evidence of the impact of systemic and institutional racism on all our lives.

I may be accused of being pie-in-the-sky but there seems to be a great deal of systemic and institutional misunderstanding throughout our nation and there is desperate need for forward thinking strategies to engage and ameliorate these issues. Another speech on personal responsibility is dead on arrival if it is not coupled with equally cogent messages about the nature and impact of systemic and institutional obstacles—oppression that is—and how they shape the contexts for individual responsibility and hard work. A move like that, perhaps, could have helped the public become more understanding of racism in presidential politics, or the charge of racism against police brutality resulting in the rise of #BlackLives-Matter movement.

Bridge to Retrenchment: Police Brutality, #BlackLivesMatter, and White Allies

On a rainy February night in Florida in 2012, a Black teenager named Trayvon Martin was visiting his dad in a Sanford, Florida gated community. During halftime of a football game on television, Trayvon went to the corner store to get some candy—a bag of Skittles—and a bottle of tea. As he walked back to his dad's house he noticed an older man following him. The man was George Zimmerman, the neighborhood watch captain. Since Trayvon was walking in the rain and wearing a hoodie, and a recent string of home break-ins had occurred, Zimmerman found suspicion with Trayvon and called in the report to the local police dispatch. The operator asked Zimmerman to stay in his car and the police would be there shortly, but Zimmerman decided to pursue Trayvon. Although there were several eyewitness and "earwitness" reports, what happened next is sketchy. What we do know, based on testimony from Rachel Jeantel, Trayvon's friend who was on the phone with him during the moments leading up to the tragedy, is that Tryavon felt fear and worry about the "cracker" (sic) who was following him. We also know, most importantly, Trayvon was unarmed. A confrontation commenced, leading to a fistfight. The fight ended with Trayvon lying dead from a gunshot wound to the chest.

As the report of the unarmed shooting spread across social media, the story caught fire on national news and launched the "Hoodie" campaign as an act of solidarity with the Martin family and an act of protest against the shooting of unarmed Black men. For many, the news of Trayvon was a surprise but not shocking. There is a long history of tragic violence against Black men—*and women*—by law enforcement that spans centuries. Eventually, a six-member jury composed of five White women and one non-White person eventually acquitted Zimmerman—who argued self-defense under the protection of Florida's controversial "Stand Your Ground" law—of both murder and manslaughter. The decision caused a maelstrom of protests and applause, largely delineated by race.

A *Washington Post*/ABC News poll conducted July 22, 2013 found while 87% of African Americans polled found the jury erroneous in their decision, 51% of White Americans polled agreed with the verdict and 18% of White Americans had no opinion. What is essential to point out here is that the poll also showed 32% of White Americans polled either somewhat or strongly disagreed with the verdict. A similar poll conducted by the Pew Research Center (Levinson, 2013) found approximately the same results, reporting 86% of African Americans showing disfavor with the verdict and 30% of White Americans lodging the same opinion. There are two key points to take away from those polling numbers. First, the idea of two nations, White and non-White, separate and unequal (Hacker, 1992), clearly persists. Second, the data also show, despite a majority of White antipathy, a significant number of White folks whom, for whatever reason, can detect racial unfairness and inequity when they see it.

In the months following the Zimmerman verdict, it seemed as though the nation was beginning to see a steady stream of instances in which an unarmed Black man was murdered by a police officer. To wit, an FBI report of officer-involved shootings between 2005 and 2012 found that nearly twice a week in the United States, a White police officer killed a Black person (Johnson, Hoyer, & Heath, 2014). Even more shocking is 18% of the African Americans killed during those seven years were under the age of 21, compared to 8.7% of Whites (Johnson et al., 2014).

During the eight-year Obama administration the phenomenon of White officer-involved shootings or murders of unarmed Black men did not subside and it seemed as though every week a new story surfaced on social media. The stories of Eric Garner, Michael Brown, Freddie Grey, Sandra Bland, Sean Bell, Alton Sterling, Philando Castille and countless others (many chronicled on camera phones or live streamed on Facebook) served as rallying cries to protest the actions of law enforcement and the historic, violent marginalization of African Americans communities. During this era, the controversial Stop and Frisk program of the New York City Police Department was also deemed unconstitutional. The statistics of the program were startling. According to the Wall Street Journal (Gardiner, 2012), 87% of those stopped and frisked were Black or Latinx, the overwhelming majority of which was not violating any crime. By comparison, even though the White population of New York City is approximately 47%, they were only 13% of all stopped and frisked (Mathias, 2012).

To aggravate this issue, in the wake of officer-involved shootings and subsequent protests in cities like Ferguson, Missouri; Baltimore; and Chicago; United States Department of Justice (DOJ) investigations found each of those cities' police departments grossly and routinely violated the civil rights of non-White citizens (United States Department of Justice Civil Rights Division, 2015, 2016, 2017). Collectively the DOJ reports showed clear patterns of profiling, disrespectful and abusive treatment toward non-White citizens, routine excessive force against non-White citizens, unlawful searches (including strip searches), unlawful arrests, distribution of racist materials through departments, and many other violations. Indeed, the reports cast a pall of shame and distrust over those departments.

The death of Trayvon Martin and subsequent acquittal of the shooter, George Zimmerman, sparked a national outcry of protests. The phoenix that rose from the ashes of the Martin tragedy was the #BlackLivesMatter Movement (#BLM), and it immediately became a lightening rod of racial activism and racial dissent. Founded by Alicia Garza, Opal Tometi, and Patrisse Cullors, #BLM is:

> ... working for a world where Black lives are no longer systematically and intentionally targeted for demise. We affirm our contributions to this society, our humanity, and our resilience in the face of deadly oppression. We have put our sweat equity and love for Black people into creating a political project—taking the hashtag off of social media and into the streets. The call for Black lives to matter is a rallying cry for ALL Black lives striving for liberation. (http://blacklivesmatter.com/about/)

The meteoric rise of #BLM served as a testament to the historic and contemporary frustrations of African Americans and the collective struggle against systemic and institutional oppression. For example, Michelle Alexander (2012) adeptly chronicled the rise of the mass incarceration of African Americans. Her now classic book, *The New Jim Crow: Mass Incarceration in the Age of Colorblindness*, challenges readers to see how law has been manipulated (intentionally and unintentionally) to perpetuate a Black underclass.

The deaths of Trayvvone Martin, Tamir Rice, Eric Garner, Laquan McDonald, Sandra Bland, and many other unarmed African Americans at the hands of police officers ushered in a new era of protests and activism. Police brutality has been a perennial problem for the United States, and African Americans have borne a significant brunt of those practices. As Ta-Nehisi Coates pointed out, "… this conversation is old, and I'm sure for many of you the conversation is quite old. It's the cameras that are new. It's not the violence that's new" (Goodman, 2015). The protests against racism that have occurred around the country have not been just seas of marginalized groups raging against the machine. In fact, the protesters have been coalitions that span the identity spectrum. Not that one would be able to tell this from traditional media representations, but considering the pictures posted on social media, the questions I have received from students, editorials and blog posts, and other indicators, it is easy to see the involvement of African Americans, Latinxs, Asian Americans, Native Americans, Middle Eastern Americans, *and* White Americans in this struggle against oppression. In fact, White perceptions and support for the #BLM movement has grown, especially among White youth (Horowitz & Livingston, 2016; Sommerfeldt, 2016). According to a poll conducted by GenForward in late 2016, 51% of White adults between 18 and 30 strongly or somewhat support the movement, a ten-point increase from June to September of 2016 (Sommerfeldt, 2016). Similarly, a Pew Research Center survey conducted between February 29 to May 8, 2016 (roughly four years after the movement's inception) found that 40% of White respondents expressed support for #BLM, while 28% said they opposed it (Horowitz & Livingston, 2016).

The fact of growing support for #BLM among White folks is an important point. It does not necessarily mean that all those White folks who support it are fully racially enlightened and committed to undoing racial oppression, but what we can say is that there is an acknowledgement of systemic and institutional injustice and oppression and there are White folks who feel something needs to be done about it. That means there are White allies who are primed to learn more and do more. The Pew poll also showed that about four in ten (38%) White respondents who have heard about #BLM do not understand the movement's goals particularly well. That means there is educating to be done and how we approach and talk about that is important. If our language is dismissive or, for lack of better terms, marginalizing, then we run the risk of losing allies and future accomplices and leaders in the struggle for racial justice.

Now consider for a moment being in a discussion with members of that 38%. What if as that discussion ensued there were questions that showed a lack of understanding about how systemic and institutional racism function, or the White person lodged counterarguments about personal responsibility, or someone grew frustrated and suddenly decided they couldn't continue in the conversation? How we then construct that person is crucial. We can say they are just wallowing in White resistance and complicit in furthering racism, finding solace in their privilege. Or, we can embrace the idea that there was an attempt to understand but dealing with that cognitive dissonance is difficult and can cause disrupture and fatigue. If the White individuals in question believe that racism is morally wrong but then displays struggle with the process of unlearning and rethinking their assumptions and knowledge that is reflective of a state of fatigue.

The binary oppositions of Black/White, minority/majority, racist/anti-racist, or resistor/ally do more destruction that anything. It is not as simple as us and them, and our society needs more inclusive and effective language for talking about the great spectrum of how individuals understand and engage race and racism, especially if we mean what we say when we call for everyone to embrace, value, and celebrate diversity and justice, social justice that is.

Back to Square One?: White Fatigue, the End of the Obama Era, and the Rise of Trump

When Donald Trump entered the over-crowded Republican primary in 2015 he was initially written off as an impossibility, but as the campaign wore on he gained more and more popularity despite the outlandish and deeply insulting comments he made about practically every historically marginalized group. It was clear that Donald Trump had little to no interest in creating a true interracial coalition similar to the one developed by President Obama, and even Mr. Trump's attempts to court the favor of non-White, historically marginalized communities (Easley, 2016) can be deemed as half-hearted and transparently opportunist. Mr. Trump did not even begin to actively campaign for so-called minority voters until late in a campaign that lasted well over a year and a half. Moreover, future President Trump had already deeply insulted many communities with his nationalist, xenophobic rhetoric. On June 16, 2015 he infamously declared about Mexican immigrants:

> When Mexico sends its people, they're not sending their best. They're not sending you. They're sending people that have lots of problems, and they're bringing those problems with us. They're bringing drugs. They're bringing crime. They're rapists. And some, I assume, are good people. (Edelman, 2016)

He brazenly spoke to African Americans, often from overwhelmingly White rallies, lumping the entire community into "the ghetto," focusing largely on gun violence and poverty, and encouraging support for his candidacy by asking, "What in the hell do you have to lose" (LoBianco & Killough, 2016)? This added insult to injury after he spent six years questioning President Obama's citizenship and academic achievements (Coates, 2017; Devega, 2016; Sanders, 2016).

What was most pernicious about Mr. Trump's campaign was the result of his unfiltered vitriol. He almost single-handedly gave license for his overwhelmingly White supporters to disregard social and political decorum and put their hate and disdain on full display. As his campaign went on and the masses grew tired of his loaded rhetoric, protests at his rallies grew and some spilled over into violence. He encouraged his supporters to berate and even use violence against protesters, claiming, "I'll defend you in court" (Howell, 2016). Standing before cheering, White crowds he painted a grim picture of the United States in decline on the heels of a socially, culturally, and politically groundbreaking presidency, and in his diatribes he went on to blame racial and religious minorities, immigrants, and political correctness (among other factors) as the reasons why all those White faces were losing jobs and status. He self-righteously stoked a fire and sparked a powder keg of White backlash that had been simmering under the surface, waiting to explode.

It was argued that President Trump's success was not an issue of racial animus but of economics (Casselman, 2017; Schiller, 2016), which is absolutely a legitimate point given an arguably sluggish economic rebound from the Great Recession of 2008 and fears of a hemorrhaging manufacturing and industrial economic sector, which impacted millions of White working class, non-college educated workers. However, White backlash against political correctness and social, economic, cultural, and political advances among historically marginalized groups has had a slow burn for decades and galvanized a White public that feels their privileged status and positionality slipping away (despite the idea that they reject the notion of privilege). Trump is not original in his strategy. Presidents Nixon, Reagan, and George H. W. Bush each used racially divisive tactics in their campaigns, and the effectiveness of these racially charged strategies is vexing. A study conducted by Valentino, Neuner, and Vandenbroek (2016) found that "Whites now view themselves as an embattled racial group, and this has led to both strong in-group identity and greater tolerance for expressions of hostility toward outgroups" (p. 28).

The problem is that some attempted to disregard race altogether as a factor in the rise of Mr. Trump, but with the combination of his impudent rhetoric, increasing attacks on political correctness and news media, and White working class fearmongering, "it's the economy, stupid" is a woefully incomplete explanation. We also cannot forget the previous eight-year's worth of racially charged disrespect toward the Obamas and the range of race-based controversies that ensued. Issac J. Bailey (2016) of *Politico* succinctly makes the point:

> Trump simply tapped into and coaxed out of America a racial angst that was already present—and which is now, thanks to him, far less shy about showing its face. As a result, this election is no longer about all Americans. It is about White Americans. The United States of America is essential undergoing a White identity crisis. By dramatic numbers, people of color have, in no uncertain terms, expressed their horror about the possibility of what a Trump victory in November would mean. It is White America that has yet to decide which way it plans to pull. (paras. 6 and 7)

And without doubt, the soul of White America is embattled. Despite Trump's victory, winning the necessary 270 electoral-college votes, he resoundingly lost the popular vote.

His election numbers among White voters are startling, though. Considering the nature of his campaign, Mr. Trump nonetheless won the White vote over his Democratic challenger, Secretary Hillary Clinton, by 21 percentage points (58% to 37%) (Tyson & Maniam, 2016). What is even more interesting is that Mr. Trump won non-college educated White voters 52%–44%. Tyson and Maniam report, "Among whites, Trump won an overwhelming share of those without a college degree; and among white college graduates—a group that many identified as key for a potential Clinton victory—Mr. Trump outperformed Sec. Clinton by a narrow 4-point margin" (para. 8).

Ferreting out the numbers is difficult since there are so many variables at play. What I focus on is the fact that Mr. Trump's victorious run was on the back of rural America; he overwhelmingly won among White, rural, men *and* women (Morin, 2016; Zitner & Overberg, 2016) and that allowed him to secure the electoral points of most of non-coastal America. Lack of exposure to others can skew how one understands the reality of others and the shared concerns of all. I also focus on the fact that Mr. Trump did not win 70%, 80%, or 90% of the White vote. Millions of White voters rejected Mr. Trump's divisive, populist rhetoric, and as Mr. Trump approached Inauguration Day, hordes of White citizens took to the streets in protest of his divisive rhetoric as part of a coalition with the historically marginalized.

I do not mean to minimize rural Trump supporters and claim they are all irredeemable racists. Struggling rural communities across the country have long-standing problems to which government has been unresponsive for decades, making the economics of the rift between White and non-White folks hard to reject. This rift can explain some racial resentment toward Barack Obama and Black folks generally. Stokley Carmichael and Charles Hamilton, back in 1967, spoke about deepening racial animus between poor Whites and Blacks. "Poor

White people are becoming more hostile—not less—toward Black people, partly because they see the nation's attention focused on Black poverty and few, if any, people coming to them" (Carmichael & Hamilton, 2008, p. 186).

J. D. Vance (2016) points out in *Hillbilly Elegy*, rural folks have grown tired of being disregarded, disrespected, downplayed, and dismissed as hateful of Black folks and other marginalized racial groups. Vance argues that White rural conservatives were not looking simply at President Obama's race but the totality of his image. For many of them he was, for lack of better terms, foreign, and his rise happened as many low-income rural Whites saw their place in the American economy and society careening toward a dead-end. Allow me to quote Vance at length:

> Many of my new friends blame racism for this perception of the president. But the president feels like an alien to many Middletonians for reasons that have nothing to do with skin color. Recall that not a single one of my high school classmates attended an Ivy League school. Barack Obama attended two of them and excelled at both. He is brilliant, wealthy, and speaks like a constitutional law professor—which, of course, he is. Nothing about him bears any resemblance to the people I admired growing up: His accent—clean, perfect, neutral—is foreign; his credentials are so impressive that they're frightening; he made his life in Chicago, a dense metropolis; and he conducts himself with a confidence that comes from knowing that the modern American meritocracy was built for him. Of course, Obama overcame adversity in his own right— adversity familiar to many of us—but that was long before any of us knew him.
>
> President Obama came on the scene right as so many people in my community began to believe that the modern American meritocracy was not built for them. We know we're not doing well. We see it every day: in the obituaries for teenage kids that conspicuously omit the cause of death (reading between the lines: overdose), in the deadbeats we watch our daughters waste their time with. Barack Obama strikes at the heart of our deepest insecurities. He is a good father while many of us aren't. He wears suits to his job while we wear overalls, if we're lucky enough to have a job at all. His wife tells us that we shouldn't be feeding our children certain foods, and we hate her for it—not because we think she's wrong but because we know she's right. (p. 191)

I appreciate Vance's insight. Through his text he humanizes the often-disregarded White poor and working class (Isenberg, 2017). Barack Obama's pedigree, beyond race alone, is so distant from the average rural American it could be challenging to see him as another person who also struggled, but Vance raises an important point in that reasoning. The fact that "Barry" Obama also had economic struggles is all but disregarded by the rural, White working class and poor. This of course raises the question of stereotypes and assumptions about the construction of African Americans (and others) in the White poor and working class imaginary. Certain politicians and media outlets went out of their way to negatively define and defame the first Black president. As Vance goes on to point out, the incessant conflicting messages and misinformation circulated through conservative and ultra-right wing news, especially talk radio, did not help at all, making it that much more logical that months prior to the 2016 election, two-thirds of Trump supporters continued to believe President Obama was Muslim (Gangitano, 2016). (I always find that funny considering where this chapter and his campaign trail of 2008 began.)

Paying attention to the influence of economics as a dividing factor is important. After all, poor White folks have been pitted against Black folks and other marginalized groups since Bacon's Rebellion in 1676 (Alexander, 2012; Battalora, 2013). However, it is without doubt, based on news reports, interviews with Trump supporters, letters to the editor of newspapers, and many other sources, there is a palpable racial animus among Trump supporters and they feel much more unfettered to publicly voice their derisions. Many of President Trump's voters, including rural voters, may say they are not racist, but German Lopez (2016) pointed out:

> The findings (of several non-partisan polls) suggest a great majority of Trump supporters hold unfavorable views of Muslims and support a policy that bans Muslims from entering the US. Most of them support proposals that stifle immigration from Mexico, and they agree with Trump comments that Mexican immigrants are criminals. And many—but not a majority—say that black people are less intelligent and more violent than their white peers.
>
> Now, the polls find majorities—even mega majorities—of Trump supporters holding such views. But that still leaves out a lot of Trump supporters who don't share bigoted or prejudiced perspectives about people based on their race, ethnicity, or religion. It's likely many are genuine conservatives who simply support the candidate they see as more conservative. (paras. 3–4)

The ascendency of Donald Trump, through his celebrity and unchecked rhetoric across the campaign trail, absolutely opened the floodgates of a wave of racial intolerance that had been simmering across the country.[2] It is troubling that "mega majorities" of Trump supporters have such antiquated and deplorable views of non-White citizens. Simultaneously, it is also clear that they do not necessarily understand how racism functions as a systemic and institutional phenomenon and they are caught up in their own self-interests. If they were more knowledgeable of the history of the ways in which a racial hierarchy was constructed and how the positioning of poor Whites literally pitted them against others for their slice of the pie then maybe they could see the nature of the oppression of others and the reality of their own economic oppression. Their knowledge of systemic and institutional oppression in all forms (including class-based oppression) is limited because of a near absence of those critical ideas in K-12 curricula across the country. We must take care in constructing these people. If we essentialize them then we run the risk of alienating those who could be allies and later accomplices or leaders in the fight against racial oppression. After all, as pointed out earlier in this book, if it is wrong to essentialize one group it is wrong to essentialize any group. White fatigue is a term that can help capture a portion of that community, recognizing not only their resistance but also their potential, and their humanity.

What is of utmost importance is how we deal with these issues in schools and how our teachers offer students engaging and critical possibilities to explore them. Unfortunately, despite the best efforts of the founders, theorists, and many practitioners of multicultural education, there seems to be an emphasis on humanist ideals and teaching tolerance without an attendant, critical exploration of the ways in which systemic and institutional actions have constrained possibilities for the historically marginalized, and the irony is that includes the ways in which socioeconomic classes have also been systemically and institutionally stratified. Because of this, and the lack of education about the ways in which Whiteness functions or a fuller consideration of the ways in which White folks have been champions of anti-oppression, there has been a systemic miseducation of White folks that must be addressed if we expect to move forward—the key idea of the coming chapter.

Notes

1. Although I do not have the space to go into Reverend Wright's sermon here I *strongly* suggest all of you read the whole sermon or watch an extended clip, delivered in the wake of the tragic events of September 11, 2001. Of course, understanding the whole context of Rev. Wright's sermon is essential. A longer clip can be easily found on YouTube.
2. In fact there were numerous editorials, articles, and exposes decrying the rhetoric and language of Mr. Trump. However, his Republican primary opponents (except Jeb Bush, Lindsay Graham, and Ted Cruz) and leaders in the Republican party did little to denounce and/ or distance themselves from Mr. Trump.

Bibliography

Alexander, M. (2012). *The new Jim Crow: Mass incarceration in the age of colorblindness*. New York, NY: The New Press.

Bailey, I. J. (2016, August 22). How Trump exposed America's White identity crisis. *Politico*. Retrieved from http://www.politico.com/magazine/story/2016/08/trump-race-white-americaidentity-crisis-214178

Battalora, J. M. (2013). *Birth of a white nation: The invention of white people and its relevance today*. Houston, Tex: Strategic Book Publishing.

Bigg, M. (2008, November 24). Election of Obama provokes rise in U.S. hate crimes. *Reuters*. Retrieved from http://www.reuters.com/article/us-usa-obamahatecrimes-idUSTRE4AN81U20081124

Black Lives Matter. (n.d.). *About the Black Lives Matter network*. Retrieved from http://blacklivesmatter.com/about/

Blake, J. (2008, July 22). Could an Obama presidency hurt Black Americans? *CNN Politics*. Retrieved from http://www.cnn.com/2008/POLITICS/07/22/obama.hurt.blacks/

Burke, L. V. (2012, January 27). The 10 worst moments of disrespect towards President Obama. *Politics365*. Retrieved from http://politic365.com/2012/01/27/the-10worst-moments-of-disrespect-towards-president-obama/#

Casselman, B. (2017, January 9). Stop saying Trump's win had nothing to do with economics. *FiveThirtyEight*. Retrieved from https://fivethirtyeight.com/features/stop-saying-trumps-win-had-nothing-to-dowith-economics/

Coard, M. (2012, January 31). Top 9 most racist things Republicans have done since President Obama has been in office. *Philadelphia Magazine*. Retrieved from http://www.phillymag.com/news/2012/01/31/top-9-racist-republicans-presidentobama-office/

Coates, T. (2013, May 20). How the Obama administration talks to Black America. *The Atlantic*. Retrieved from https://www.theatlantic.com/politics/archive/2013/05/how-the-obamaadministration-talks-to-black-america/276015/

Coates, T. (2017). My president was Black: A history of the first African American White House—And of what came next. *The Atlantic*. Retrieved from https://www.theatlantic.com/magazine/archive/2017/01/my-president-wasblack/508793/

Craven, J. (2017, January 11). Obama is Black, but that wasn't enough. *The Huffington Post*. Retrieved from http://www.huffingtonpost.com/entry/barack-obama-blackamericans_us_586d1824e4b0de3a08fa54fc

Crenshaw, K. (1991). Mapping the margins: Intersectionality, identity politics, and violence against women of color. *Stanford Law Review, 43*(6), 1241–1299.

Crenshaw, K., Gotanda, N., Peller, G., & Thomas, K. (1995). *Critical race theory: The key writings that formed the movement*. New York, NY: The New Press.

Cullors, P., Tometi, O., & Garza, A. (n.d.). Guiding principles [Website]. Retrieved from http://blacklivesmatter.com/guiding-principles/

Devega, C. (2016, September 20). Trump's attack on Black America: Birtherism was always about more than Obama's birth certificate. *Salon*. Retrieved from http://www.salon.com/2016/09/20/trumps-attack-on-black-america-birtherism was-always-about-more-than-obamas-birth-certificate/

Easley, J. (2016, August 23). Trump courts minority voters. *The Hill*. Retrieved from http://thehill.com/homenews/campaign/292267-trump-courts-minority-voters

Edelman, A. (2016, August 31). A look at Trump's most outrageous comments about Mexicans as he attempts damage control by visiting with country's president. *New York Daily News*. Retrieved from http://www.nydailynews.com/news/politics/trump-outrageous-comments mexicans-article-1.2773214

Gangitano, A. (2016, May 10). Poll: Two-thirds of Trump backers think Obama is Muslim. *Roll Call*. Retrieved from http://www.rollcall.com/news/politics/poll two-thirds-trump-supporters-think-obama-muslim

Gardiner, S. (2012, February 14). Stop and frisk hit record in 2011. *The Wall Street Journal*. Retrieved from https://www.wsj.com/articles/SB10001424052970204795304577221770 75263312

Goodman, A. (2015). Ta-Nehisi Coates on police brutality: "The violence is not new, it's the cameras that are new." *Democracy Now*. Retrieved from https://www.democracynow. org/2015/11/27/ta_nehisi_coates_on_police_brutality

Hacker, A. (1992). *Two nations: Black and White, separate, hostile, and unequal*. New York, NY: Scribner.

Horowitz, J. M., & Livingston, G. (2016, July 8). How Americans view the Black Lives Matter movement. *Pew Research Center*. Retrieved from http://www.pewresearch.org/ fact-tank/2016/07/08/how-americans-view-theblack-lives-matter-movement/

Howell, K. (2016, March 5). Donald Trump gives supporters permission to be violent at rallies: "I'll defend you in court." *The Washington Times*. Retrieved from http://www. washingtontimes.com/news/2016/mar/5/donald-trump-givessupporters-permissions-be-viole/

Isenberg, N. (2017). *White trash: The 400-year untold history of class in America* (Reprint ed.). New York, NY: Penguin Books.

Johnson, K., Hoyer, M., & Heath, B. (2014, August 14). Local police involved in 400 killings per year. *USA Today*. Retrieved from https://www.usatoday.com/story/news/nation/ 2014/08/14/police-killingsdata/14060357/

Kopan, T. (August 31, 2016). What Donald Trump has said about Mexico and vice versa. *CNN Politics*. Retrieved from http://www.cnn.com/2016/08/31/politics/donald-trump-mexico-statements/index.html

Levinson, A. (2013). Polls show wide racial gap on Trayvon Martin case. *NPR*. http://www. npr.org/sections/itsallpolitics/2013/07/22/204595068/polls-showwide-racial-gap-on-trayvon-martin-case

LoBianco, T., & Killough, A. (2016, August 19). Trump pitches to Black voters: "What the hell do you have to lose?" *CNN Politics*. Retrieved from http://www.cnn.com/2016/08/19/ politics/donald-trump-african-american-voters/

Lopez, G. (2016, September 12). Polls show many—even most—Trump supporters really are deeply hostile to Muslims and nonwhites: Hillary Clinton said, "You could put half of Trump's supporters into what I call the 'basket of deplorables.'" Is she right? *Vox*. Retrieved from http://www.vox.com/2016/9/12/12882796/trump supporters-racist-deplorables

Lowen, J. (2007). *Lies my teacher told me: Everything your American history textbook got wrong* (Revised ed.). New York, NY: Touchstone.

Massey, D., & Denton, N. (1993). *American apartheid: Segregation and the making of the underclass* (Reprint ed.). Cambridge, MA: Harvard University Press.

Mathias, C. (2012, May 15). NYPD stop and frisk: 15 shocking facts about a controversial program. *The Huffington Post*. Retrieved from http://www.huffingtonpost.com/2012/05/13/nypd-stop-and-frisks-15-shockingfacts_n_1513362.html

McCaskill, N. D. (2017, January 19). Obama's parting letter to America: Thank you. *Politico*. Retrieved from http://www.politico.com/story/2017/01/obama-letter-toamerica-233841

McWhorter, J. (2008, December 30). Racism in America is over. *Forbes*. Retrieved from https://www.forbes.com/2008/12/30/end-of-racism-opedcx_jm_1230mcwhorter.html

Mehlhorn, D. (1998). A requiem for blockbusting: Law, economics, and race-based real estate speculation. *Fordham Law Review, 67*(4), 1145–1161.

Merica, D. (2013, May 13). Blacks outvoted Whites in 2012, the first time on record. *CNN Politics*. Retrieved from http://politicalticker.blogs.cnn.com/2013/05/09/blacks-outvoted-whites-in-2012the-first-time-on-record/

Mooney, A. (2008, July 14). *New Yorker* defends controversial Obama cover. *CNN Politics*. Retrieved from http://www.cnn.com/2008/POLITICS/07/14/obama.cover/index.html?iref=topnws

Morin, R. (2016, November 19). Behind Trump's win in rural White America: Women joined men in backing him. *Pew Research Center*. Retrieved from http://www.pewresearch.org/fact-tank/2016/11/17/behind-trumps-win-in-ruralwhite-america-women-joined-men-in-backing-him/

No Author. (n.d.). Trayvon Martin shooting and verdict: Huge racial gaps. *The Washington Post*. Retrieved from https://www.washingtonpost.com/politics/trayvon-martinshooting-and-verdict-huge-racial-gaps/2013/07/22/2b8ca5be-f307-11e2-8505bf6f231e77b4_graphic.html?utm_term=.14a52283254d

Nagourney, A. (2008, November 4). Obama elected president as racial barrier falls. *The New York Times*. Retrieved from http://www.nytimes.com/2008/11/05/us/politics/05elect.html

Norman, J. (April 11, 2016). U. S. worries about race relations reach a new high. *Gallup News*. Retrieved from http://news.gallup.com/poll/190574/worries-race-relations-reach-new-high.aspx

Obama, B. (2004). *Dreams from my father: A story of race and inheritance*. New York, NY: Broadway Books.

Obama, B. (2008). *A more perfect union* [speech]. Retrieved from http://www.npr.org/templates/story/story.php?storyId=88478467

Oremus, W. (n.d.). Did Obama hug a radical: What's "critical race theory," and how crazy is it? *Slate*. Retrieved March 1, 2017 from http://www.slate.com/articles/news_and_politics/explainer/2012/03/derrick_bellcontroversy_what_s_critical_race_theory_and_is_it_radical_.html

Peralta, E. (2013, May 19). Two excerpts you should read from Obama's Morehouse speech. *National Public Radio*. Retrieved from http://www.npr.org/sections/thetwo-way/2013/05/19/185348873/two-excerpts_you-should-read-from-obamas-morehouse-speech

Race relations. (n.d.). *Gallup News*. Retrieved from http://news.gallup.com/poll/1687/race-relations.aspx

Sanders, S. (2016, October 16). For much of Black America, election 2016 has been rough. *NPR.* Retrieved from http://www.npr.org/2016/10/16/497841789/for much-of-black-america-election-2016-has-been-rough

Schiller, B. (2016, November 9). Why did Trump win? The economy, stupid. *The Los Angeles Times.* Retrieved from http://www.latimes.com/opinion/op-ed/la-oe schiller-trump-victory-economy-20161109-story.html

Senior, J. (2015, October 7). The paradox of the first Black president. *New York Magazine.* Retrieved from http://nymag.com/daily/intelligencer/2015/10/paradox-of-the-first-black-president.html

Sheppard, D. (2012). *Def Sheppard: Observatins from the intersection of religion, science, politics, and culture.* Retrieved June 27, 2016 from http://www.defshepherd.com/2012/10/racism-is-alive-and-well-35 incredibly.html

Sommerfeldt, C. (2016, September 6). Majority of young White people support Black Lives Matter: Poll. *The Daily News.* Retrieved from http://www.nydailynews.com/news/national/majority-young-whites-support black-lives-matter-poll-article-1.2779291

Stewart, J (Executive producer). (2015, March 11). *The daily show with Jon Stewart* [Television show]. United States: Comedy Central.

Teaching Black Historical Facts America Doesn't Want You to Know 99%. (2015). *In Facebook* [Group page]. Retrieved March 23, 2015 from https://www.facebook.com/groups/1458629974415864/

Tyson, A., & Maniam, S. (2016, November 9). Behind Trumps victory: Divisions by race, gender, education. *Pew Research Center.* Retrieved from http://www.pewresearch.org/fact-tank/2016/11/09/behind-trumps-victorydivisions-by-race-gender-education/

United States Department of Justice Civil Rights Division. (2015). *Investigation of the Ferguson Police Department.* Washington, DC: Author.

United States Department of Justice Civil Rights Division. (2016). *Investigation of the Baltimore Police Department.* Washington, DC: Author.

United States Department of Justice Civil Rights Division. (2017). *Investigation of the Chicago Police Department.* Washington, DC: Author.

Valentino, N. A. Neuner, F. G., & Vandenbroek, L. M. (2016). *The changing norms of racial political rhetoric and the end of racial priming* (Working Paper). Retrieved from https://www.research-gate.net/publication/310230276_The_Changing_Norms_of Racial_ Political_Rhetoric_ and_the_End_of_Racial_Priming

Vance, J. D. (2016). *Hillbilly elegy: A memoir of a family and culture in crisis* (Kindle ed.). Retrieved from Amazon.com.

Weiner, R. (2013, April 29). Black voters turned out at a higher rate than White voters in 2012 and 2008. *The Washington Post.* Retrieved from https://www.washingtonpost.com/news/the-fix/wp/2013/04/29/black-turnout-was higher-than-white-turnout-in-2012-and-2008/?utm_term=.1d90560dc239

Wise, T. J. (2009). *Between Barack and a hard place: Racism and white denial in the age of Obama.* San Francisco, CA: City Lights Books.

Woodson, C. G. (1933/1993). *The miseducation of the Negro* (African World Press ed., 6th Printing). Washington, DC: African World Press.

Zinn, H. (2015). *A people's history of the United States* (Reissue ed.). New York, NY: Harper Perennial Modern Classics.

Zitner, A., & Overberg, P. (2016, November 9). Rural vote fuels Trump; Clinton loses urban grip. *The Wall Street Journal.* Retrieved from https://www.wsj.com/articles/rural-vote-helps-donald-trump-as-hillary-clintonholds-cities-1478664251

CHAPTER FOUR

The Miseducation
of White Folks

The Success and Failure of the
Multicultural Education Movement

What do students learn about race in K-12 education? Understanding the ways in which historical narratives have been hijacked and manipulated to repeat lullabies that bolster White privilege is essential. Even today, the national curriculum on race is largely stalled on advancing human relations, often without critical examinations of the economic, political, social, and cultural impact racism has on all our lives. Wendy Brown Scott (2002) pointed out, "… the miseducation of White America is less often acknowledged as a consequence of the perpetuation of a racial hierarchy from slavery to the present day" (p. 74). Not calling attention to the historic and contemporary ways in which Whiteness is privileged through the curriculum of American public education—and through the public curriculum via media and other institutions—makes both the legitimizing of counternarratives about Whiteness and the amelioration of racism that much more daunting.

Much against the intentions of multicultural educators, the centering of Whiteness in the American curriculum and multicultural education produced practices that minimized racial literacy and often skirted deeper explorations of systemic and institutional racial oppression (alongside other forms of oppression), and White students bring those uncritical perspectives into higher education/ teacher education classes. The critical challenge and exposure of a more nuanced retelling of history and sociopolitical phenomenon adds to the frustrations of many White students, leaving them wondering "why didn't we learn this in school" and reinforces feelings of White fatigue.

Multicultural Education: The Struggle to Name Others in the American Curriculum

In 1933, Carter G. Woodson, one of our most significant African American historians and activists, released his classic text, *The Miseducation of the Negro*. The basic premise of his text is American education (at the time and arguably since then) grossly misrepresented peoples of African descent while lionizing those of European descent (i.e., White Americans). The marginalized framing of those of African, Indigenous, and Asian descent resulted in a minimization of their roles in American history and culture, let alone world history. Moreover, this minimization promoted not only the marginalization and denigration of historically marginalized groups but also reinforced a sense of racial superiority for White Americans and maintenance of the racial system of oppression along with the White racial framing (Feagin, 2013) of the United States.

Although Woodson's points are crucial for understanding African American educational history, as his focus rests squarely on the Black experience, the book reveals the miseducation of White folks too, for the rhetoric and lessons learned in schools were and are learned by not only marginalized groups but also White folks. If one group receives misinformation through curriculum then everyone receives misinformation. For example, if your world history teacher tells you that the cradle of civilization rests in ancient Greece and Rome at the expense of great African empires that predate Greece and Rome—like Egypt, Carthage, Kush, and Punt—then all students are receiving a distorted understanding of world history. The distorted and self-inflated sense of history from White educators during the 19th and 20th centuries was crucial in the maintenance of an imposed White cultural superiority and the systemization and institutionalization of White racism. Recognizing and voicing this miseducation is especially important since White students are rarely afforded the opportunity to learn alternative histories of White folks' role in actively resisting racial oppression (Wise, 2012). Again, along with the fact that White folks were making decisions that maintained a system of advantage based on race, they were also reproducing those conditions for future generations. Breaking out of that cycle requires both an intervention that signifies the maintenance of a cycle and sustained engagement with how that cycle functions with the encouragement of the moral obligation to rectify those oppressive practices. In short, students must be exposed to not only introductory information about historically misrepresented marginalized groups but also an understanding of how *and why* those groups are marginalized, the role White folks have in perpetuating marginalization, and the role White folks have in challenging marginalization.

Although many educators had been arguing for more accurate inclusion of African Americans and other marginalized groups, the modern Multicultural

Education movement began in the 1960s and 1970s with the Ethnic Studies Movement (Banks, 2004). The push for multicultural education attempted to challenge the notions of Eurocentric thought and values dominant in American curriculum (McCarthy, 1993). At its impetus, multicultural education was meant to challenge the dominance of Whiteness and Eurocentricity in the U.S. curriculum and canon. McCarthy states:

> ... Canonical knowledge was official knowledge, which undergirded official stories about social stratification and minority educational marginalization. In contrast to the dominant preoccupation of traditional educators, African American and other minority groups emphasized a variety of transformative themes, instituting that curriculum and educational policy address the vital questions of community control, the distribution of power and representation in schools, and the status of minority cultural identities in curriculum organization and arrangements. (p. 290)

With regard to race, this meant both an examination of Whiteness as a system of thought that furthered acts of domination and subordination and a reengagement of the histories, cultures, contributions, and constructions of non-White groups and other historically marginalized groups. According to Sonia Nieto (1995):

> Multicultural education challenges and rejects racism and other forms of discrimination in schools and society and accepts and affirms the pluralism (ethnic, racial, linguistic, religious, economic, and gender, among others) that students, communities, and teachers represent. Multicultural education promotes the democratic principles of social justice. (p. 307)

This new wave in education manifested in the dramatic increase in classes dedicated to exploring marginalized cultures across disciplines. For example, beginning in the latter 1960s through the 1970s there was a sharp increase in ethnic and gender studies courses. In higher education, departments dedicated to Black Studies, Asian Studies, Women's Studies, Queer Studies, and the like exploded, providing evidence that a tide of curricular change was coming. Eventually these ideas trickled down into secondary and elementary school curricula, giving rise to the inevitable resistance to the challenge.

Backlash: The Eventual Rise of the Anti-Multiculturalists

The growth in multicultural education was met with considerable backlash as the 20th century moved closer to an end. There was a growing contingent of conservative educators, policy makers, and pundits that considered the multicultural education movement as a "watering down" of the core curriculum and was undermining the Eurocentric canon and common American culture and ideals (Hirsch, 1988). Education commentators such as D'Souza (1991), Brann (1993), Schlesinger (1992), and Webster (1997) among others aided in mounting strident attacks against the goals of multicultural education curricula, and some attempted to restore Eurocentrism back to the center of the American curriculum (a somewhat deceptive idea since Eurocentrism never truly moved from the center of the American curriculum but was only challenged).

Employing dog whistles like separatist education, reverse discrimination, victim's revolution, liberal education, and affirmative action fostered an irritation with multicultural education efforts and shifted the tide back toward pedagogies of Eurocentricity and the notion of cultural literacy (Hirsch, 1988) rather than pedagogies of cultural relevance (Ladson-Billings, 1994) and oppression (Freire, 1970). Explaining the "victim's revolution," ultra-conservative scholar Dinesh D'Souza (1991) stated:

> Many campuses have witnessed the somewhat strange phenomenon of various minority groups—(B)lacks, Hispanics (sic), American Indian, foreign students, feminists, homosexuals, and so on—climbing aboard the victim bandwagon. ... By converting victimhood into a certificate of virtue, minorities acquire a powerful moral claim that renders their opponents defensive and apologetic, and immunizes themselves from criticism and sanction. Ultimately, victimhood becomes a truncheon with which minority activists may intimidate nonminorities—thus the victim becomes the victimizer while continuing to enjoy superior moral credentials. (pp. 242–243)

The notion of "reverse discrimination" distorts not only the purpose of multicultural education but also the perspectives of historically marginalized groups. Moreover, it subtly shifts equity and social justice discourses back into the favor of Whites (or the dominant group) by truncating critical discussions regarding power, privilege, positionality politics, and hegemony (Apple, 1990; Gramsci, 1971).

Conservative rhetoric furthered by D'Souza, Schlesinger, Hirsch, and many others legitimated feelings of entitlement on behalf of White Americans by constructing Whiteness as under attack by often undeserving, complaining so-called minorities. As Fine (1997) pointed out, "We hear Whiteness, again, being produced and narrated in contrast to Blackness and in response to an alleged 'scarcity of opportunities.' This rhetoric relies upon fetishistic opposition and denigration" (p. 63).

Eller (1997) illuminates the principle arguments "anti-multiculturalists" attempted to further. First, emanating from the desire of multicultural education's goal of pointing out differences and relations among cultural groups, there was a belief that multiculturalism would, in the words of Schlesinger (1992), disunite

America and pushed for the furthering of a common culture. Second, there was concern that offering alternatives or revisions to the academic canon would "constitute not scholarly advances but personal commitment or even over-wrought emotion posing as knowledge and reason" (Eller, 1997, p. 250). Third, there was a fear of cultural essentialism or provincialism. Eller explains, "Provincialism comes in the form of ethnic studies courses and programs and all the accouterments, in which people only learn about and interact with 'their own kind,' thus failing to prepare for a multicultural world and undoing two generations of integrationism" (p. 251). Finally, anti-multiculturalists were concerned that education would become a "battlefield" where identities become weapons.

Indeed the concerns voiced here are legitimate, but Eller goes on to argue that the concerns voiced by anti-multiculturalists are exaggerated and based on some serious assumptions. For example, they assume that America is already "united," a point that could be argued against strongly. Related to this point is the belief that "America or 'The West' is one culture" (p. 253). What anti-multiculturalists are missing is the idea that Western culture could not exist without multiple cultures. Finally there is the assumption that engaging with examinations of Whiteness and Western culture, or investigating the cultural perspectives of "others" in the attempt to challenge assumptions and constructions, would ultimately fragment and dismantle American culture, a sort of perpetuation of the zero-sum game. Eller's criticism can best be summarized by the following:

> The worries of anti-multiculturalists come down to this: multiculturalism is contesting their culture, the traditionally privileged position of Western scholarship, history, and culture. Anti-multiculturalists quite reasonably see this cultural contestation as cultural crisis. It is a loss of power for some, certainly, but it is more fundamentally a loss of faith. They fear the loss of European and Western cultural supremacy in the school curriculum because these things are real and true and valuable to them. (p. 254)

The issue that tends to be overlooked when detractors rail against multiculturalism, diversity, equity, and social justice is that all perspectives *are* political constructions, borne out of both personal interests *and* power relations. What emerged in the 1960s and 1970s was the culmination of centuries and generations of struggle and resistance against the dominant culture in American society (i.e., Whiteness). Like James Baldwin (1984/1998) once wrote, "No one was White before he/she came to America. It took generations, and a vast amount of coercion, before this became a White country" (p. 178). As a result, the ensuing backlash attempted to construct rhetorics of purity and naturalness without giving credence and voice to "other" ways of understanding and experiencing the world, how "others" add to scholarship and American culture, and in effect sustaining privilege for some and continuing to marginalize others.

Delpit (1988) wrote about the notion of a "culture of power" that operates in classrooms (in fact all institutions) and that some individuals have acquired the codes to succeed in those contexts and others have not. She states, "The codes or rules I am speaking of relate to linguistic forms, communicative strategies, and presentations of self; that is, ways of talking, ways of writing, ways of dressing, and ways of interacting" (p. 283). Delpit goes on to say that "those with power are frequently least aware of—or least willing to acknowledge—its existence" (p. 282). This is of particular importance because it shows how discourses (in this case Whiteness) are normalized to the point that they are seldom questioned.

McIntosh's (1988) exploration of White and male privilege also spoke to this phenomenon. Defining White privilege as "an invisible package of unearned assets which (one) can count on cashing in each day, but about which I was *meant* to remain oblivious" (p. 10) (Emphasis is in the original text). What is fascinating when considering the similarities of McIntosh's and Delpit's ideas is Whiteness and the power that comes with it is meant to be normalized, unquestioned, unconsidered, and uncontested, reflections of a long-standing hegemony that has been challenged in the American curriculum (considering public education has been in place in the United States since the 1800s).

The ideas presented by the anti-multicultural theorists quickly gained currency in the 1980s and 1990s. Institutions, especially media outlets such as talk radio, seized onto the rhetoric, enforcing and encouraging narratives of White men as victims of minority advances and losers in the new progressive reform agendas in education and politics. Pundits like Rush Limbaugh, Laura Ingram, Sean Hannity, and many other lesser-known ultra-conservative pundits mounted a full-on attack against multicultural education, and their banter distorted the ideas and values multicultural education attempted to further. Their ideas fundamentally missed the point.

To Critique but Not Criticize nor Essentialize: Missed Lessons on Whiteness

Critical multicultural education theorists were not necessarily interested in capriciously attacking *White people*. They were (and are) interested in an examination of *Whiteness* and Eurocentricity and how those influences shape inequitable power relations, resulting in the furthering of systemic and institutional oppression. The difference between *Whiteness* and *White people* is fundamental; although they are related they are nonetheless distinct ideas. "Whiteness is a racial discourse, whereas the category of white people represents a socially constructed identity, usually based on skin color" (Leonardo, 2002, p. 31). Whiteness is a system of thoughts, values, and beliefs that shape the ways in which an individual interacts with and interprets her/his environment. As a historically and socially constructed discourse, Whiteness has come to be identified with a number of signifiers. Fine, Weis, Powell, and Wong (1997) explain the construction of Whiteness as: "objectivity, normality, truth, knowledge, merit, motivation, achievement, and trustworthiness; it accumulates invisible supports that contribute unacknowledged to the already accumulated and bolstered capital of Whiteness. Rarely, however, is it acknowledged that Whiteness demands and constitutes hierarchy, exclusion, and deprivation" (p. viii). When White students begin wrestling with those realities of hierarchy, exclusion, and deprivation, once brought to the fore, feelings of White guilt can manifest for some, and that is sensible since those are painful realities K-12 education tends to skirt (Richardson & Johanningmeier, 2003). As children progress through K-12 education and do not have significant, sustained, interdisciplinary, and cross-curricular opportunities to critically explore the relationship between Whiteness and racial domination they establish the quietly held belief that other ways of seeing the world are less valid since they do not fit into the hegemony constructed through Whiteness and furthered through curriculum, in effect validating practices of exclusion and domination.

Anti-racist educator Gary Howard (1999), however, warned us against "academic rhetoric that equates Whiteness with oppression" (p. 110). Howard asks, "If Whiteness is theorized to be synonymous with oppression, then how do we provide White educators with a positive racial identity and include them in the work of social transformation" (p. 111)? Similarly, Henry Giroux (1997) called for the need to be sensible in investigating Whiteness and warns against essentializing Whiteness. His words work best here and I must quote at length:

> While it is imperative that a critical analysis of "Whiteness" address its historical legacy and existing complicity with racist exclusion and oppression, it is equally crucial that such work distinguish between "Whiteness" as a racial identity that is nonracist or anti-racist and those aspects of "Whiteness" that are racist. Where "Whiteness" has been dealt with in educational terms the emphasis is almost exclusively on revealing "Whiteness" as an ideology of privilege mediated largely through the dynamics of racism. While such interventions are crucial in developing antiracist pedagogy, they do not go far enough. I am concerned about what it means educationally for those of us who engage in an antiracist pedagogy and politics to suggest to students that "Whiteness" can only be understood in terms of the common experience of White domination and racism. What subjectivities or points of identification become available to White students who can only imagine White experience as monolithic, self-contained, and deeply racist? What are the educational and political stakes in rearticulating "Whiteness" in anti-essentialist terms so that White youth can understand and struggle against the long legacy of White racism while using the particularities of their own culture as a resource for resistance, reflection, and empowerment? (p. 91)

We must be vigilant to not essentialize Whiteness and White people, like any other group. McCarthy further states, "… to predicate multicultural education on the basis of static definitions of what White people are like and what minorities are like can lead to costly miscalculations that can undermine the goal of race relations reform in education itself" (McCarthy, 1993, p. 298). In the spirit of critically oriented multicultural education pedagogy and practice, Whiteness must be examined in order to understand the construction of systemic and institutional racial oppression, privilege, and the complexity of culture as an idea and lived experience. Moreover, critically engaging with Whiteness allows practitioners and others to also understand how Whiteness, White people, and Western European ancestry are connected and historically created a worldview that promoted and protected a racial hierarchy that reverberates today. Unfortunately, the practice of multicultural education in k-12 schools has been focused largely on teaching tolerance and explorations of racial and ethnic "others." That focus centered Whiteness and White people as merely recipients of these lessons and not equal objects of critique and understanding. Richardson and Johanningmeier (2003) say:

> Multicultural education in the United States is commonly taught as an isolated, superficial exercise lacking historical context for both the subject and the object of study. The dominant culture remains the subject and minority cultures silent objects. At its best this constitutes a relatively safe exercise in reconstruction; at its worst it is fundamentally reproductive of inequality. (p. xi)

In short, as students—particularly White students—progress through k-12 education they learn very little about Whiteness and the construction of our nation's racial hierarchy, the hierarchy's roots, and its persisting impact.

As stated above, multicultural education as a movement began in the 1960s, but that does not necessarily mean battles over the cultural guise of America is a new development. The struggle for the cultural construction and cultural center of America has been on-going since the formation of the first colonies. According to Spring (2001), early European Americans fought hard to define America as a nation for White people through the process of deculturalization. Spring defines deculturalization as "the educational process of destroying a people's culture and replacing it with a new one" (p. 4). In the early days of America what was accepted as legitimate cultural practices emanated from Protestant, English notions of what was good and proper, wrapped in the mission of civilizing others. Spring writes:

> Reflecting the attitudes of English colonists, the founding fathers rejected the idea of a multicultural society and advocated the creation of a unified American culture. … When English colonists and later educators and officials of the U.S. government considered the deculturalization of Native Americans, they included replacing cultural

values related to family structures, gender roles, child-rearing practices, sexual attitudes, economic relationships, and government. (pp. 7–8)

This process of deculturalization was not unique to only Native Americans but
also Africans, Puerto Ricans, Asians, and Eastern Europeans.

The spirit of multicultural education is not to further marginalize groups and
perspectives, including White people and Whiteness. The anti-multiculturalists
claim that multiculturalism makes education a political battlefield *is* truly on the
mark, as any curricular decision—education itself—is laden with politics (Apple,
1990; Aronowitz & Giroux, 1994 Cherryholmes, 1991; Freire, 1970; McLaren,
2007). However, Eller (1997) points out a crucial point that redresses both camps:

> When anti-multiculturalists bemoan the descent of scholarship and culture as a whole
> into political competition, they fail to realize that the politics was always there but that
> they dominated the scene with little noise or opposition. Of course, multiculturalists
> must accept the right of anti-multiculturalists to enter the foray and defend their
> positions, too. (pp. 254–255)

This point is useful in reminding us that education is political. Multicultural education, critical or not, is not a panacea for ameliorating the serious issues of systemic
and institutional oppression, racism, or social justice, but as long as multicultural
education is widely a discussion on the heroes and holidays of "other" groups, a
White hegemony will be sustained and by extension White racial dominance will
ensue unfettered. This is at the heart of White fatigue in that students are not
provided the opportunity to develop a critical eye about issues of diversity, race, and
social justice. By the time those students arrive in our classes, where there tends to
be far greater critical engagement, they have had twelve years of formal education
and eighteen or more years of media and personal messages that promoted a pano-
ply of misrepresentations, half-truths, and unchallenged ideas that sustain oppressive hierarchies and practices, namely Whiteness and racial oppression.

What Is Multicultural Education and Why Does It Need to Be "Critical?": Issues of Discourse, Pedagogy, and Practice

Gay (1992) and Banks (2004) have asserted a disconnection between the theory
and practice of multicultural education. The body of work expounding on theoretical approaches to multicultural education has grown while practical application
and widespread adoption of critical, multicultural education practices are fledgling.
There is a fairly simple explanation for this dilemma. The place of multicultural
education has shifted in teacher preparation programs and there is rising emphasis

in addressing issues of race, ethnicity, gender, class, sexual orientation, and physical ability. As the United States writ large pays more attention to its growing diversity (i.e., the shift toward a majority minority nation and the advances in the acceptance of the LGBTQ+ community), the need to pay particular attention to critical and culturally relevant pedagogies and the sociopolitical context of education practice is gaining more currency in teacher preparation programs in the hopes of strengthening connections among democracy, pluralism, empowerment, and student achievement (Aronowitz & Giroux, 1993; Delpit, 1996; Duncan-Andrade & Morrell, 2008; Giroux, 2011; Howard, 1999; Ladson-Billings, 1994, 1998; McLaren, 1994/2004; Nieto, 2004). The resulting paradigm shift has relocated the emphasis of multicultural education and in turn has caused a revolution in the ways in which teachers think not only the role of multicultural education but also the elements of curriculum in light of standards based reforms, shifts in the responsibilities of teachers, and arguments around the purposes of schooling.

Again, the major problem with narrow interpretations of multicultural education, specifically understanding it as content integration (Banks, 2004), is that the narrow view dismisses the demand for more critical conversations about how knowledge is constructed, illuminating motives, interests, and effects of the construction of canons and cultural literacy (Hirsch, 1988). Equally important is that narrow constructions of multicultural education eclipse the notion of the school as a cultural system or institution that can work both for *and* against students.

With that in mind, Banks (2004, 2015) asserts there is a high level of consensus concerning the aims and goals of multicultural education. He suggests for successful implementation of multicultural education the following must be altered: changes in the curriculum; the teaching materials; teaching and learning styles; attitudes, perceptions, and behaviors of teachers and administrators; and the goals, norms, and culture of the school. Many schools fall short because reform centers primarily on curriculum change that encourages inclusion of more gender, racial, ethnic and linguistic groups. Banks argues that this common practice is a result of strong calls for curricular reform by scholars and later activists while overshadowing the other key components of multicultural education.

Banks (2004) delineates the dimensions of multicultural education as the following:

- *Content integration*: This deals explicitly with teachers' use of "examples, data, and information from a variety of cultures and groups to illustrate key concepts, principles, generalizations, and theories in their subject area or discipline" (p. 4). This is what is commonly focused on in the popular discourse about multicultural education. It is also the point that confounds many science and math teachers, since due to the assumption that their disciplines are not necessarily culturally bound, or the state curricular guidelines do not offer space to address other cultural constructions of science or math.

- *Knowledge construction*: "The knowledge construction process describes the procedure by which social, behavioral, and natural scientists create knowledge, and the manner in which the implicit cultural assumptions, frames of reference, perspectives, and biases within a discipline influence how knowledge is constructed within it" (p. 4). This is a key aspect of multicultural education since it engages students in how knowledge is constructed and has the potential of uncovering racial, ethnic, gender, and social class influences of individuals and groups. In other words, knowledge constructions challenges dominant paradigms and allows students the opportunity to see how power functions and why women and groups of color do not seem to "contribute as much" to the history of knowledge and disciplines.
- *Prejudice reduction*: This aspect focuses on student perspectives about race, gender, and other related issues and is intended to offer students strategies for the development of democratic perspectives.
- *Equity pedagogy*: As Banks explains: "equity pedagogy exists when teachers use techniques and methods that facilitate the academic achievement of students from diverse racial, ethnic, and social class groups" (p. 5).
- *Empowering school culture and social structure*: Schools must be restructured to ensure that diverse students are in fair and equitable environments. Particular attention is paid to grouping practices, labeling practices, social climate of the school, and teacher expectations.

Although these dimensions are well defined, the reality is that they do not always translate into practice.

In *Making Choices for Multicultural Education*, Sleeter and Grant (2011) outline five pedagogical approaches to multicultural education, including: teaching the exceptional and culturally different; human relations; single-group studies; multicultural education; and multicultural social justice education. Of the five approaches they ultimately favor multicultural social justice education because the others do not help students understand the social, cultural, economic, and institutional constraints that shape opportunities for and representations of groups, nor do the other approaches help students move to "praxis," or learning about, reflecting upon, and then acting to change one's condition, environment, and community (Freire, 1970/2000). Teachers who practice a multicultural social justice education approach "engage students in the process of challenging historical norms and existing power structures in order to advance local and global change, promote critical thinking, and validate diverse community funds of knowledge" (Stanton, 2015, p. 182). This is a much deeper exploration of diversity and oppression than what is commonly offered in schools. Christine Sleeter (2010) encourages educators at all levels "to think critically about the power relationships locally and globally today, power relationships on which society was historically constructed, and alternative relationships and ways of conceiving life are possible" (p. 201). In order to teach at that depth, educators must be willing to invest themselves in the challenge of being more critical, including being more critical about their own identities and positionality.

For example, it is essential that educators do more than merely introduce luminaries and great stories. Those people and incidents must be contextualized and challenged. If you treat things as ahistorical then you will perpetuate the system already in place and continue to do harm (Cherryholmes, 1991). Schools that decorate the main bulletin board with ethnic and racial luminaries during celebration months may think they are doing a good service for students (especially the students who are the focus of the celebration month). For all intents and purposes, such efforts are important, especially since exposure to others unlike oneself is an approach championed in multicultural education. However, when pictures of people are posted with no attendant discussion or exploration of the larger social, cultural, economic, and political contexts of their time, then we continue to avoid deeper investigations about how *systems of advantage*—including racism—function. Again, exposure is essential, but exposure at the expense of critical engagement can be destructive.

Cameron McCarthy (1993) argues that multiculturalism has taken on a humanist perspective and is largely guided by arguments about content, texts, and attitudes. In the current popular conception of multiculturalism, more substantive issues regarding institutional racism, unequal power distribution, and glib, essentialist constructions of dominant and subordinate groups are not challenged and this lack of critique reproduces Whiteness and Eurocentricity in the United States' curriculum, in spite of honest efforts to challenge the dominant discourse.

McCarthy outlines three popular discourses of multicultural education that largely guide the ways in which educators think about and act on multicultural education: cultural understanding, cultural competence, and cultural emancipation. Discourses of *cultural understanding* are evidenced in human relations programs in high schools and universities, promoting the idea that there is an inherent equality among various cultures, ethnicities, and races. The stress of these discourses is an acceptance of differences; in other words, "We are all the same but different." An unintended consequence of these programs is the assertion of various ethnic identities by White Americans, such as Polish, Irish, Italian, etc. and the voicing of the "struggles" of immigration these groups endured as an equivocation or understanding of the marginalization of African Americans, Latinxs, Native Americans or other subordinated groups in American history and contemporary society.

The second discourse, *cultural competence*, attempts to frame multicultural-ism in terms of cultural pluralism. By restructuring curriculum to focus on ethnic studies and language differences, cultural competency programs are assumed to help bridge gaps between various ethnic groups. With an emphasis on language and identity of different groups, White students are allowed the opportunity to become more familiar with non-White groups while students of color have the opportunity of representation in the curriculum.

The third discourse, *cultural emancipation*, rests on an economic model and asserts that reframing school curricula can boost the academic success and eco-nomic futures of students of color. Injecting the curriculum with knowledge about the history and achievements of people of color would "reduce the dissonance and alienation from academic success that centrally characterize minority experiences in schooling" (p. 292).

In a similar typology, McLaren (1994) also criticizes what he sees as prevail-ing discourses of multicultural education that fall short in addressing notions of racism and social justice. He highlights conservative or corporate multiculturalism, liberal multiculturalism, and left-liberal multiculturalism. Each has its own subtle difference in the conception of culture. For instance conservative multicultural-ism disavows racism and prejudice. Liberal multiculturalism embraces a notion of cultural sameness. Finally, left-liberal multiculturalism exoticizes diverse cultures. The essential problem with the three constructs is that each ignores substantive issues of power and structural inequity, and the three types tend to fragment the struggles for equity that marginalized groups face.

As Banks (1988) expresses, popular multicultural education discourses attempt to further a "prejudiceless goal" without seriously interrogating the institutional and representational practices that foster Eurocentric hegemony and social stratifi-cation. What is particularly troubling about these discourses is they do not attempt to uncover hidden notions of systemic and institutional racism, intergroup power relations, and inequitable distribution of resources. McCarthy states, "Within these frameworks school reform and freedom in race relations depends almost exclusively on the reversal of values, attitudes, and the human nature of social actors understood as individuals" (pp. 292–293). Racism is constructed through these discourses as a problem with the individual, and the individual only needs exposure to new ideas and perspectives for the problems of racism to diminish. For example, the cultural emancipation discourse discussed by McCarthy rests heavily on the assumption that increased academic achievement for students of color will automatically translate into better opportunities in the economic marketplace.

MacLeod (1995) counters this conclusion. Drawing on the spectrum of social reproduction theory as his conceptual framework, his ethnography of poor and working class Whites and Blacks in an urban housing project focused on the formation of aspirations and educational attainment. MacLeod found that despite Black participants' more favorable engagement with and outcomes in school they fared no better in job attainment than their White counterparts whom prided themselves on their disdain for school and getting into trouble with criminal activity. Explaining this phenomenon, MacLeod emphasizes the positionality of different ethnic and racial groups in the economic marketplace and exposes structural and cultural impediments to success. MacLeod summarized the intersection of race and class:

> Like class, race has an objective dimension rooted in the structure of opportunities. Educational attainment, annual earning, rates of employment, and a host of other measures confirm that African Americans are disadvantaged relative to Whites. Yet race exists not just in material differences but also in subjective dimension—in individuals' minds as a category that shapes they way they view themselves and the social world. As with class, the subjective articulation of race seldom lines up with its objective dimension. (p. 250)

MacLeod's ethnography, along with others, like Paul Willis' *Learning to Labor* (1981), uncover the complexity of these issues. Grasping texts that explicate the complex dynamics of success and failure is a challenge for many students, including teacher education students. Would this be the case if students were learning about these issues at earlier stages in their academic, intellectual, social, and spiritual development? White fatigue is an individual's response to recognizing the real complexity—and intellectual challenge of understanding that complexity—in her effort to understand how racism and other forms of oppression function, especially if they hope to be a teacher capable of creating experiences that can empower all students.

Employing a critical multicultural pedagogy allows educators to engage larger notions of structure, power, and the construction of "self" and "others" through the curriculum. These issues may come up in examination of literature and history, but that assumes that students will necessarily make these connections and that they will know what to do with that knowledge. Equally, this also assumes teachers are prepared and willing to take up these challenging issues.

Unfortunately, many teachers feel unprepared to teach multicultural or antibias curriculum (Au & Blake, 2003; Derman-Sparks, Ramsey, & Edwards, 2011; Ukpokodu, 2004). Fehr and Agnello (2012) in a study examining the use of the *Cultural Diversity Awareness Inventory*, originally created by Gertrude Henry (1986) and updated by Fehr and Agnello for today's context, found that 56% of the preservice teachers surveyed—whom were overwhelmingly White and female—indicated "a superficial understanding of multicultural education."

According to Fehr and Agnello this superficial understanding of multicultural education "falls short of even describing the 'tourist approach' to multicultural education" (p. 37).

A critical multicultural education program has a better chance at helping not only students but also future teachers engage with the complexities of race, ethnicity, culture, structural inequality, oppression, and other substantive issues that shape American culture and education. Critical multicultural education asks educators to not only consider these thematic issues but also act upon them to help change lives and communities. If we are not helping students learn to be change agents in their communities then what exactly is the point, especially in the standards dominated environment that education has become? Finally, employing critical multicultural education pedagogy and practice may challenge the notions of cultural essentialism and provide teachers and students with a new language in which to engage issues.

It is not so much that any given approach to multicultural education is flatly wrong. All can be useful. Rather, the engagement of multicultural education has had the tendency to focus on explanations about exoticized or unknown others. A more concerted effort to historically, economically, politically, and culturally situate historically marginalized groups across the history of the United States has been minimized until fairly recently. This fixes Whiteness and White people at the center of the discussion and inadvertently further marginalizes non-White groups. The inverse is the White institutionalized mainstream continues to be held at arm's length from the very groups they are trying to engage, like exhibits in a museum to gaze upon and question rather than neighbors to dialogue with and understand as both unique and common.

Drifting From the Point: Silences and Misrepresentation in Multicultural Curriculum

Today in 2017, as a result of the rise of standards based reform, the demands of No Child Left Behind, and the burden of standardized testing, talk about multicultural education has receded. It is as though multiculturalism is seen as a persistent norm in schools—an "obvious" consideration, if you will. After all, what teacher do you know who would openly admit to the notion that only certain students can learn or that it is alright to marginalize any student based on identity, despite what their actual teaching practices may convey. You would be hard-pressed. You can see this mindset in statements like, "I treat all my kids the same," another misplaced sensibility born out of colorblind ideologies (Bonilla-Silva, 2013).

For students fighting White fatigue, this is a fundamental point. They understand the basic idea that racism is wrong but are not yet fully understanding of how racism functions. Understanding this is essential to preparing future teachers to be savvy enough to engage their own students and create opportunities for critical engagement, either through explicit curricular opportunities or through impromptu situations that often erupt on school grounds or in popular culture. The state of fatigue occurs in light of grappling with their own misunderstandings and lack of (or budding) criticality, despite their stated and felt desires for racial equity. But, equity takes work, and learning the full scope of issues of oppression can be equally demanding.

Multicultural education not keeping pace with the theory that guided it fostered a sort of cult of personality that furthered traditional ideals of the American dream, most specifically the notion of bootstrapping (Villanueva, 1993). I imagine many have heard the cliché, "you've gotta pull yourself up by your bootstraps." This sensibility, reflective of the Protestant work ethic that undergirds the American odyssey and fuels the machine of capitalism (Spring, 2001; Weber, 1930/2001), renders any structural, systemic, or institutional constraints null and void. In K–12 classrooms, there is an overemphasis on discourses of the strong, independent individual that fomented change out of their own will. For instance, popular recounts of the Civil Rights Movement of the 1950s and 1960s all but erase the amazing display of collective strategizing, grass roots organizing, and bravery by thousands of lesser, unknown women and men (Branch, 1988; Williams & Bond, 1993). There is a tendency to talk about the luminaries of the Movement, specifically Dr. Martin Luther King and Mrs. Rosa Parks. However, a number of important issues are left in the margins of the teacher's handbook.

In the case of the story of Mrs. Parks, young students are not engaged in the fact that she was not the first to sit at the front of a Montgomery, AL bus, nor that she was intimately involved with the Montgomery, Alabama NAACP, nor that she had attended a Freedom School, nor that she was part of a coordinated, strategized movement (Kohl, 1995). In short, the most important parts of her story (strategizing, mobilizing community, collaboration, along with self sacrifice) are silenced—leaving kids to believe that she just "pulled herself up by her bootstraps" and made change happen, as though she was the very first to resist Jim Crow.

Similarly, millions know Dr. King's quote, "I have a dream that my four little children will one day live in a nation where they will not be judged by the color of their skin but by the content of their character" (King, 1963, p. 5) from his historic *I Have a Dream Speech* at the March on Washington for Jobs and Freedom in 1963. The contemporary memory of that speech misses the more sober and critical metaphor that "America has given Negro people a bad check, a check which has come back marked 'insufficient funds'" (p. 2). Moreover, the national lionization of Dr. King has come at a significant cost. The persistent memory of the human-ist, beloved community rhetoric of his message is indispensible; however, his cou-pling of racial and economic justice is eclipsed in the popular collective memory of Dr. King. The effect of this selective national memory is that the idea of the indi-vidual and how we *think* about one another supersedes the larger challenge of systemic and institutional reform that ameliorates marginalizing practices against African Americans and other historically marginalized groups. From the extent of the devastation of the continental Indigenous at the hands of Columbus and others, to the resistance against Women's suffrage, to the interracial reality of the struggle against racial oppression, truncated stories are pervasive in the American mythos. Even when I talk to graduate students about them, many are shocked at the details left on the editing room floor of popular American history, and the textbooks used in American schools do more harm than good (Lowen, 2007) when perpetuating such myths or half-truths.

While knowing great individuals is important, the ways in which these lumi-naries are often decontextualized from their historic realities of community, grass roots organizing, and common struggle against racial oppression. The retelling of Civil Rights Movement stories all but erase the presence of White folks who were not only supportive of the cause for racial justice but also participated actively in the struggle. It is without doubt, and none should ever be cast, that the Civil Rights Movement was fomented and lead by African Americans, but erasing White allies and accomplices from the story, like Gary Howard (1999), Henry Giroux (1997), and Tim Wise (2012) pointed out, leaves White students without role models of racial justice and a positive racial identity, and further reifies the idea that the struggle for racial justice is "their" struggle, not "ours." Moreover, the omission of White allies and accomplices—let alone leaders—creates a cultural context that reinscribes discourses of opposition, making it that much more challenging for non-Whites and Whites to form coalitions.

White fatigue settles in for White students when they are confronted with deeper elements of the backstories of these great events, and when they are con-fronted with messages that position White folks as only the problem that needs to be fixed and not agents of change. Both of these issues of positioning are flawed, as neither encourages *all* learners to consider the nature of systemic and institutional racism and how it functions to further hierarchy and marginalization, adding to not only the miseducation of Black students but also all students. In regards to Mrs. Park's story, I ask my students, after they express frustration about not being taught "the real" story, "Whose interests are served by perpetuating the lone frus-trated woman who decided to sit at the front of the bus story? And, what does it mean for our understanding of both the African American community *and* the reality of the Movement when we frame Mrs. Park's story as we popularly do?" I have watched the faces of many White students turn from innocent ignorance, to frustration, to withdrawal. Like the great Johnny Rotten, lead singer of the punk rock group the Sex Pistols, once asked, "Have you ever gotten the feeling you were being cheated" (Temple, 2005)?

Advancing the Struggle Against Oppression: Considerations on Social Justice Education

In light of accrediting and academic organizations promoting standards that encourage attention to diversity and critical thinking, the ideas of multicultural education can now be seen as just another brick in the foundation of both teacher education and general education in the United States. The problem, though, is that talk and instruction about these issues does not necessarily promote the empowerment of students nor an understanding of how systems and institutions serve as conduits of oppression. In the case of White fatigue, the oftentimes uncritical and cursory approaches to curricular inclusion (heroes and holidays) do not provide White students (all students for that matter) with a deeper understanding of the historic development and positionality of Whiteness and White people, and when they find themselves in "diversity courses" that are critical and social justice oriented, those White students are exposed to a bevy of previously told half-truths and misconstructions. That new knowledge adds to their confusion and frustration, and although that cognitive and spiritual dissonance is necessary for growth it is dissonance nonetheless.

As standards and accreditation organizations include words like diversity and inclusion into their standards, the proliferation of these concepts have become hackneyed and common. The result is a palpable frustration from all stakeholders in the process of teacher education, especially students. Their derision appears as a form of tacit knowledge (Berliner, 1994). In the case of teacher education, it is as though many preservice and practicing teachers "get it" and feel that one or two "diversity courses" is sufficient to understand the complexities of undoing the primacy of Eurocentric canons, cultural capital, and social expectations embedded in schools and curriculum.

I have encountered many students who express frustration at having to "learn this stuff" again, or they argue that they "covered these issues in another class." Multicultural education and the attendant ideas are often deemed as items to cross off a checklist toward certification or professional development rather than an essential component of the foundations of pedagogy, curriculum, and practice. Constructing those responses as resistant is convenient. However, it is not entirely fair to place those tendencies at the feet of teacher education students. Rather, teacher education programs have not necessarily helped because of the historic proclivity of programs to offer the "diversity course" and only until the last decade have programs en masse begun to rethink their curricular options and infuse multicultural education principles across the curriculum. After all, a single class or two are not sufficient for offering students at any level the exposure necessary to understand diversity as a human condition and central determinant in the success and failure of children, youths, and communities. It can be legitimately argued that, for example, the National Council for the Accreditation of Teacher Education (NCATE) Standard 4 on diversity was helpful in promoting attendance to diversity. The standard states:

> The unit designs, implements, and evaluates curriculum and provides experiences for candidates to acquire and demonstrate the knowledge, skills, and professional dispositions necessary to help all students learn. Assessments indicate that candidates can demonstrate and apply proficiencies related to diversity. Experiences provided for candidates include working with diverse populations, including higher education and P–12 school faculty, candidates, and students in P–12 schools.

That is all fine and good, but the issue here is that this is not a promotion of critical perspectives that help teacher education students, who are largely White females, understand how our national history of racial oppression began, was furthered by law, policy, and social practices, and persists today. Again, we can teach about diversity and the "needs" of various groups, but that is not the same as teaching for social justice or how to be an agent for change.

The New Frontier: The Rise of Social Justice Education in Teacher Education

The term multicultural education has devolved into a buzzword. As talk about how multicultural education has fallen out of favor we have seen an increase in social justice and social justice education. Miller and Kirkland (2010) define social justice education as the "unpack(ing) of truths that challenge master narratives and unveils counter-narratives that often go untold or ignored altogether" (p. 3). Similarly, Diane Goodman (2011) states that social justice education "involves addressing issues of equity, power relations, and institutionalized oppression … changing unjust institutional structures, policies, and practices, and challenging the dominant ideology" (p. 4). Social justice and multicultural education are two sides of the same coin. While both have the project of promoting the empowerment of historically marginalized groups, there is an important distinction between the two. Banks (2004) points out that "A major goal of multicultural education ... is to reform the schools and other educational institutions so that students from diverse racial, ethnic, and social-class groups will experience educational equality" (p. 3). Social justice education is a conceptual strategy that promotes the interrogation of key issues related to the larger umbrella of multicultural education. Social justice education gives multicultural education a clearer mission and debalkanizes multicultural education by encouraging a focus on the larger, common issues of systemic and institutional oppression and their amelioration, across groups and interests. Regardless of the ways in which social justice education has risen in popularity, the reality is that it continues to lie at the fringes of curriculum reform and debate, especially in the k-12 milieu.

Lee Ann Bell (2016) explains that the primary goal of social justice education is to promote the "full and equal participation of all groups in a society that is mutually shaped to meet their needs" (p. 3). In other words, social justice educators inject notions of equity, equality, inclusion, and empowerment in the educational imaginary and further offer students opportunities to critically consider how various forms of power tacitly and explicitly shape marginalization. In this effort, social justice educators promote critical examinations of systems and institutions—particularly but not limited to education—and the ways in which oppression functions. In essence, social justice educators operate from the basic premise that trends of failure used to describe marginalized groups are not products of laziness, ineptitude, ignorance, or cultural differences but are products of systemic and institutional practices that all but ensure trends of inequity and the norm of Whiteness in all areas. However, social justice education has its detractors, as any aspect of multicultural education has.

Kathy Hytten (2006) illuminates an important point about social justice education and the popular resistance to it. She states:

> While there have always been educators calling for a social justice approach toward education, this vision has never been the dominant one. This is especially true in our current climate, where teachers are increasingly asked to focus on a very narrow set of goals, in particular, raising standardized test scores. (p. 224)

Despite the deeply humanist underpinnings of social justice education and its goal of dismantling oppression in all its forms, the reality is social justice education is a tough sell in schools in the United States. Definitely, there are many schools (both K-12 and teacher education) scattered across the country that openly promote a social justice education curriculum, but by and large they are anomalies. Practitioners of social justice education are often maligned and lampooned as being socialists, communists, touchy-feely, and reverse racist. Social justice education and its goals do not fit the American project, as social justice educators regularly challenge long-standing assumptions about the United States, like the veracity of the Protestant work ethic, the impact of and challenge against equity based policies, Eurocentric canons, the privileging of the White racial framing of the United States (Feagin, 2013), and other issues. The challenge of social justice education is that its very nature is antagonistic to the status quo. If a primary goal of social justice education is the dismantling of all forms of systemic and institutional oppression, then challenges toward those positioned as "more powerful" or privileged are indispensible.

Recognizing the role teachers play in shaping their students' identities, beliefs, and expectations is essential and substantial (Freire & Macedo, 1987; Miller, 2007). Miller (2007) states, "Teachers should become aware of how their own biases and presuppositions of students based on family background, appearance, and discourse can disenfranchise and marginalize potential learners" (p. 159). The pedagogies and practices perpetrated in schools have a profound impact on students, and when those pedagogies and practices reflexively and uncritically promote the status quo, discourses of power and identity that promote marginalization infect the minds of youth, rendering them unwitting accomplices in the furthering of oppression. In short, the choices teachers make about not only what to teach but also how to teach that material is fundamental to the maintenance of inequity and oppression, and when White students who may show seemingly resistant behaviors are summarily constructed as part of the problem that hampers more progressive possibilities. Framing their resistance as fatigue is a way of recognizing their struggle while also continuing to hold their feet to the fire to learn this fundamentally important material, as future teachers and/or citizens.

As I am writing this, I recognize that I may be committing an act of racial heresy, but the great W. E. B. DuBois (1904/1969) asked, "How does it feel to be a problem" (p. 43)? DuBois was asking that question specifically of African Americans, and the query can be aimed toward any historically marginalized group. However, a critical approach to multicultural and social justice education can ask the same question of Whiteness and White people, which for them is not necessarily the most comfortable cognitive nor emotional nor spiritual position, but like the historically marginalized, exploring this question is a necessary step in the development of a positive racial identity and aligning oneself with the values of social justice. Curriculum must be purposefully designed for an educative experience (Dewey, 1938/2015) that draws on experiences and fosters dialogue with all members of the community. Merely finding out how we are similar in order to tolerate one another is a pedestrian goal. Rather, investigating how we are similar in order to understand how groups have been systematically pitted against each other to create and sustain a racial hierarchy is the goal of social justice education. In that end, we must examine how Whiteness has been used as a tool to ensure hierarchy and hegemony.

Exposure to these more complex ideas, which could have been introduced at much younger grade levels, shows students that their assumptions about "treating each other with respect" or exercising colorblind ideologies are ultimately discursive and curricular practices that render projects of criticality disengaged. Yes, White folks, there is a great deal to own up to, but as curriculum planners with an eye toward social justice rethink how we engage these issues we can counter-balance the acts of marginalization by White folks with the acts of active resistance against marginalization. That is the most effective means to thwart fatigue: provide students with a critical eye and a positive, alternative construction of the racial self. Unlearning the messages of racial hierarchy is challenging and the notion of habitus from Pierre Bourdieu can be helpful in understanding why.

Bibliography

Apple, M. (1990). *Ideology and curriculum* (2nd ed.). New York, NY: Routledge.

Aronowitz, S., & Giroux, H. A. (1994). *Education still under siege*. Westport, CT: Bergin & Garvey.

Au, K., & Blake, K. (2003). Cultural identity and learning to teach in a diverse community. *Journal of Teacher Education, 54*, 192–205.

Baldwin, J. (1998). On being White ... and other lies. In D. Roediger (Ed.), *Black on White: Black writers on what it means to be White*. New York, NY: Schocken Books.

Banks, J. (1988). *Multicultural education: Theory and practice*. Boston, MA: Allyn and Bacon.

Banks, J. (2004). Multicultural education: Historical development, dimensions, and practice. In J. A. Banks & C. McGee Banks (Eds.), *Handbook of research on multicultural education* (pp. 3–29). San Francisco, CA: Jossey Bass.

Banks, J. A. (2015). *Cultural diversity and education* (6th ed.). New York, NY: Routledge.

Bell, L. A. (2016). Theoretical foundations for social justice education. In M. Adams & L. A. Bell (Eds.), *Teaching for diversity and social justice* (3rd ed., pp. 3–26). New York, NY: Routledge.

Berliner, D. C. (1994). Expertise: The wonder of exemplary performances. In J. N. Mangieri & C. C. Block (Eds.), *Creating powerful thinking in teachers,* (pp. 161–186). Fort Worth, TX: Harcourt Brace College.

Bonilla-Silva, E. (2013). *Racism without racists: Color-Blind racism and the persistence of racial inequality in America*. Lanham, MD: Rowman & Littlefield.

Bowles, S., & Gintis, H. (2011). *Schooling in capitalist America: Educational reform and the contradictions of economic life* (Reprint ed.). Chicago, IL: Haymarket Press.

Branch, T. (1988). *Parting the waters: America in the King years, 1954–1963.* New York, NY: Simon and Schuster.

Brann, E. (1993). Liberal education and multiculturalism: Friends or enemies? *Vital Speeches of the Day, 59,* 221–224.

Cherryholmes, C. H. (1991). *Power and criticism: Poststructural investigations in education.* New York, NY: Teachers College Press.

D'Souza, D. (1991). *Illiberal education: The politics of race and sex on campus.* New York, NY: Free Press.

Delpit, L. D. (1988). The silenced dialogue: Power and pedagogy in educating other people's children. *Harvard Educational Review, 58*(3), 280–298.

Delpit, L. D. (1996). *Other people's children: Cultural conflict in the classroom.* New York, NY: New Press.

Derman-Sparks, L. O., Ramsey, P. G., & Edwards, J. O. (2011). *What if all the kids are White?* (2nd ed.). New York, NY: Teachers College Press.

Dewey, J. (1938/2015). *Experience and education.* New York, NY: Free Press.

DuBois, W. E. B. (1904/1969). *The souls of Black folk* (Signet Classic ed.). New York, NY: Penguin Books.

Duncan-Andrade, J., & Morrell, E. (2008). *The art of critical pedagogy: Possibilities for moving from theory to practice in urban schools* (New edition ed.). New York, NY: Peter Lang.

Eller, J. D. (1997). Anti-anti-multiculturalism. *American Anthropologist, 99*(2), 249–256.

Feagin, J. (2013). *The White racial frame: Centuries of racial framing and counter framing* (2nd ed.). New York, NY: Routledge.

Fehr, M. C., & Agnello, M. F. (December 01, 2012). Engaging in diverse classrooms: Using a diversity awareness survey to measure preservice teachers' preparedness, willingness, & comfort. *Multicultural Education, 19,* 2, 34–39.

Fine, M. (1997). Witnessing Whiteness. In M. Fine, L. Weis, L. C. Powell, & L. M. Wong (Eds.), *Off White: Readings on power, privilege, and resistance* (pp. 57–65). New York, NY: Routledge.

Fine, M., Weis, L., Powell, L. C., & Wong, L. M. (1997). Preface. In M. Fine, L. Weis, L. C. Powell, & L. M. Wong (Eds.), *Off White: Readings on power, privilege, and resistance* (pp. vii–xi). New York, NY: Routledge.

Freire, P. (1970/1997). *Pedagogy of the oppressed* (New revised 20th anniversary ed.). New York, NY: Continuum.

Freire, P., & Macedo, D. (1987). *Literacy: Reading the word and the world.* New York, NY: Routledge.

Gay, G. (1992). The state of multicultural education in the United States. In K. Adam Moodley (Ed.), *Education in plural societies: International perspectives* (pp. 47–66). Calgary, Alberta, Canada: Detselig Enterprises.

Giroux, H. A. (1997). *Channel surfing: Race talk and the destruction of American youth.* New York, NY: St. Martin's Press.

Giroux, H. A. (2011). *On critical pedagogy.* London: Continuum International Publishing Group.

Goodman, D. J. (2011). *Promoting diversity and social justice: Educating people from privileged groups*. London: Routledge.

Gramsci, A. (1971). *Selections from the prison notebooks*. New York, NY: International.

Henry, G. B. (1986). *Cultural diversity awareness inventory*. Hampton, VA: Hampton Mainstreaming Outreach Services.

Hirsch, E. D. (1988). *Cultural literacy: What every American needs to know*. New York, NY: Vintage.

Howard, G. R. (1999). *We can't teach what we don't know: White teachers, multiracial schools* (1sted.). New York, NY: Teachers College Press.

Hytten, K. (2006, May 1). Education for social justice: Provocations and challenges. *Educational Theory, 56*(2), 221–236.

King, M. L. (1963). *I have a dream* [speech]. Retrieved from https://www.archives.gov/files/press/exhibits/dream-speech.pdf

Kohl, H. (1995). *Should we burn Babar?: Essays on children's literature and the power of stories*. New York, NY: New Press.

Ladson-Billings, G. (1994). *Dreamkeepers: Successful teachers of African American children*. San Francisco, CA: Jossey-Bass.

Ladson-Billings, G. (1998, January 1). Just what is critical race theory and what's it doing in a nice field like education? *International Journal of Qualitative Studies in Education, 11*(1), 7–24.

Leonardo, Z. (2002, March 1). The Souls of White Folk: Critical pedagogy, whiteness studies, and globalization discourse. *Race Ethnicity and Education, 5*(1), 29–50.

Lowen, J. (2007). *Lies my teacher told me: Everything your American history textbook got wrong* (Revised ed.). New York, NY: Touchstone.

MacLeod, J. (1995). *Ain't no makin' it: Aspirations and attainment in a low income neighborhood* (2nd ed.). Boulder, CO: Westview Press.

McCarthy, C. (1993). After the canon: Knowledge and ideological representation in the multicultural discourse on curriculum reform. In C. McCarthy & W. Crichlow (Eds.), *Race, identity, and representation in education* (1st ed., pp. 289–305). New York, NY: Routledge.

McIntosh, P. (1988). White privilege and male privilege: A personal account of coming to see correspondences through work in women's studies. In M. L. Anderson & P. Hill-Collins (Eds.), *Race, class, and gender: An anthology* (pp. 70–81). Wellesley, MA: Wellesley College Center for Research on Women.

McLaren, P. (1994). *Life in schools: An introduction to critical pedagogy in the foundations of education* (2nd ed.). Harlow, UK: Longman.

McLaren, P. (2007). *Life in schools* (5th ed.). Boston, MA: Allyn & Bacon.

Miller, s. j. (2007, January 1). Social justice and sociocultural issues as part of the loaded matrix. *Counterpoints, 311*, 157–203.

Miller, s. j., & Kirkland, D. E. (2010). *Change matters: Critical essays on moving social justice research from theory to policy*. New York, NY: Peter Lang.

Nieto, S. (1995). *Affirming diversity: The sociopolitical context of multicultural education*. New York, NY: Longman.

Nieto, S. (2004). *Affirming diversity: The sociopolitical context of multicultural education* (MyLab-School ed., 4th ed.). Boston, MA: Allyn & Bacon.

Richardson, T. R., & Johanningmeier, E. V. (2003). *Race, ethnicity, and education: What is taught in school*. Greenwich, CT: Information Age Publishing.

Schlesinger, A. M. (1992). *The disuniting of America: Reflections on a multicultural society*. New York, NY: W. W. Norton.

Scott, W. B. (2002, January 1). The miseducation of White America. *Widener Law Symposium Journal, 9*, 73–80.

Sleeter, C. E. (2010). Decolonizing curriculum: An essay review of *The Sacred Hoop*. *Curriculum Inquiry, 40*(2), 193–203.

Sleeter, C. E., & Grant, C. (2011). *Making choices for multicultural education: Five approaches to race, class, and gender* (6th ed.). Hoboken, NJ: John Wiley & Sons.

Spring, J. (2001). *Deculturalization and the struggle for equality: A brief history of the education of dominated cultures in the United States*. New York, NY: McGraw-Hill.

Stanton, C. R. (2015, October 2). Beyond the margins: Evaluating the support for multicultural education within teachers' editions of U.S. History textbooks. *Multicultural Perspectives, 17*(4), 180–189.

Temple, J (Director). (2005). *The filth and the fury: A Sex Pistols film* [DVD]. New Line Home Video.

Ukpokodu, O. (2004). The impact of shadowing culturally different students on preservice teachers; disposition toward diversity. *Multicultural Education, 12*, 19–28.

Villanueva, V. (1993). *Bootstraps: From and American academic of color*. Urbana, IL: National Council for the Teachers of English.

Weber, M. (1930/2001). *The protestant ethic and the spirit of capitalism*. New York, NY: Routledge.

Webster, Y. (1997). *Against the multicultural agenda: A critical thinking alternative*. Westport, CT: Praeger.

Williams, J., & Bond, J. (1993). *Eyes on the prize: America's civil rights years, 1954–1965* (Reprint ed.). New York, NY: Penguin Books.

Willis, P. (1981). *Learning to labor: How working class kids get working class jobs*. New York, NY: Columbia University Press.

Wise, T. (2012). *Dear White America: Letter to a new minority*. San Francisco, CA: City Lights Books.

Woodson, C. G. (1933/1993). *The miseducation of the Negro* (African World Press, Inc. ed., 6th Printing). Washington, DC: African World Press.

CHAPTER FIVE

Breaking Bad Habit(u)s

Considerations on the Reproduction of Worldviews

Why does it seem so difficult to teach about race and racism, especially to White students? Teaching about issues related to race is unlike most other bodies of knowledge. As pointed out previously, subjects like calculus, physics, geology, and even psychology rarely see the same kind of resistance from students as race. It is literally as though the notion of highly rigorous studies is incidental when it comes to the academic exploration of race, and this sentiment is not lost in teacher education. Many of my colleagues and I routinely lament how we can show students decades of data and historical analysis that clearly show the consistent marginalization of non-White groups and some students will respond by saying, "Well, in my opinion." Imagine being in a chemistry class and telling the professor, "Well, in my opinion I just don't believe this whole protons and neutrons thing!" However, it is common to hear a students say, "I don't buy this whole mass incarceration and slavery thing; that's a stretch."

Now, I recognize that some may argue that oftentimes issues of race are discussed in the *soft sciences* and I am comparing apples and oranges. To that point, think about how students readily embrace the legitimacy of classical philosophy, like Plato's *Allegory of the Cave*. I regularly use the *Allegory of the Cave* to explore the nature and project of critical thinking and the notion of truth. If you are not familiar with Plato's *Allegory* it is quite simple, yet deeply complex. Plato creates a scenario: a group of people are chained and shackled in a cave, facing the back wall and seeing an incessant stream of shadows projected onto the wall. They cannot see the source of the projections, but they are exposed to them nonetheless. Eventually, one of the prisoners breaks free of the shackles and escapes the cave. The escaped prisoner first realizes that the images projected onto the wall are manipulations. Then, as the prisoner emerges from the darkness, the natural light is blinding, but as the escaped prisoner's eyes acclimate to the natural light of the sun, the prisoner begins to see things as they are. Now that the prisoner *sees* that the projections are manipulated and there is a whole new world outside the cave, the prisoner eventually returns to the cave to encourage the others to break their shackles. Unfortunately, the freed person is jeered and heckled. The key point of the allegory is what is often represented as truth are manipulations, and one must turn to the light (truth) in order to understand one's reality. Students tend to point to the media and the ways in which media constructs and manipulates messages to promote particular positions.

Students *see* so much truth in the allegory and make many connections without ever challenging its legitimacy. However, when I have them grapple with Lisa Delpit's (1988) "The Silenced Dialog: Power and Pedagogy in Educating Other People's Children" and her notion of the culture of power, some students will retort with, "I don't think this is true at all," and some have even dismissed Delpit as angry and divisive. It is as though the ancient supersedes the contemporary when it comes to legitimacy.

The point of contention I have is that students' resistance is not always about challenging simple opinions but rigorous research. Their resistance is often couched in blind adherence to an idiosyncratic belief rather than an embrace of what has been studied and validated by professionals and experts. Why? The consistent challenge and dismissal of research about race and racism simply reproduces our current racial status quo. Not embracing what we have learned over the past 100-plus years about how race and racism function in American society reproduces particular worldviews of marginalization, and this often happens without an acknowledgement of those worldviews and how they reproduce a particular social structure.

Although there are many theories of social reproduction in education (Bernstein, 1971/2003; Bourdieu & Passeron, 1990; Bowles & Gintis, 1976/2011; Giroux, 1983; Heath, 1983; MacLeod, 2004; Willis, 1977/1981) French sociologist Pierre Bourdieu's (Bourdieu, 1977; Bourdieu & Passeron, 1990) concepts are particularly helpful in understanding how perspectives are reproduced from generation to generation. Bourdieu's notion of cultural capital has attained a sacred space in the sociology of education and has been quite useful in helping explain the nature of cultural and racial disparities in schools (Leonardo, 2013; MacLeod,

2008; Morrow & Torres, 1995). Regardless, his notion of habitus affords us the ability to talk about group trends and individuals' experiences simultaneously (Hiller & Rooksby, 2005). Simply stated, habitus can be considered as the sum total of an individual's experience and the ideals, values, dispositions, codes, etc. that form how that individual understands and interacts with any given social context. This phenomenon can occur for both individuals and larger groups.

Recognizing the power of habitus is important since some habitus is privileged and some is marginalized in social practices. In a conversation with Leslie David Burns, we considered the connection between aspects of habitus that are privileged and tied Bourdieu's idea to Gramsci's concept of hegemony (Chou, Lee, & Ho, 2012; Gramsci, 1971; Harker, 1984). A simplified way of thinking about hegemony is as though it is an umbrella of ideals, beliefs, rules, codes, expectations, and ways of being that govern behaviors in any given context, large and small. Gramsci posits that hegemonies are social constructions that are at least initially willful and conscious to some degree. Hegemonies are built to serve certain groups and maintain power relations such that, when effective, they often appear to become unconsciously accepted over time to the point that people feel they are normal or natural states of being even though they are not. Structurally, as such, hegemonies such as Whiteness seem likely to move toward an even deeper, subconscious level at which societies may begin to not recognize them as purposeful in their origins at all, making those hegemonies less apparent to the point of subconsciousness. They become unexamined and unquestioned "common sense," especially for those who may benefit most from maintaining them. This is complementary and consonant with habitus (L. D. Burns, personal communication, November 2, 2016).

Understanding the connection between habitus, hegemony, and the maintenance of worldviews is useful for explaining why they are not so easily unlearned. This is key to understanding why learning about race and racism, which often challenges deep-seated worldviews, is such a contested enterprise, the primary hurdle for the fatigued.

Breaking and Racializing Habitus: Considering Bourdieu's Vague Idea

French sociologist Pierre Bourdieu released his groundbreaking text *Outline of a Theory of Practice* in 1977. At the time of release, Marxist and neo-Marxist interpretations of a structural-deterministic understanding of human interaction and social reproduction dominated French sociological thought. In other words, there are structures in society (like schools, the economy, and politics) and groups are *assigned* roles in that structure. Depending on your role, you are pre-determined for specific outcomes. The primary problem with structural-deterministic theories is that there is little consideration of human agency—the ability for humans to make their own choices and actions that may challenge the structure. So, for example, it is confounding in structural-deterministic theories to explain why a student from an underperforming, low income neighborhood can grow up to become one of the wealthy elite.

Bourdieu considered himself a structural Marxist, but he also had a higher goal in the development of his theory of practice framework as outlined in his 1977 text. Specifically, his ideas attempted to thread a thin needle between structure and agency (Nash, 1999). As Shilling (2004) describes:

> Pierre Bourdieu's writings constitute a powerful attempt to construct a corporeal sociology, an approach towards the structuring of human relationships and identities centered around the socially shaped embodied subject (Crossley, 2001; Shilling, 2003). This approach was developed by Bourdieu in order to avoid those "theoretically debilitating" dualisms (the object/subject, structure/agency, culture/nature and public/private divisions) that fragmented the study of society into artificially divided segments. (Bourdieu, 1980, p. 25; 1990a; 1999, pp. 613, 620). (p. 473)

If a person speaks a certain way, that speech may or may not gain that person access to particularly economically privileged spaces. But, is that necessarily true under all circumstances? For example, Samuel Bowles and Herbert Gintis' *Schooling in Capitalist America* (1976/2011) offered a Marxist analysis of how schooling reproduces class relations through the *correspondence principle*. According to Bowles and Gintis' correspondence principle, "the relationships of authority and control between administrators and teachers, teachers and students, students and students, and students and their work replicate the division of labor which dominates the work place" (p. 12). Jean Anyon's (1981) study of the pedagogical and instructional differences among high schools in different economic strata does support Bowles and Gintis' structural determinism, but these analyses neglect to factor in the infinite diversity of individual possibilities that could change the trajectory of a student's life, like a low-income student being extended a scholarship for an elite preparatory school, or an upper-middle class student having to leave her private school to attend the local public school after her parents lost considerable money in the wake of a national economic crisis. Structuralist constructions are definitely useful, as they can elegantly help us understand how our social world—societies, communities, and institutions—is constructed. However, structuralist theories also tend to be fixed and operate as a series of declarations of how things are and will be (Cherryholmes, 1988; Eagleton, 1983), minimizing the possibility of human agency. Bourdieu sought to resolve the structural-determinism/agency trap through his theory of practice. There are three primary components of Bourdieu's

(Bourdieu, 1977, 1992, 1993) theory of practice: *social field, cultural capital, and habitus*. Although habitus is the focus of this chapter, it is necessary to consider field and cultural capital for a moment.

Field

Bourdieu's notion of social fields refers to organized or structured sets of spaces where issues of power and identity are negotiated (Bourdieu, 1992, 1993). As Hargrove (2009) explains, "Across the field, agents and/or institutions battle for power over the distribution of the specific capital that has accumulated (Bourdieu, 1993), and it is these struggles and their outcomes that heavily influence subsequent strategies for domination and control employed by those in the loftiest positions" (p. 95). In effect, fields can be thought of as discrete spaces (or ideas of organized reality) where meaning is produced, and as Bourdieu further points out, "all agents within the field must share a certain number of fundamental interests, namely everything that is linked to the existence of the field" (Bourdieu, 1993, p. 73). For example, everything from academic disciplines, genres of art and cultural production, to particular manifestations of racial experience (i.e., Whiteness, Blackness, etc.) can be constructed as social fields, but a field would be nothing without those "fundamental interests." This is where cultural capital becomes an issue.

Cultural Capital

As Jay MacLeod (2004) states in *Ain't No Makin' It*, "Bourdieu's most important contribution to reproduction theory is the concept of cultural capital, which he defines as the general background, knowledge, dispositions, and skills that are passed from one generation to the next" (p. 13). This is the simplest part of Bourdieu's ideas to grasp. As children we all learn a set of knowledge, dispositions, values, beliefs, mannerisms, and skills that can help us advance in our cultural and social contexts. We learn what clothes to wear in different situations; how to talk; when to talk; which fork to use; what is of value. Depending on a host of factors, we learn, for example, the value of particular schools compared to others. Since social reproduction theory initially focused on class-based reproduction in light of its Marxist origins, Bourdieu (1977) gave particular focus to the ways in which forms of capital reproduced inequity in schools. McLeod (2004) further explains:

> By embodying class interests and ideologies, schools reward the cultural capital of the dominant classes and systematically devalue that of the lower classes. Upper class students, by virtue of a certain linguistic and cultural competence acquired through family upbringing, are provided with the means of appropriation for success in school. (p. 13)

Cultural capital is a theoretical means for understanding the value of our ideals, beliefs, dispositions, mannerisms, etc. It helps us to answer the question of why speaking what is called Standard English is so crucial to academic and economic success, or why having an advanced degree is considered impressive, or why knowing which fork to use at a formal banquet is important (at least to some). Not having that cultural capital can marginalize a person and ultimately hold that person at arm's length from accessing power and privilege. Acquiring capital is a life-long, immersive process and happens across multiple fields. This is where Bourdieu's notion of habitus becomes central to his theory of practice.

Habitus

Habitus is arguably Bourdieu's most contested idea (Reay, 2004), but it is also the piece of his theory that helps us understand why it seems so difficult to "change" the ways in which people understand and interact with their social worlds. In *Outline of Theory of Practice* (1977) Bourdieu defined habitus as "a system of lasting, transposable dispositions which, integrating past experiences, functions at every moment as a matrix of perceptions, appreciations, and actions" (pp. 82–83). Building on that definition Bourdieu wrote of the embodied nature of habitus:

> It is a socialized body. A structured body, a body which has incorporated the immanent structures of a world or of a particular sector of that world—a field—and which structures the perception of that world as well as action in that world. (Bourdieu, 1998, p. 81)

More to the point, each of us inhabits habitus. As we live, grow, and socialize into our respective contexts a "matrix of perceptions, appreciations, and actions" shapes each of us in an infinite number of ways across fields. The connection between habitus and social fields is essential to understanding Bourdieu's idea:

> The relation between habitus and field operates in two ways. On one side, it is a relation of conditioning: the field structures the habitus, which is the product of the embodiment of the immanent necessity of the field (or of a hierarchy of intersecting fields). On the other side, it is a relation of knowledge or cognitive construction: habitus contributes to constituting the field as a meaningful world, a world endowed with sense or with value, in which it is worth investing one's energy. (Bourdieu, as cited in Wacquant, 1989, p. 44)

Another way to put this is that habitus is embodied within individuals, and the field (location or context) is where that embodiment plays out. The habitus, composed of accumulated cultural capital, projects a set of values, beliefs, dispositions, skills, etc. (Bourdieu, 1980; Shilling, 2004). Again, the most succinct way of operationalizing habitus is to think of it as the sum total of what an individual learns—implicitly and explicitly—about her context across time and shapes how she goes on to think about and interact socially. In short, "it is through the workings of habitus that practice (agency) is linked with capital and field (structure)" (Reay, 2004, p. 432).

Structure With Agency: Habitus and the Individual

Bourdieu refutes arguments about the deterministic nature of habitus by positing that even though there is a collective nature to habitus, at the individual level there are variances based on the experiences of the individual. He states, "Just as no two individual histories are identical so no two individual habituses are identical" (Bourdieu, 1990, p. 46). That simple point is essential in considering how two White students who may be from the same neighborhood, attending the same school, with similar incomes and opportunities can have divergent understandings of racial oppression and social justice.

Implicit in Bourdieu's idea is the reality that competing social trajectories can result in divergent realities, despite a collective habitus. As Reay points out, "Implicit in the concept is the possibility of a social trajectory that enables conditions of living that are very different from initial ones" (p. 435). In other words, because each of us have different experiences, those experiences can have a profound impact on the ways in which we develop new dispositions or how we interact with our social worlds. For example, let's consider the fictional White students, Nora and Diane. Both Nora and Diane were socialized in an all-White, rural environment. However, Nora's parents migrated into the all-White environment from a racially and ethnically diverse metropolitan area and had many non-White friends who regularly visited their home for parties, dinners, and vacations or extended visits. Also, Nora's parents have access to resources that offered more opportunities for travel, domestically and internationally, among other opportunities that allowed greater exposure to ideas and people of diverse backgrounds. These experiences may challenge the collective habitus of the rural community, and the divergent trajectory of Nora presents new possibilities that reshape *her* habitus. If these opportunities happen across the life span of the student, the result is an individual who may be more informed and more open to appreciating how others experience the world and are constructed through popular culture, curriculum, and society writ-large. By the same token, if Diane's only exposure is through mediated images in popular culture, without any substantial flesh and blood humans to engage, it may be much more difficult to change those notions once Diane enrolls in a "diversity" course as a general elective or a required teacher education course. This is precisely why considering habitus, both individual and collective habitus, is key for understanding why it is challenging to teach White students about race and racism, specifically systemic and institutional forms of racism. Yes, I just threw a curveball. There are both an individual's habitus and a collective's habitus. Remember, we all, whether we intend it or not, belong to larger groups, and due to structural and systemic factors, there are varied experiences of larger groups in which individuals are a part. This will be explored more shortly.

Systemically, we all are exposed to particular structures that shape constructions, impressions, judgments, opportunities, and experiences. Racism is but another field in which individuals' habituses are constructed. If racism is a system of advantage then Bourdieu's structural-deterministic nature is well positioned to explain the development of a collective habitus that hides, while also reinscribing, Whiteness and its superiority. At the same time, and Bourdieu recognizes this, individuals act independently. However, as pointed out, those actions are always limited by a number of factors that contribute to the development of one's habitus, which is always functioning within a context. Habitus allows us to recognize the permanence of structures while challenging individuals' functioning within those structures. So it figures that any given White American can be sympathetic toward or even understanding of the problem of African American men being detained or killed by a police officer without substantive cause. Simultaneously, other White Americans (if not the majority) may respond to that reality (borne out by statistical and anecdotal data) by questioning the tone, dress, emotions, or stereotypes of young Black men or promoting the argument of Black on Black crime, dismissing any historically systemic and institutional underpinnings of the problem.

Using Habitus to Explore Race and Racism

Although Bourdieu's concepts are couched in a class-based analysis, employing the notion of habitus for considering racial issues is supported by many theorists and researchers (Cicourel, 1993; McClelland, 1990; Reay, 1995). As a construct that seeks to consider the sum total of an individual's experiences within a particular context, habitus allows for an analysis of the ways in which privilege and marginalization play themselves out. All aspects of identity—gender identity, able-bodiness, ethnicity, social class and race, language, etc.,—influence such dispositions (McClelland, 1990). Reay argues the effectiveness of using the notion of habitus to explore smaller yet complicated spaces like classrooms. She states:

> Habitus is a way of looking at data which renders the "taken-for-granted" problematic. It suggests a whole range of questions not necessarily addressed in empirical research; How well adapted is the individual to the context they find themselves in? How does personal history shape their responses to the contemporary setting? What subjective vocations do they bring to the present and how are they manifested? Are structural effects visible within small-scale interactions? What is the meaning of non-verbal behaviour as well as individuals' use of language? These questions clearly raise issues of gender and "race" alongside those of social class. (Reay, 1995, p. 369)

I further extend those research agenda to consider why it is such a challenge to teach students, specifically White students, about understanding race and racism. McNay (1999) further adds, "(Habitus) can also provide a corrective to 'socio-logical naive claims about the transformation of social (and sexual) identities' by highlighting the rootedness of class, gender and ethnic divisions" (p. 106).

Those identity divisions are essential to consider. As pointed out earlier, habitus is a phenomenon of both the individual *and* the collective (groups). Drawing on Bourdieu, the work of Eduardo Bonilla-Silva (2003) introduced the idea of White habitus. He defined White habitus as a "racialized, uninterrupted socialization process that conditions and creates Whites' racial tastes, perceptions, feelings, and emotions and their views on racial matters" (p. 104). In a study using data from both the 1997 *Survey of College Students' Social Attitudes* and the 1998 *Detroit Area Study on White Racial Ideology*, Bonilla-Silva, Goar, and Embrick (2006) draw out three key themes about the White habitus.

First, White Americans continue to experience a great deal of racial segregation and isolation. Due to trends of White flight Bonilla-Silva, Goar, and Embrick's point has been persistent over time, despite efforts toward desegregation (Brown, 2016; Massey & Denton, 1998; Semuels, 2015). Second, Bonilla-Silva et al.'s (2016) research showed that White respondents resisted connecting their racial isolation to the effects of systemic or institutional racism. What is more shocking about their findings is that "in the color-blind era of race relations, when Whites are asked about their social interactions with minorities, they present a view of their social world that contradicts this isolationist reality" (Bonilla-Silva et al., 2006, p. 248). Finally, their research also found White respondents were "very unlikely to engage in interracial unions with Blacks" (p. 248). Although this research was conducted in 2003, the resistance to interracial marriage remains significant in 2016.

Interracial relationships and marriage definitely are more socially accepted and common, but there remain many detractors, as evidenced by the uproar about a 2013 Cheerio's commercial featuring an interracial family (Goyette, 2013). According to a Pew Research Center analysis (Wang, 2015) of the most recently available census data, in 2013 12% of newlyweds married someone of a different race and

6.3% of all marriages were interracial. However, the data analysis also shows that only 7% of White Americans interracially married in 2013. African Americans were the next highest group, at 19%, nearly three times more likely to enter into an interracial marriage than Whites. Despite increasing social acceptance, the data shows that interracial marriage is not as pervasive as one may assume.

Taken together, Bonilla-Silva et al.'s (2006) research shows the persistence of both White isolation/segregation and a White habitus. They summarize the importance of their findings as follows:

> Because the White habitus creates a space in which White's extreme isolation is normalized, Whites do not experience troubling doubts or second thoughts as to their lack of interaction with Blacks. This affords Whites the luxury of non-reflexivity, enabling them to proudly espouse the virtues of color-blindness and unity. However, their responses to questions concerning their interracial lives (or lack thereof) betray them, suggesting that Whiteness is accompanied by a particular lifestyle that allows individuals to simultaneously cling to a color-blind ideology while retaining a vigilant distance from Black others. (Bonilla-Silva et al., 2006, p. 249)

The White habitus creates an umbrella that covers all aspects of the White experience and furthers particular notions of truth and reality. As Bonilla-Silva (2003) later points out, one strategy that emerges for them is the notion of color-blindness as a rhetorical and conceptual strategy for mitigating and insulating themselves from larger, intractable problems associated with race and racism.

Unless there are strong, intervening acts and experiences that challenge young White folks to critically think about their relationships (or lack thereof) with historically marginalized groups then half-baked assumptions about how racism functions persist. Although Bonilla-Silva et al.'s idea of White habitus has been represented in the literature for over a decade, the reality is that it is a notion that is not regularly employed in helping students and citizens understand how and why Whiteness and White people are privileged. The problem is that the capital learned through a White habitus emerges in schools, furthering a set of hegemonies that reinscribe White privilege at the expense of other ways of being and knowing.

From Habitus to Hegemony: Privileging Whiteness in Schools

In his classic text, *Ideology and Curriculum*, Michael Apple (1990) stated:

> It is important to realize that while our educational institutions do function to distribute ideological values and knowledge, this is not all they do. As a system of institutions, they also ultimately help produce the type of knowledge (as a kind of commodity) that

is needed to maintain the dominant economic, political, and cultural arrangements that now exist. (p. x)

This is an important point about schools, schooling, and teaching about race. There is a dominant narrative about race that is furthered in schools, one that minimizes the systemic and institutional construction of a racial hierarchy since the beginning of the original thirteen colonies. The reality of understanding race is that it is an intersectional and contested story wherein issues of race collide with class, gender, and sexuality in oftentimes-complex ways. Whether members of a course are considering the genocide and land annexation (theft) of Indigenous Americans, the enslavement of Africans and the subsequent de jure and de facto segregation of African Americans, or the exploitation of Asians, the forms of violence perpetrated by the group of people that named themselves White is troubling and disturbing. When considering the role of schools and the cultural capital privileged and promoted in schools largely serve to further the proclivities of dominant groups, in this case White people.

Key to Apple's argument, and essential for understanding the connection between habitus and schooling, is the notion of hegemony. First coined by Italian neo-Marxist Antonio Gramsci (1971), the idea of hegemony is a way of describing the lived experience of the dominant group(s), in the case of the United States that is White, male, wealthy, heterosexual, and Christian. Apple says that hegemony "refers to an organized assemblage of meanings and practices, the central effective and dominant system of meanings, values, and actions which are *lived*" (emphasis in original text) (Apple, 1990, p. 5). The cultural capital gained through one's habitus is consistently held up against the hegemony and that is where one finds legitimacy and illegitimacy in who one is, how one is, and what one is.

Case in point. I knew of a young African American woman from the south side of Chicago who was in her clinical teaching placement in an elementary grade classroom. By all accounts she was a wonderful student and on her way to being a highly qualified teacher. For a clinical placement—in a predominantly White, middle class school—she assisted an elementary classroom teacher. As she was reading aloud to the students one day, her cooperating teacher overheard her read "ax" instead of "ask." The teacher immediately reported the "infraction" to the principal and the student was subsequently pulled from the site. The young lady's "punishment" was compounded by the fact that her teaching institution did not come to her defense and point out that such shifts in language were actually insignificant and did not deter her from being a good Language Arts teacher (National Council for the Teachers of English, 1974).

It does not stop there. I have heard of preservice teachers removed from placements for smelling like cigarettes, wearing clothes that were too tight, being too "touchy-feely" with kindergartners, questioning cooperating teachers' approaches too much, and other reasons, all of which are defined as negative dispositions, which of course begs questions: If a disposition is negative, who makes those judgments? Whom do they privilege? And, whom do they marginalize? After all, if you are raised in a particular neighborhood, perhaps a low-income, African American neighborhood, and you are socialized into speaking African American Language (also known as Ebonic or African American Vernacular English, among other names) being more loud in tone, quick in speech, openly affectionate, etc., does that mean you are inherently wrong or incapable of being a good teacher? This is how hegemony works. Hegemony creates a norm to which all are held under scrutiny. If your cultural capital and habitus reflects the dominant hegemony in a given context then you are in effect privileged in that context. If your cultural capital and habitus does not reflect the dominant hegemony in a given context then you can be marginalized and held up as suspect.

I describe hegemony as an umbrella of reality. If you reflect certain values, ideals, dispositions, actions, etc., you are covered by that umbrella. If you do not reflect them, then you are literally left out in the rain. Apple (1990) draws upon the work of cultural studies pioneer Raymond Williams to explain the concept of hegemony. I must quote at length:

> (Hegemony) is a whole body of practices and expectations; our assignments of energy, our ordinary understanding of man and his world. It is a set of meanings and values which as they are experienced as practices appear as reciprocally confirming. It thus constitutes a sense of reality for most people in the society, a sense of absolute because experiences [as a] reality beyond which it is very difficult for most members of a society to move in most areas of their lives. But this is not, except in the operation of a moment of abstract analysis, a static system. On the contrary we can only understand an effective and dominant culture if we understand the real social process on which it depends: I mean the process of incorporation. The modes of incorporation are of great significance, and incidentally in our kind of society have considerable economic significance. The educational institutions are usually the main agencies of transmission of an effective dominant culture, and this is now a major economic as well as cultural activity; indeed it is both in the same moment. Moreover, at a philosophical level, at the true level of theory and at the level of the history of various practices, there is a process which I call the *selective tradition*: that which, within the terms of an effective dominant culture, is always passed off as 'the tradition', *the* significant past. But always the selectivity is the point: the way in which from a whole possible area of past and present, meanings and practices are neglected and excluded. Even more crucially, some of these meanings are reinterpreted, diluted, or put into forms which support or at least do not contradict other elements within the effective dominant culture

> The process of education; the process of a much wider social training within institutions like the family; the practical definitions and organizations of work; the selective tradition at an intellectual and theoretical level: all these forces are involved in a continual making and remaking of an effective dominant culture, and on them, as experienced, as built into our living, reality depends. If what we learn were merely an imposed ideology, or if it were only the isolable meanings and practices of the ruling class, or of a section of the ruling class, which gets imposed on others, occupying merely the top of our minds, it would be—and on would be glad—a very much easier thing to overthrow. (Raymond Williams as cited in Apple, 1990, pp. 5, 6)

I recognize that was quite a bit of information, but it was necessary to cite William's explanation of hegemony in full, as the full scope of his words draw out some deeply fundamental points.

First, hegemony is a way of thinking about how we engage the world, completely. In the above examples I cited isolated incidents, which does not give hegemony its full scope. Rather, hegemony is a totality. We may be able to talk about discreet incidents or moments or characteristics or dispositions, but that is akin to explaining one dot on Georg Seurat's *Sunday on La Grande Jatte*, the classic post-impressionist painting in which Seurat used the technique of pointillism (mixing tiny pin-point dots of color rather than brush strokes). Up close you only see dots, but as you pull away you see a magnificent, undeniable portrait. Discreet examples of hegemony are merely pinpoints. You must pull back and look at the whole to more fully grasp hegemony at work.

Second, since hegemony is a complete portrait, if you will, it ultimately seems like reality, or "just the way it is." Some may say hegemony reflects "common sense," but what is common to some may not be common to others. The idea of common sense is a product constructed through social relations mediated by power, politics, and culture. The ways in which our institutions and systems reinforce particular ways of being dismissed what is uncommon or undesirable to dominant groups. Racially, in the context of the United States that dominant group is White folks, filtered through a White habitus.

Third, hegemony is not a static construct. To the contrary, it is dynamic and ever changing, following the trends of the dominant group. More importantly, since it is not static it is necessary to incorporate people into the hegemony. Some may call that assimilation. I like to ask students when teaching about cultural capital, habitus, and hegemony, if immigrants have to assimilate, what are they assimilating into? What do they have to learn? What do they have to abandon in that process of incorporating themselves into the new society?

We can see this most notably in Americanization programs for European immigrants in urban schools in the early to middle 1900s (Tyack, 1974). While Tyack focused his historical analysis on the East, Sanchez (1993) aimed his analysis toward California and that state's efforts at the Americanization of Mexicans. Sanchez pointed out "the efforts to alter the immigrant generation itself were abandoned in favor of school-based programs which sought to teach American born children a culture different from that of their immigrant parents" (p. 105). Key to these "lessons" included changes in diet, hygiene, language, work habits, family planning, and family roles and responsibilities. To the point of hegemony, there is a totality to it and that totality is dynamic across time, and individuals must be incorporated/assimilated into that reality.

Finally, this totality is learned not simply through schooling alone; rather it is experienced across, within, and throughout our matrix of institutions. We learn hegemony through popular culture and media, political institutions, law, church, family, and on, most notably in schools. Expectations of "proper" behavior is circulated throughout and across society, and children are expected to acquiesce to those lessons: This is how you do x, y, and z. This is how you speak in x, y, and z situations. This is how you dress. This is how you defer.

Anti-racist educator Judith Katz (1999) delineated a typology of the general aspects and dispositions of Whiteness. In her typology (and she describes this as general) she considers such notions as: rugged individualism; the Protestant work ethic; considerations of status, power, and authority; the nature of competition; emphasis of the scientific method, objectivity, linear thought, and rationality; rigidity of time, a future orientation and delayed gratification; the nuclear family structure; hierarchical decision making; modes of communication, privileging of the written tradition, avoidance of conflict, and minimizing of emotions; Christian and White/European based holidays; an action orientation; notions of justice; Western-based history; and European aesthetics. Considering the broadness of her typology, it is clear that all those aspects are learned inside and outside school. Furthermore, those aspects and dispositions of Whiteness span across the social experience. We all are immersed into hegemonic structures, and each of us, despite our unique backgrounds, is expected to assimilate into those hegemonies, lest we receive a backlash for our resistance or ignorance.

Another way of thinking about this is to consider Delpit's (1988) notion of the culture of power. She delineates five key aspects of power in classrooms:

- Issues of power are enacted in classrooms.
- There are codes or rules for participating in power; that is, there is a "culture of power."
- The rules of the culture of power are a reflection of the rules of the culture of those who have power.
- If you are not already a participant in the culture of power, being told explicitly the rules of that culture makes acquiring power easier.

- Those with power are frequently least aware of—or least willing to acknowl-edge—its existence. Those with less power are often most aware of its exis-tence. (p. 283)

The point most crucial to this discussion is her final aspect of power; "those with power are frequently least aware of—or least willing to acknowledge—its exis-tence." This reflects the way in which hegemony works. Essentially, Delpit is illuminating the often "silenced" notion that there are expectations and codes of behavior that function in classrooms and those expectations and codes are institu-tionalized, in the case of the United States, through the lens of Whiteness.

Considering the connection between habitus and hegemony is central because the cultural capital gained through one's habitus becomes privilege within hege-monies. This is what makes teaching White students about race so challenging. There are assumptions about what is common sense and assumptions about which ways of being (and doing) are "right." Observation and recognition of that ten-dency is actually pretty simple and many students I have worked with have been understanding of the notion that some of their ways of being are privileged in and out of school. But *recognition* does not necessarily mean *change*. The challenge lies in the frustrating permanence of habitus. As we attempt to challenge habitus and recognize that the lessons we learn as we are "raised" by our families and social-ized (incorporated) into institutions, those processes are mediated by overarching hegemonies that reinforce many aspects of their cultural capital as the norm. This is especially true for schooling.

Speaking Fatigue: Considerations of Discourse, Language, and Habitus in Classrooms

It is without doubt that schooling is one of the single most powerful and perva-sive institutions we encounter. For most of the country, schooling is a compulsory activity from the age of five to sixteen, give or take a year. Despite its perva-siveness, citizens are not necessarily concerned with what is actually taught in schools—short of any keenly controversial issues like sex education or Darwin's theory of evolution. More importantly, though, citizens do not seem all that con-cerned with how decisions about what our children and youth are taught and why. As Labaree (1997) has pointed out, there is an overemphasis on the social mobil-ity of schooling. This thirst for social mobility eclipses a collective need to criti-cally interrogate the implications of the hidden curriculum furthered in American schools. What is often most taken for granted is the privileging of Whiteness in American schools.

With regards to race, American textbooks tend to offer uncritical portraits of race relations, sanitized of the depth of strife between White and non-White groups (Brown & Brown, 2010; Lowen, 2007; Sleeter & Grant, 1991). Tosolt and Love (2012) point out "previous studies examining school textbooks argue that textbooks reaffirm the status quo and fail to help students understand the complicated structures of racism, sexism, and classism which are embedded within American society" (p. 47). The state of Texas caused a firestorm of controversy when they adopted a textbook that described enslaved Africans as "workers" (Fernandez & Hauser, 2015). The publisher, McGraw-Hill Education, quickly issued apologies, began to redraft the passage in question, and suggested supplemental materials to teachers for accuracy. However, it does not stop there.

In a subsequent op-ed piece for the *New York Times*, Ellen Bressler Rockmore (2015) further critiqued how Texas has altered historical representations. She pointed out the 2010 Texas Board of Education decision to minimize the role of slavery as a root cause of the Civil War, but her critique that is more substantial is the ways in which textbooks are written. As she states:

> (It) is not only the substance of the passages that is a problem. It is also their form. The writers' decision about how to construct sentences, about what the subject of the sentence will be, about whether the verb will be active or passive, shape the message that slavery was not all that bad. (para. 6)

To illustrate this phenomenon, she included the following passage:

> Some slaves reported that their masters treated them kindly. To protect their investment, some slaveholders provided adequate food and clothing for their slaves. However, severe treatment was very common. Whippings, brandings, and even worse torture were all part of American slavery. (para. 9)

In her analysis she pointed out the benevolence of slaveholders and that the enslaved could have "fond" feelings about their treatment. The third sentence, however, the sentence that speaks to specific cruelties of slavery, is devoid of people, divorcing the brutality of slaveholders (largely White folks) toward the enslaved. Similarly, Rockmore also includes the sentence, "Families were often broken apart when a family member was sold to another owner" (para. 11). As she notes, the use of the passive voice in the sentence allows the slave owner to escape the responsibility of his actions. For youth, especially those not familiar with the history of slavery, direct statements are essential. Families were not "broken apart" by happenstance; rather, a real human being (more often than not a White male), purposefully decided to "break apart" families of enslaved Africans. The perpetuation of those misrepresentations adds to habitus and creates a particular and popular way of remembering our racial history. This makes it much more challenging to undo the messages, perceptions, and assumptions we have about what is arguably the most powerful and persistent social, economic, and cultural organizing mechanism in our nation's history. Alongside this phenomenon these curricular and pedagogical actions minimize the importance of a critical examination of Whiteness and shores particular hegemonies of Whiteness, for Whiteness is either erased or at the very least assumed when the conversation turns to the inhumane.

Sometimes Teachers Have No Clue: Learning and Acquiring Habitus

As we progress through K-12 education, we all are constantly exposed to a range of messages and pedagogical acts that reinforce a White racial and cultural hegemony, and these messages and pedagogical acts are often unchecked, as standards reforms often skirt the promotion of anti-racist and anti-oppressive pedagogies and practices. Morrow and Torres (1995) commented on this *pedagogic authority* and virtually unfettered autonomy teachers have in furthering particular messages, both expressly and inadvertently:

> This relative autonomy of pedagogic authority allows cultural reproduction to contribute most effectively to the overall process of social reproduction, given that pedagogic actions "tend to reproduce the system of cultural arbitraries characteristic of that social formation, thereby contributing to the reproduction of power relations which put that cultural arbitrary into the dominant position" (Bourdieu & Passeron, 1977, p. 10). … In short, pedagogic work is a substitute for repression and external coercion and works, most fundamentally by masking the underlying realities of power to both the dominant and subordinate groups in society. (p. 183)

Our understanding about race is learned through formal processes and institutions, like schools. However, they are also acquired informally, which can also happen in schools. Noted linguist and literacy scholar, James Gee (2012), differentiates between the two:

> Acquisition is a process of acquiring something (usually subconsciously) by exposure to models, a process of trial and error, and practice within social groups, without formal teaching. It happens in natural settings that are meaningful and functional in the sense that the acquirers know that they need to acquire the thing they are exposed to in order to function and they in fact want to so function. This is how most people come to control their first language.

Learning is a process that involves conscious knowledge gained through teaching (though not necessarily from someone officially designated a teacher) or through certain life-experiences that trigger conscious reflection. This teaching or reflection involves explanation and analysis, that is, breaking down the thing to be learned into its analytic parts. It inherently involves attaining, along with the matter being taught, some degree of meta-knowledge about the matter. (pp. 166–167)

Gee's differentiation is crucial, as he is legitimating the idea that we are always learning, either through direct, formal instruction from a teacher or one operating as a teacher, or acquiring from virtually anyone in our social and institutional worlds. Particular messages about thought and action are reinforced consistently, and if that reinforcement says, for example, "we must be tolerant of others but we are all individuals and responsible for our own success and failure," then deeper analysis of confounding institutional and systemic variables can be rendered ineffective. After all, we all may have institutional hurdles, but you still have to work hard and overcome them. Language, arguably one of the most important elements of identity and culture, is not exempt from these lessons.

Gee (2012) reflected on the discourse analysis of two seven year old girls' stories during a sharing-time activity and their White teacher's reception of those stories. Leona, an African American girl who "comes from a culture that has retained substantive ties with an 'oral culture' past" (p. 127), and Mindy, an Anglo-American middle class girl. His discourse analysis showed Leona's sharing-time story was deeply complex and rooted in her cultural experience and oral traditions. However, Leona's delivery was not what her teacher was expecting. Gee explains:

Leona's language is an invitation to the other children to participate with her in sense-making, to achieve solidarity with her, and they readily accept this invitation. The teacher did not. Leona was regularly told to sit down because she was either "rambling on" or "not talking about one important thing" (a sharing-time rule in the class). (p. 141)

By contrast, Mindy's stories were supported by the teacher. Mindy and her teacher share the verbal interactions of middle class homes (Heath, 1983). As Gee (2012) describes, Mindy and her teacher were "in sync" (p. 143) with one another, and the teacher, although she frequently interrupted Mindy, was able to sync with Mindy and help the student develop a "lexically explicit, coherent, and school-based account of a complex activity" (p. 144). In other words, the exchange between Mindy and the teacher matched the teacher's expectations of delivery and performance, resulting in a positive evaluation of Mindy's sharing-time story. By extension, a particular mode of communication was privileged and modeled in real time for the other students in class.

In contrast, although Leona's story possessed a much more complex and community-engaging structure and delivery, the teacher's lack of understanding denigrated her performance and home culture. Gee notes:

> What is striking about the poor reception that Leona's stories received ... is that her stories have deep meanings when she tells them in her own community or when we situate them in the interpretive setting of "poetics" and "linguistic stylistics" ... Yet they have no very deep meaning when they are situated in school at sharing-time. Sharing-time in these classrooms was early essayist (reportive, linear, "the facts") "literacy" training. Leona's text does not "resonate" well with that practice, while other sorts of texts do. (p. 145)

The troubling thing here is that the very ways in which individuals speak can be privileged and marginalized and further particular assumptions about what is right and what is wrong. Over time, these forms of capital become cemented in consciousness and add to the creation of a habitus, to the extent that other forms of speech are immediately constructed as undesirable or flat-out wrong.

In school, oftentimes what we learn is not necessarily through direct instruction. Rather, behavioral expectations are communicated through teacher responses and invectives. Language is most recognizable in this. Has a teacher ever told you, "Don't say ain't. Ain't isn't a word," or "Please only speak English in my classroom?" More crudely, has a teacher ever told you the way you speak is wrong or improper? This is actually a common occurrence, especially for students whose home language is African American Language, a point briefly alluded to earlier in this chapter.

African American Language (AAL), formerly known by many names, including Ebonics and African American Vernacular English is a valid, rule-governed system of communication spoken by millions of African Americans at some point in their lives (Rickford & Rickford, 2000; Smitherman, 1994, 1999, 2006). Rigorous study of the legitimacy and structure of AAL has been conducted by linguist for decades (Dillard, 1972; Labov, 1972; Smith, 1994; Smitherman, 1981; Turner, 1973; Wolfram, 1969), but despite the professional legitimation of AAL, the popular opinion continues to cast AAL in a negative light. To this point, the Linguistic Society of America, a leading professional organization dedicated to the study of linguistics states:

> The variety known as "Ebonics," "African American Vernacular English," (AAVE), and "Vernacular Black English" and by other names is systematic and rule-governed like all natural speech varieties. In fact, all human linguistic systems—spoken, signed,

and written—are fundamentally regular. The systematic and expressive nature of the grammar and pronunciation patterns of the African American vernacular has been established by numerous scientific studies over the past thirty years. Characterizations of Ebonics as "slang," "mutant," "lazy," "defective," "ungrammatical," or "broken English" are incorrect and demeaning. (Linguistic Society of American, 1997, para. 2)

I have taught many classes in which we discussed the selective marginalization of African American culture and have encouraged my students to consider African American Language. In many instances, despite reading many articles about the legitimacy of the language and while having the above quote projected on the screen behind me, students will continue to say, "Well in my opinion it's just slang." So, despite the best evidence available from the most knowledgeable people on the subject (in this case linguistics) students can eschew rigorous research and professional judgment for their own "opinion." The thing is, it is not simply opinion. (And some of you right now are wondering if AAL is a language or a dialect; linguists use the term language varieties in place of dialects and find debates about language v. dialect matters of politics and power).

Each of us brings a lifetime of codes and messages about how one should behave, act, and engage in social and institutional spaces. The cultural capital of White middle class language styles translates directly into school language and the economic marketplace (Brice-Heath, 1983, 2012). That is systemically and institutionally reiterated and produces a key part of White habitus, which is then constructed as the norm—or hegemony—privileged in school contexts, among others. Language is merely one example of this, but the reality is that this cuts across the entire matrix of our lives; it is all-pervasive and near impossible to avoid.

Habitus organizes all our lives, and when it comes to issues of race, those lessons are long and deep. This makes it fundamentally challenging for White students coming into our classes to learn about race. Challenging the development of their cultural capital and habitus is, in effect, challenging their entire identity, and we should not take that lightly. That struggle—especially when many, if not most, of our White students are considerate of the moral imperative of anti-racism—is complex, intellectual, and spiritual. Given that complexity, it is sensible that many White students have times of fatigue. The challenge we now face is how do we create educational spaces that recognize this struggle.

Bibliography

Anyon, J. (1981). Social class and school knowledge. *Curriculum Inquiry, 11*(1), 3–42.
Apple, M. (1990). *Ideology and curriculum* (2nd ed.). New York, NY: Routledge.

Bernstein, B. (1971/2003). *Class, codes, and control: Theoretical studies toward a sociology of language*. New York, NY: Routledge and Kegan Paul.

Bonilla-Silva, E. (2003). *Racism without racist: Colorblind racism and the persistence of racial inequality in the United States*. Lanham, MD: Rowman & Littlefield.

Bonilla-Silva, E., Goar, C., & Embrick, D. (2006). When Whites flock together: The social psychology of White habitus. *Critical Sociology, 32*(2–3), 229–253.

Bourdieu, P. (1977). *Outline of a theory of practice*. New York, NY: Cambridge University Press.

Bourdieu, P. (1980). *The logic of practice*. Cambridge: Polity.

Bourdieu, P. (1990a). *In other words*. Cambridge: Polity.

Bourdieu, P. (1990b). *Sociology in question*. Cambridge: Polity.

Bourdieu, P. (1992). *The logic of practice*. Cambridge: Polity.

Bourdieu, P. (1993). *The field of cultural production: Essays on art and literature*. Cambridge: Polity.

Bourdieu, P. (1998). *Practical reason: On the theory of action*. Palo Alto, CA: Stanford University Press.

Bourdieu, P. (1999). *The weight of the world: Social suffering in contemporary society*. Cambridge: Polity.

Bourdieu, P., & Passeron, J.-C. (1990). *Reproduction in education, society and culture* (Revised ed.). London: Sage Publications.

Bowles, S., & Gintis, H. (1976/2011). *Schooling in capitalist America: Educational reform and the contradictions of economic life*. Chicago, IL: Haymarket Press.

Brice Heath, S. (2012). *Words at work and play: Three decades in family and community life*. Cambridge: Cambridge University Press.

Brown, A. L., & Brown, K. D. (2010). Strange fruit indeed: Interrogating contemporary textbook representations of racial violence towards African Americans. *Teachers College Record, 112*(1), 31–67.

Brown, E. (2016, May 17). On the anniversary of Brown v. Board, new evidence that U.S. schools are resegregating. *The Washington Post*. Retrieved from https://www.washingtonpost.com/news/education/wp/2016/05/17/on-the-anniversary-of-brown-v-board-new-evidence-that-u-s-schools-are-resegregating/

Cherryholmes, C. (1988). *Power and criticism: Poststructural investigations in education*. New York, NY: Teachers College Press.

Chou, R. S., Lee, K., & Ho, S. (2012). The White habitus and hegemonic masculinity at the elite southern university: Asian Americans and the need for intersectional analysis. *Sociation Today, 10*(2). Retrieved from http://www.ncsociology.org/sociationtoday/v102/asian.htm

Cicourel, A. V. (1993). Aspects of structural and processual theories of knowledge. In C. Calhoun, E. Lipuma, & M. Postone (Eds.), *Bourdieu: Critical perspectives*. Cambridge, UK: Polity.

Crossley, N. (2001). *The social body*. London: Sage.

Delpit, L. D. (1988). The silenced dialogue: Power and pedagogy in educating other people's children. *Harvard Educational Review, 58*(3), 280–298.

Dillard, J. L. (1972). *Black English: Its history and usage in the United States*. New York, NY: Vintage Press.

Eagleton, T. (1983). *Literary theory: An introduction.* Minneapolis, MN: University of Minnesota Press.

Fernandez, M., & Hauser, C. (2015, October 5). Texas mother teaches textbook company a lesson on accuracy. *The New York Times.* Retrieved from http://www.nytimes.com/2015/10/06/us/publisher-promises-revisions-after-textbook-refers-to-african-slaves-as-workers.html

Gee, J. (2012). *Social linguistics and literacies: Ideology in discourses* (4th ed.). New York, NY: Routledge.

Giroux, H. A. (1983). *Theory and resistance in education: A pedagogy for the opposition.* London: Heinemann Educational.

Goyette, B. (2013, May 31). Cheerios commercial featuring mixed race family gets racist backlash. *Huffington Post.* Retrieved from http://www.huffingtonpost.com/2013/05/31/cheerios-commercial-racist-backlash_n_3363507.html

Gramsci, A. (1971). *Selections from the prison notebooks.* New York, NY: International.

Hargrove, M. D. (2009). Mapping the *social field of Whiteness*: White racism as habitus in the city where history lives. *Transforming Anthropology, 17*(2), 93–104.

Harker, R. K. (1984). On reproduction, habitus and education. *British Journal of Sociology of Education, 5*(2), 117–127.

Heath, S. B. (1983). *Ways with words: language, life, and work in.* Cambridge, MA: Cambridge University Press.

Hiller, J., & Rooksby, E. (2005). Introduction to the first edition. *Habitus: A sense of place* (pp. 19–43). Aldershot: Ashgate.

Katz, J. (1999). *White culture and racism: Working for organizational change in the United States* (p. 5) (The Whiteness Papers, 3). Roselle, NJ: Center for the Study of White American Culture.

Labaree, D. (1997). Public goods, private goods: The American struggle over educational goals. *American Educational Research Journal, 34*(1), 39–81.

Labov, W. (1972). *Language in the inner city: Studies in Black Vernacular English.* Philadelphia, PA: University of Pennsylvania Press.

Leonardo, Z. (2013). *Education and racism.* New York, NY: Routledge.

Linguistic Society of America. (1997). *Resolution on the Oakland "Ebonics" issue unanimously adopted at the annual meeting of the Linguistic Society of America.* Retrieved from http://www-personal.umich.edu/~jlawler/ebonics.lsa.html

Lowen, J. (2007). *Lies my teacher told me: Everything your American history textbook got wrong.* New York, NY: Touchstone.

MacLeod, J. (2004). *Ain't no makin' it: Aspirations and attainment in a low income neighborhood* (2nd ed.). Boulder, CO: Westview Press.

MacLeod, J. (2008). *Ain't no makin' it: Aspirations and attainment in a low income neighborhood* (3rd ed.). Boulder, CO: Westview Press.

Massey, D. S., & Denton, N. A. (1998). *American apartheid: Segregation and the making of the underclass.* Cambridge, MA: Harvard University Press.

McClelland, K. (1990). Cumulative disadvantage among the highly ambitious. *Sociology of Education, 63,* 102–121.

McNay, L. (1999). Gender, habitus, and the field: Pierre Bourdieu and the limits of reflexivity. *Theory, Culture, and Society, 16*, 95–117.

Morrow, R. A., & Torres, C. A. (1995). *Social theory and education: A critique of theories of social and cultural reproduction.* Albany, NY: State University of New York Press.

Nash, R. (1999, June 1). Bourdieu, "Habitus", and educational research: Is it all worth the candle? *British Journal of Sociology of Education, 20*(2), 175–187.

National Council of Teachers of English. (1974). *Students' right to their own language.* Urbana, IL: National Council of Teachers of English.

Reay, D. (1995). Using habitus to look at race and class in primary school classrooms. In M. Griffiths & B. Troyna (Eds.), *Anti-racism, culture and social justice in education*(pp. 115–132). Stoke-on-Kent: Trentham Books.

Reay, D. (2004). It's all becoming a habitus: Beyond the habitual use of habits in educational research. *British Journal of Sociology of Education, 25*(4), 431–444.

Rickford, J. R., & Rickford, R. J. (2000). *Spoken soul: The story of Black English.* New York, NY: Wiley Publishing.

Rockmore, E. B. (2015, October 21). How Texas teaches history. *The New York Times.* Retrieved from http://www.nytimes.com/2015/10/22/opinion/how-texas-teaches-history.html

Sánchez, G. (1993). *Becoming Mexican American: Ethnicity, culture, and identity in Chicano Los Angeles, 1900–1945.* New York, NY: Oxford University Press.

Semuels, A. (2015, July 30). White flight never ended. *The Atlantic.* Retrieved from http://www.theatlantic.com/business/archive/2015/07/white-flight-alive-and well/399980/

Shilling, C. (2003). *The body and social theory* (2nd ed.). London: Sage.

Shilling, C. (2004). Physical capital and situated action: A new direction for corporeal sociology. *British Journal of Sociology of Education, 25*(4), 473–487.

Sleeter, C. E., & Grant, C. A. (1991). Textbooks and race, class, gender, and disability. In M. W. Apple & L. K. Christian-Smith (Eds.), *The politics of the textbook* (pp. 78–110). New York, NY: Routledge.

Smith, E. (1994). *The historical development of African American language.* Los Angeles, CA: Watts College Press.

Smitherman, G. (1994). *Black talk: Words and phrases from the hood to the amen corner.* Boston, MA: Houghton Mifflin.

Smitherman, G. (1999). *Talkin that talk: African American language and culture.* New York, NY: Routledge.

Smitherman, G. (2006). *Word from the mother: Language and African Americans.* New York, NY: Routledge.

Smitherman, G. (Ed.). (1981). *Black English and the education of Black children and youth.* Boston, MA: Houghton Mifflin.

Tosolt, B., & Love, B. L. (2012, March 7). Racial harmony & heroes: A content analysis of the Pearson reading program "good habits, great readers". *Critical Questions in Education, 2*(1), 44–51.

Turner, L. D. (1973). *Africanisms in the Gullah dialect.* Ann Arbor, MI: University of Michigan Press.

Tyack, D. (1974). *The one best system: A history of American urban education.* Cambridge, MA: Harvard University Press.

Wacquant, L. (1989). Towards a reflexive sociology: A workshop with Pierre Bourdieu. *Sociological Theory, 7,* 26–63.

Wang, W. (2015, June 12). Interracial marriage: Who is "marrying out"? *Pew Research Center.* Retrieved from http://www.pewresearch.org/fact-tank/2015/06/12/interracial-marriage-who-is-marry ing-out/

Willis, P. (1977/1981). *Learning to labor: How working class kids get working class jobs.* New York, NY: Columbia University Press.

Wolfram, W. (1969). *A linguistic description of Detroit Negro speech.* Washington, DC: Center for Applied Linguistics.

CHAPTER SIX

Concluding Thoughts

Promoting Racial Literacy, Standards, and Reconstructing White Folks for Social Justice

Through this text I have introduced, defined, and explore the idea of White fatigue, a quasi form of White resistance that manifests for individuals who may seem tired of talking and learning about race and racism despite an understanding of the immorality of racism. Along with White fragility and White guilt, White fatigue provides language to talk about the spectrum of the ways White folks grapple with the subject matter of race and racism. Incorporating the idea of White fatigue may be a way of minimizing the often-used binary opposition of racist/ally by recognizing the challenges of *unlearning* uncritical messages about race circulated through school curriculum and the public curriculum via media and popular culture. Minimizing this binary is necessary as it can be alienating for many, especially those who see themselves as not racist but are not yet fully understanding of how racism functions as a systemic and institutional form of oppression, therefore not fully understanding or mindful of how their own actions can be deemed racist. That alienation, whether inadvertent or deliberate, can have the unintended consequence of deterring the nurturing of allies, accomplices, and leaders in anti-racism, and racial oppression cannot subside without the activism and efforts of committed and understanding White allies, accomplices, and leaders.

White fatigue is simply an effort to continuously humanize all actors in our interracial community, for White folks are actors in this system of advantage based on race, and they have their role to play, and through virtually every institution they are prompted to blindly accept their privilege, including through school curricula. Despite decades of multicultural education theory and critically inspired pedagogies, the practice of multicultural education in schools has been largely successful at encouraging humanist notions of tolerance rather than promoting sustained critical examinations of the ways in which racial oppression permeates all areas of life in the United States and has consistently deleterious effects on historically marginalized groups. White fatigue as a concept promotes the fundamental idea that the process of learning about race and racism is challenging for all of us, regardless of your racial identification, and if we do not take the fundamental step of prefacing the humanity in each of us—especially those not understanding of how systemic and institutional racial oppression functions—then we will continuously struggle with our national racial consciousness. This requires a reconsideration of the ways in which we engage race and racism and that reengagement must begin in our educational institutions, for ideas about race and racism must be addressed in schools through both instruction and policy. This must begin with the promotion of racial literacy at all levels in education, the preparation of our nation's teachers, and the reconsideration of how we construct White folks in our educational and public discourses.

Encouraging Racial Literacy

It is without doubt that education, public and private, is one of the most substantial and pervasive institutions in the United States. Our system annually educates millions of students, pre-kindergarten through college, and schooling is compulsory in most states for children six to sixteen years of age, with some slight age variations and exceptions depending on the state. Therefore, if there is one space that touches millions of Americans, school is one such space. The primacy of schooling is obvious, considering the political rancor that swirls around schooling. Despite the oftentimes-contentious political squabbles about schooling, schools can continue to be spaces of democratic, humanist, progressive, and critical engagement, and they can be sites in which we, as a society, learn how to talk about race and work to ameliorate ideas that promote, either tacitly or implicitly, racist practices. In other words, schools are a prime site to gain racial literacy (Skerrett, 2011; Stevenson, 2014; Twine, 2004).

According to Stevenson (2014), racial literacy is "the ability read, recast, and resolve racially stressful social interactions. The teaching of racial literacy skills protects students from the threat of internalizing negative stereotypes that undermine academic critical thinking, engagement, identity, and achievement" (p. 4).

Stevenson makes the point that "schools and families fail at teaching racial coping because teachers, administrators, parents, and students are not trained to properly do so, do not approach it as a competency topic, nor do they have a rationale for engaging in such a 'risky' practice" (p. 4). The goal of racial literacy is simple yet complex. Vetter and Hungerford-Kressor (2014) say the goal of racial literacy "is to develop a set of social proficiencies that attempt to make sense of the discursive and performative systems of race" (p. 84).

This is a move far beyond the human relations sensibilities and objectives of many educators' attempts at multicultural education. Rather, this is an attempt to help students not only understand how to identify and address issues of interpersonal discrimination and prejudice but also to make connections to larger systemic and institutional functions of racial oppression. Vetter and Hungerford-Kressor go on to quote another racial literacy scholar, Allison Skerret (2011) as she further describes the goal of racial literacy. "Specifically, racial literacy develops an understanding of how race shapes the 'social, economic, political, and educational experiences of individuals and groups' (Skerrett, 2011, p. 314)" (as cited in Vetter & Hungerford-Kressor, 2014, p. 84). Again, what is key here is the push to see race and racism as more than issues of not liking someone because they are of a different race but understanding the ways in which race functions to radically frame one's worldview and life chances (Guinier, 2004; Ladson-Billings & Tate, 1995; Twine, 2004).

As I have pointed out throughout this book, ameliorating racism requires far more than simply treating each other with more respect. Although that interpersonal imperative is important, it is merely a prelude to the more challenging work of undoing systemic and institutional practices that promote racism. However, without changing our national consciousness about race and racism we will be mired in debates about whether or not racism, beyond personal behaviors, is even real! Beginning these lessons in Kindergarten and continuing through high school would have a profound effect on the ways our society considers and engages issues of marginalization, exploitation, and oppression.

I have found that oftentimes when broaching the subject of teaching children about race and racism many scoff at the idea, claiming that children do not need to engage in such matters or that it is too complicated, or too upsetting. I have also found that those statements are more about the unease of adults rather than of children. In the case of teachers, as pointed out in earlier chapters, the theory of multicultural education continues to outpace its practice, and comfort with (let alone belief in) topics related to forms of oppression is central to that disjuncture. Some adults' reasons for avoiding courageous conversations (Singleton, 2014) about race, arguing children's discomfort and protecting their innocence, is disingenuous at best and complicity in maintaining systems of oppression at worst. If *Sesame Street* can teach children about 9/11 and incarceration then we can figure out how to age-appropriately teach them about racism, not just prejudice and discrimination but racism.

Curriculum theorist Jerome Bruner in *The Process of Education* (1960/1996) posited the notion of the *spiral curriculum*. The spiral curriculum promotes the perspective that concepts of subjects are introduced and regularly returned to with greater depth and complexity as the child advances through education, and this consideration ought to be the basis for curriculum. As a matter of fact, Bruner's ideas are reflected in our current approach to K-12 curriculum development. Bruner argues, "… any subject can be taught effectively in some intelligently honest form to any child at any stage of development" (p. 33). Specifically, Bruner describes the spiral curriculum this way:

> A curriculum as it develops should revisit these basic ideas repeatedly, building upon them until the student has grasped the full formal apparatus that goes with them. Fourth-grade children can play absorbing games governed by the principles of topology and set theory, even discovering new "moves" or theorems. They can grasp the idea of tragedy and the basic human plights represented in myth. But they cannot put these ideas into formal language or manipulate them as grownups can. (p. 13)

Understanding race, racism, and any other form of oppression, is subject to the same scaffolding. Although as a nation we have done a fine job of encouraging children and youth to be nice and respectful to one another—tolerant—that does not mean we are teaching them that larger systems and institutions are at play and there are significant histories of oppression and marginalization that have had real and lasting consequences. As my dear colleague David Stovall suggested in a lecture at Northern Illinois University in 2017, what if we introduced to kindergarteners ideas like oppression, land annexation, genocide, or disenfranchisement? What if?

Are these lessons painful? Perhaps. But, what then do we make of the distortions and half-truths we tend to perpetuate? My mom always told me, "Son, I can handle the truth; its a lie that tears me up." After all, why celebrate Columbus Day when we know he did not "discover" America and was responsible for enslaving, raping, and killing hundreds of thousands of indigenous children, women and men? Why do we, as a nation, not have any considerate depth of understanding about the institution of American chattel slavery? After all, American chattel slavery was a historically unique form of slavery; it built the southern economy and greatly contributed to the northern economy; and it framed social relations in what became the United State for centuries. Why can't we teach children about mass incarceration and trace its roots to the *Thirteenth Amendment* of the *Constitution*, especially since the United States incarcerates more people than any other nation on the planet? Engaging children and youth in these crucial lessons about systemic and institutional racism and other forms of oppression is key in advancing a national anti-racist, anti-oppressive consciousness. Bruner summarizes the point:

> If one respects the ways of thought of the growing child, if one is courteous enough to translate material into his logical forms and challenging enough to tempt him to advance, then it is possible to introduce him at an early age to the ideas and styles that in later life make an educated man. (p. 52)

However, in order for this to happen, we must take a radical reconsideration of our teaching and learning standards, most importantly to the standards governing the teachers we produce. After all, standards documents are like the federal budget; they reflect our true priorities.

The Hope of Anti-Racism and Curriculum and Professional Teaching Standards

I am not interested in litigating the efficacy of the Common Core State Standards (CCSS). They have their strengths and weaknesses, intentional and unintentional outcomes, explicit and covert purposes. Some states have opted out of using the CCSS. At the same time there are teachers and administrators that feel the standards have pushed them to be better teachers and help frame instruction beyond basic subject matter knowledge. I bring up the CCSS because of what they do not say. If standards reflect our (or at least the drafters') learning priorities, then social justice and anti-oppression in all its forms is regrettably absent. Now, this does not mean that teachers cannot create social justice and/or anti-oppression curricula. After all, one of the virtues of the CCSS is that they do not tell teachers how they *must* teach, but frame the objectives for learning. Through a multistate, qualitative study, Dover (2015) showed that justice-oriented curricula could be aligned with the CCSS, especially standards relating to critical and higher-ordered thinking.

The issue is if ideals like anti-racism, anti-oppression, and social justice are not explicitly encouraged through educational standards then there is no systemic and institutional pressure to make sure teachers and administrators engage their students in learning about these issues. There is also no pressure to ensure that there is effective teacher education and professional development to aid preservice teachers, teachers, and administrators in understanding of how systemic and institutional racial oppression works and how our various silos can engage those issues in our curricula. If there is an expectation for K-12 educators to be more critically engaged and committed to helping children and youth understand how these phenomena function, it is essential for teacher education and professional standards to also encourage attendance to these ideas. Attending to issues of anti-racism, anti-oppression, and social justice ought to be part of a teacher's DNA in a pluralistic, democratic society—a society that has had a clear and persistent history of maltreatment of marginalized, minority groups.

Since many preservice teachers enter teacher education programs with a wide array of understanding about the nature of social justice (Miller, 2014), it is indispensible for teacher preparation programs to promote an understanding of not only diversity but also social justice as high values for highly qualified teachers. Unfortunately, the Council for the Accreditation of Educator Preparation (CAEP), the primary accrediting organization for teacher education, has not offered a standard for such a mission. In its latest version of standards (CAEP, 2013) there is no mention of racism, social justice, anti-racism, anti-oppression, etc. Within the standards, the word diverse is mentioned only once, and that is in relation to the recruitment of students. The organization does point out that "diversity must be a pervasive characteristic of any quality preparation program" (CAEP, 2013, p. 21), but diversity and social justice are not the same things. Social justice absolutely requires an understanding of diversity, but diversity does not require an understanding of social justice. Similarly, according to the National Board for Professional Teaching Standards (NBPTS), "the Five Core Propositions—comparable to medicine's Hippocratic Oath—set forth the profession's vision for accomplished teaching" (NBPTS, 2016, para. 1). Despite the gravitas, the Propositions do not have any language about social justice, anti-oppression, nor teachers as agents of change. In effect, the two primary professional standards organizations that have an incredible amount of power in shaping the teaching and professional development of teachers offer little credence toward social justice and/or anti-oppression in its standards. This is a significant statement and one that reverberates across teacher education. On the other hand, the National Council for the Social Studies National Standards for the Preparation of Social Studies Teachers (2015) has language that speaks specifically to social justice. Standard 5: Professional Responsibility and Informed Action states, "Candidates reflect and expand upon their social studies knowledge, inquiry skills, and civic dispositions to adapt practice, promote social justice, and take informed action in schools and/or communities" (p. 17). What is so impressive about the language of this standard is that it not only promotes content knowledge but also action or activism.

One organization that is unique in their commitment to social justice is the National Council for the Teachers of English. In their document *Standards for Initial Preparation of Teachers of Secondary English Language Arts, Grades 7–12*, the National Council for the Teachers of English, in conjunction with the National Council for the Accreditation of Teacher Education (NCATE)[1] (2012), the importance of teachers teaching for social justice is incorporated into their standard regarding Professional Knowledge and Skills of English/Language Arts teachers. They state, "Candidates demonstrate knowledge of how theories and research about social justice, diversity, equity, student identities, and schools as institutions can enhance students' opportunities to learn in English Language Arts" (p. 2). This is crucial in the development of teachers. This is beyond simply promoting surface understanding of so-called others, and NCTE's standard makes an unprecedented move. They argue requirements for promoting social justice as an aspect of highly effective teachers is not only justice-oriented but also sound teaching practice (Burns & Miller, 2017).

Unfortunately, neither the National Council for the Teachers of Mathematics nor the National Science Teachers Association has either teacher preparation or academic standards highlighting attention to the ways in which math and science intersects with social justice or anti-oppression issues. This is a travesty considering the notion that the history of mathematics is a multicultural history that includes Egyptians (i.e. Africans), Persians, and Asians—a move that can decenter the Eurocentric hegemony. Environmental racism and climate change are rife with opportunities for scientific investigation that promotes social justice and anti-racism. Burns and Miller summarize the importance of social justice in the teacher education curriculum:

> … groups like NCATE, NCTE, and other SPAs should unabashedly require teacher educators and K–12 teachers to know, understand, and *realize* that social justice is not merely a nice idea. It is a scientifically proven construct and theory of pedagogy that also happens to be moral and ethical with regard to the health of our education system, the children it serves, and the society they will sustain when they inherit it. (p. 33)

Although detractors may say that social justice is just more liberal hogwash or a way of making White people feel bad—which totally misses the point and is an aberration of the goals of social justice and anti-racism—one thing that cannot be argued: The literature, theory, pedagogies, and practices of social justice is fundamentally about the uplift of all human beings.

Naming is everything, and if our professional organizations do not speak specifically about or explicitly promote issues like social justice, anti-oppression, or anti-racism, then those issues become trivial proclivities of individual teachers rather than a foundational priority in the identities and pedagogies of educators and foundational knowledge for students. Although social studies and English/language arts promotes attention to social justice, in many if not most places math and science do not, and it is vital that ideas of social justice and anti-oppression are represented as transdisciplinary values, especially during the elementary grades, when learning is most formative. But with naming also comes responsibility, and it is just as destructive for organizations and institutions to talk-the-talk of social justice while in practice merely co-opting the language like the latest flavor-of-the-month. It becomes the responsibility of our institutions to also reflect the values of social justice through all institutional practices and policies.

If we, as a society, are truly invested in ameliorating the legacy of racism and redirecting our country toward a justice orientation, then we must begin to teach our children and youth about not only the history of race and racism but also the ways in which race and racism permeate our systems and institutions, today. We must move past simple curriculum inclusion and help our children and youth learn how knowledge is constructed and institutions and systems promote inequitable and racist practices, oftentimes despite the best intentions of individuals (Banks, 2004).

Curbing the Demonization of White Folks

Stop for a second for an activity. Name as many African American, Latinx, Indigenous American, or Asian American champions for social justice as you can. Take your time. Think about if for five minutes ... an hour ... a day (and don't cheat by doing a Google search). ... Now, name as many White American champions for social justice you can think of, besides Abraham Lincoln or John Brown. Take your time. Think about if for five minutes ... an hour ... a day (and don't cheat by doing a Google search). ... Coming up with a lot more for the former than the latter? Of course.

Now, I am no better because I was exposed to the same curriculum in elementary and high school as many of you. The fact of the matter is I too struggle with naming historic White champions of racial justice. The first that come to mind are Michael Schwerner and Andrew Goodman, who along with James Chaney (a Black man) were murdered in Mississippi trying to register African Americans to vote during Freedom Summer, 1964. They left their comfortable, middle class lives in New York to be accomplices in the cause. I have a particular affinity for Michael since we both attended Michigan State University. I give much respect to Tim Wise (Earp, Jhally, & Morris, 2013) for encouraging us in the documentary

White Like Me: Racism and White Privilege in America to learn about people like: Bob Broussard, Bill Clifford, Robert McDole, Jim Zwerg, Will Campbell, Jeremiah Everetts, John Fee, Helen Hunt Jackson, Angelina Grimkey, Matilda Gage, Juliette Hampton Morgan, Jessie Daniel Ames, and Lydia Child. I refuse to perpetrate in my own book: I have more learning to do as well, but the list offered by Tim is a good place to start.

My hope is that historians and others can rediscover more White folks throughout our nation's history who allied themselves with racial justice and stood up as leaders against racial injustice. Why is it important to rediscover these luminaries? Simple. It helps us show that there is choice. They provide us solid, human examples of how White folks too are part of the struggle against this system of advantage based on race. These citizens stood up against ridicule and violence and the comfort of privilege to stand for the higher ideal of the *privileging of humanity* in all living beings that occupy not only this space called the United States but also globally. Today we see this spirit reflected in people like Virginia Foster Durr (1903–1999), Morris Dees, John Greenberg, and Anne Braden (1924–2006), Frances Kendall, Robin DiAngelo, and Ruth Frankenberg (1957–2007), Tim Wise, Heather Hackman, Father Michael Pfleger, Peggy McIntosh, Sam Hamlin, Dara Silverman, Carla Wallace, and many others. I like to remind my students that the majority of anti-racist scholars are in fact White folks. I purposely have not offered mini-biographies of these people in hopes that you seek out them and their histories on your own. (Google is a beautiful creation).

In addition to these individuals there are many anti-racist organizations organized and led by White folks: Challenging White Supremacy, the Catalyst Project, European Dissent, the Rural Organizing Project, the Heads Up Collective, the Anti-Racist Working Group and many others across the nation. A Google search of these organizations and people will lead you to a bold and strong community of White folks who humbly align themselves as part of the fight against racial oppression. The challenge is to create a space in K-12 curriculum for those people and organizations so that all our youth can see the reality of White folks as allies, accomplices, and leaders in the fight against racial oppression. Without that presence, it will continue to be much more challenging for White youth to develop a positive racial identity and no longer use the notion of colorblindness as a band-aid to deeper systemic and institutional challenges.

It is easy to talk about White folks writ large as "the problem," but the fact of the matter is there are millions of White folks that think racism is a moral abomination, and there *always* have been. Plain and simple. Now, does that mean that all White folks fully "get it"? Of course not, but that begs the question of our responsibility as educators (and citizens) to help those struggling through the process of learning about how racism functions. After all, knowing that racism is wrong is a pretty good place to start. Unfortunately, as part of a system of advantage based on race, it is sensible to systematically hide alternative constructions of White folks as champions and leaders of racial justice as a means of continuing to divide us. It is easy to follow the popular discourses and reproduce divisive rhetoric about how "they" are. It is much more difficult to see the humanity of the "other" and consider how this system of advantage based on race has established conditions in which we are perpetually at antagonistic positions. This is by no means easy work. It takes a great deal of knowledge, honesty, humility, and love, but if we as a profession advocate for pedagogies, curricula, and practices that promote these ideas as fundamental to the identity of highly qualified teachers and administrators we can move in a new direction. But this is a long game; its chess, not checkers.

We should take a lesson from September 11, 2001, when two hijacked airplane crashed into the World Trade Center in New York City. It took *less than an hour* for both of those towers, magnificent models of human ingenuity and icons to an iconic city, to come crashing to the ground. In its wake, it took *fifteen years* to rebuild on that site, which during that time endured a flood of lower Manhattan, not to mention all the political and corporate wrangling surrounding the rebuilding. Likewise, we should remember it took centuries to build this system of advantage based on race. It will take some time to dismantle it and rebuild a system/society in which the *humanity* of all individuals is privileged and not a particular race or identity. We are in that process, as we are seeing more and more people from across the racial and identity spectrum engage differently, especially our youth. But again, just knowing that racism is wrong, or stereotyping each other is wrong, does not necessarily equate to a fundamental understanding of how systemic and institutional racism functions. For without an understanding of the social, political, economic, cultural, and educational factors that perpetuate this system of advantage based on race, it is impossible to make substantive change.

White fatigue may just be a term, another iteration to describe a type of White resistance. What is most important about White fatigue rests in the fact that there are millions of White brothers and sisters who are *trying* to understand and work for a more beloved community because of an intuitive understanding that racism is wrong. It is frustrating for them. The process of understanding and developing a positive racial identity is frustrating. After all, for those of us from historically marginalized groups, we have spent years in states of frustration at learning how to navigate a world in which Whiteness is privileged. But as expressed earlier, this system of racial reality was built over hundreds of years and its architecture is solid, reinforced through multiple institutions. Learning how to rethink those messages is deeply challenging, for all of us. Education (including teacher education), no matter what, is part of that mission, and the question for us is how do we want to be aligned?

Over the past fifty years there has been a groundswell of thoughtful, critical scholars and activists working to rehabilitate the sickness planted into our national consciousness, and even though their work has been incredibly powerful we still have the tendency to marginalize White students through declarations of tacit racist behavior via resistance. As such it is necessary for us to consider how we communicate resistance while also honoring the challenge of understanding how race and racism function, which is fundamental to developing the acumen to be not simply allies but accomplices and leaders for racial justice.

I was in an Italian restaurant recently. As I walked through the facility I noticed (like Buggin' Out in *Do the Right Thing*) that there were no "brothas on the wall." Jokingly I said it to my family and we just chuckled, but it took me back twenty plus years to when a roommate and I got into a debate about the lack of representation of "others" in J Crew catalogs and how that was emblematic of racism. The argument was a stalemate; at the time I was just beginning to developed the language to talk about such things, beyond my straight up emotions. My roommate was in a state of her own flux. The talk went something like this:

"So what? There are no Black people in the catalog. Why is that racist?"

"Yo, it's like we don't exist, like Black folks don't wear khakis or something!"

"That's ridiculous; we know Black people exist."

"Then why can't they show us along with all these White people? Hell, at least Bennetton showed all shades of people. I get sick of never seeing me in their thick ass catalogs ..."

Years later, she reminded me of the dialogue and acquiesced, pointing out what she had gone on to learn in her graduate program in social work and critical reflections on of her life. This is what White fatigue is all about. She could have closed herself off from learning more. I could have dismissed her as part of the problem. However, despite her frustrations she continued to be inquisitive and search for answers, leaving herself open to new critical ideas, and growing to understand that racism is about much more than whether or not we are "nice" to each other. At the same time, I saw her humanity and knew her heart. I knew she had an innate sense of justice but did not quite understand how concepts connected or why some actions—like erasing the reality of different racial groups in a catalog—could perpetuate racism.

White fatigue is not a strategy. White fatigue is not a panacea. White fatigue is a pedagogical consideration to remind us that for our students—preservice teachers and otherwise—what they are learning about race, racism, and oppression in general is challenging. It is a quintessentially human enterprise. Embrace that humanity, which we must do, lest we hamper the possibilities of allies, accomplices and new leaders in the struggle against racial oppression.

Until the end...

Epilogue: A Final Note on Reaching the Promised Land, by Any Means Necessary ...

On April 3, 1968, Rev. Dr. Martin Luther King delivered his prescient "I've Been to the Mountain Top" speech at the Mason Temple in Memphis, Tennessee. I have always been fascinated by this speech since it was the last before his assassination, the next day on a balcony at the Lorraine Motel (my Aunt Shirley and Uncle Lee drove me by the hotel a few times before it became a museum). You see, MLK is so important to me because, despite the personal connection, he is so revered in the American imaginary but also painfully misrepresented. In that historic sermon he said that he had been to the mountaintop and seen the Promised Land:

> Like anybody, I would like to live a long life. Longevity has its place. But I'm not con-cerned about that now. I just want to do God's will. And He's allowed me to go up to the mountain. And I've looked over. And I've seen the Promised Land. I may not get there with you. But I want you to know tonight, that we, as a people, will get to the Promised Land. (King, 1968, para. 55)

That is the historic passage from the sermon, and rightfully so. Not only is it brilliant oratory but also prescient, hopeful, and bittersweet. In those words, Rev. Martin promoted the idea of a shared destiny. At the end of it all, we die, but while we ramble through this world we should be doing God's work—another way of saying we should be working to ensure justice for *all* our brothers and sisters. If we *work together*, if we help one another see through the lies, half-truths, distortions, ill-messages, and manipulations promoted through the systems that function to perpetuate this system of advantage based on race, then perhaps we can see the promised land, together.

I like to imagine that he did not see a utopia, a sort of terrestrial heaven. Rather he saw, a process, us working together to solve our most burdensome and divisive problems. I like to imagine that what he saw was a coalition of millions in concert, in dialogue, working together to create a society in which the humanity in each of us is held as eternally sacred, and not only our ideals but also our actions reflect the desire and commitment for liberty and justice for all, through social practices *and* policies. But that desire is both a goal and a process. That is the ultimate point: the struggle for social justice—whether that be for race, gender, ability, age, class, language, or any other aspect of human identity and experience—is not just about the destination but the journey itself. How we conduct ourselves and model behaviors of anti-racism is the key to knowing the Promised Land when we reach it.

Like the *I Have a Dream* speech, key thematic passages of Dr. King's last speech have been overshadowed in popular history. In the *Mountaintop* speech he also said the following in reference to the assassination attempt on him by Izola Curry, in New York City, in 1958, a decade before his actual assassination, ironically:

> It came out in the *New York Times* the next morning, that if I had merely sneezed, I would have died. Well, about four days later, they allowed me … to read some of the mail that came in, and from all over the states and the world, kind letters came in. I read a few, but one of them I will never forget … a little girl, a young girl who was a student at the White Plains High School. It said simply,

> Dear Dr. King,

> I am a ninth-grade student at the White Plains High School. *While it should not matter, I would like to mention that I'm a white girl.* I read in the paper of your misfortune, and of your suffering. And I read that if you had sneezed, you would have died. And I'm simply writing you to say that I'm so happy that you didn't sneeze.

Dr. King went on to say:

> … I want to say tonight that I too am happy that I didn't sneeze. Because if I had sneezed, I wouldn't have been around here in 1960, when students all over the South started sitting-in at lunch counters. And I knew that as they were sitting in, they were really standing up for the best in the American dream, and taking the whole nation back to *those great wells of democracy which were dug deep by the Founding Fathers in the Declaration of Independence and the Constitution.* (paras. 40–50) (Emphasis added)

He then recounts key events he was involved in during the Civil Rights Movement of the 1950s and 1960s and the grave triviality of a sneeze. The success of the Freedom Rides … The Civil Rights Bill … The *I Have a Dream* speech … Selma. … The moment of the *Mountaintop* speech, a garbage workers strike in Memphis.

Since he did not name the little White girl her presence is a footnote in a larger history, but what do we make of her, back in 1958, expressing her concern for a man who at the time was one of the most despised men in White America? An ally? An accomplice? A leader?

CONCLUDING THOUGHTS | 171

What has been left by the wayside of history has had the deleterious effect of dividing us rather than unifying us, despite the intentions of our leaders for social and racial justice. By popularly focusing only on the humanist, universal aspects of Dr. King's messages—as furthered through our school and public curriculum—we have missed his larger systemic and institutional recriminations and in many ways trivialized his message and those of others.

Similarly, people forget that as his life was rapidly approaching its own tragic end, the great Minister Malcolm X's ideas were beginning to merge with Rev. King's and he too understood that White folks had a role in fighting for racial justice. In *The Autobiography of Malcolm X* (Malcolm & Haley, 1966/1990), Minister Malcolm shared a letter he wrote while on his hajj to Mecca. He shared:

> During the past eleven days here in the Muslim world, I have eaten from the same plate, drunk from the same glass, and slept on the same rug—while praying to the same God—with fellow Muslims, whose eyes were the bluest of blue, whose hair was the blondest of blond, and whose skin was the whitest of white. *And in the words and in the deeds of the white Muslims, I felt the same sincerity that I felt among the black African Muslims of Nigeria, Sudan and Ghana.*
>
> We were truly all the same (brothers)—because their belief in one God had removed the white from their minds, the white from their behavior, and the white from their attitude.
>
> I could see from this, that *perhaps if white Americans could accept the Oneness of God, then perhaps, too, they could accept in reality the Oneness of Man*—and cease to measure, and hinder, and harm others in terms of their "differences" in color.
>
> With racism plaguing America like an incurable cancer, the so-called "Christian" white American heart should be more receptive to a proven solution to such a destructive problem. Perhaps it could be in time to save America from imminent disaster— the same destruction brought upon Germany by racism that eventually destroyed the Germans themselves.
>
> Each hour here in the Holy Land enables me to have greater spiritual insights into what is happening in America between black and white. *The American Negro never can be blamed for his racial animosities—he is only reacting to four hundred years of the conscious racism of the American whites.* But as racism leads America up the suicide path, *I do believe, from the experiences that I have had with them, that the whites of the younger generation, in the colleges and universities, will see the handwriting on the walls and many of them will turn to the spiritual path of truth—the only way left to America to ward off the disaster that racism inevitably must lead to.* (pp. 340–341) (Emphasis added)

And here we stand in 2017 in the wake of the election of a president who, in part, won the office by stoking the racial and xenophobic fears of millions of White

Americans, and simultaneously millions of other White Americans rejected that nefarious strategy. Now more than ever we must be prudent in how we engage one another. Most importantly, we educators must be attentive in how we construct and engage White folks when they show signs of resistance. We must be considerate of the range of reasons why they may sit quietly, or show discomfort, or become argumentative, or wholly disengage. We must be willing to create a rhetorical out rather than, through our language, isolate them in a rhetorical corner wherein they are just resistant, and by extension racist for struggling through the challenge of learning and understanding racism.

We all, *each of us*, have been manipulated by the same system that was constructed and perpetuated by generations that predate us by hundreds of years, and that manipulation has impacted us, as groups and individuals, in different ways, constructing different realities. It is crucial for all of us, educators and citizens, to recognize how this system of advantage based on race—one that has created a racial hierarchy in which Whiteness has been constructed as the norm—has hobbled the opportunities to crest the apex of that mountaintop and actually see the magnificent vision MLK saw, but left ill-descript. Learning how to navigating the struggle is just as beautiful as the destination in itself. Learning how to navigate the struggle is prelude to the destination.

That apex is within each of us, if we only understand that we all have been assigned roles in a system and be willing to critically reconsider those roles and the assumptions we make in light of those assignments. It is time to shift our discourses about race and truly see the humanity in one another. *Not to move into a post-racial society, but a post-racism society.* In order to see that vision we must rely on both the power of education and the role of teachers to help us navigate that terrain, like watchpersons with vigilant eyes on a chilly dawn, and vanguards riding forward into the bracing light of a new day, together.

Note

1. In 2013 NCATE merged with Teacher Education Accreditation Council (TEAC) to form the Council for the Accreditation of Teacher Preparation (CAEP).

Bibliography

Banks, J. (2004). Multicultural education: Historical development, dimensions, and practice. In J. A. Banks & C. McGee Banks (Eds.), *Handbook of research on multicultural education* (pp. 3–29). San Francisco, CA: Jossey Bass.

Bruner, J. (1960/1996). *The process of education.* Cambridge, MA: Harvard University Press.

Burns, L. D., & Miller, S. J. (2017). Social justice policymaking in teacher education from conception to application: Realizing Standard VI. *Teachers College Record, 19*(2), 1–38.

Council for the Accreditation of Educator Preparation. (2013). *2013 CAEP Standards.* Retrieved from http://caepnet.org/standards/introduction

Dover, A. (2015). Teaching for social justice and the common core: Justice-oriented curriculum for language arts and literacy. *Journal of Adolescent and Adult Literacy, 59*(5), 517–527.

Earp, J., Jhally, S., & Morris, S. (2013). *White like me: Race, racism, and White privilege in America.* Northampton, MA: Media Education Foundation.

Guinier, L. (2004). From racial liberalism to racial literacy: Brown v. Board of Education and the interest-divergence dilemma. *Journal of American History, 91*(1), 92–118.

King, M. L. (1968). *I've been to the mountaintop* [speech]. Retrieved from http://www.american-rhetoric.com/speeches/mlkivebeentothemountaintop

Ladson-Billings, G., & Tate, W. (1995). Toward a critical race theory of education. *Teachers College Record, 97*(1), 47–68.

Miller, S. J. (2014). Cultivating a disposition for sociospatial justice in English teacher preparation. *Teacher Education and Practice, 27*(1), 44–74.

National Board for Professional Teaching Standards. (2016). *Five core propositions.* Retrieved from http://www.nbpts.org/five-core-propositions

National Council for the Social Studies Task Force on Teacher Education Standards. (2015). *National standards for the preparation of social studies teachers.* Retrieved from http://www.socialstudies.org/sites/default/files/NSPSST-NCSS%20Website%20DRAFT.pdf

Singleton, G. (2014). *Courageous conversations about race: A field guide for achieving equity in schools* (2nd ed.). Thousand Oaks, CA: Corwin Press.

Skerrett, A. (2011, June 1). English teachers' racial literacy knowledge and practice. *Race Ethnicity and Education, 14*(3), 313–330.

Stevenson, H. (2014). *Promoting racial literacy in schools: Differences that make a difference.* New York, NY: Teachers College Press.

Twine, F. W. (2004, January 1). A white side of black Britain: The concept of racial literacy. *Ethnic and Racial Studies, 27*(6), 878–907.

Vetter, A., & Hungerford-Kressor, H. (2014). "We gotta change first": Racial literacy in a high school English classroom. *Journal of Language and Literacy Education, 10*(1), 82–99.

X, M. & Haley, A. (1990). *The autobiography of Malcolm X* (27th printing). New York, NY: Ballantine Books.

Afterword

BY EDWARD MOORE JR.

White fragility, White guilt, White resistance, White privilege, White supremacy, *White fatigue*. The congruent interweaving of these concepts mingles and inter-twines with the humanity and empathy called for, not just in the field of social jus-tice, but as an essential component of teacher education. How can White teachers truly educate students of color whom they have been socialized to view as inferior? How do educators slog through the murk of an educational system built for White people by White people? And how do educators survive beyond the "savior men-tality" they are indoctrinated by in teacher educator programs? If readers do not find the answers in this book (which they will if they look), at least they will be confronted with many of the essential questions, and without asking the questions, the answers will remain in the hands of the oppressor.

White fatigue. What an interesting and necessary concept. On the one hand, why do people of color once again have to worry about how White people feel about social justice? But on the other hand, as is so eloquently stated by the author, it is imperative for future educators to confront and engage in "a process of unlearning and learning" and there is nothing that can be accomplished if fatigue outweighs fragility which outweighs guilt. Addressing the system of racism in this country that was founded by and for White people head on is inescapable.

Those of us who work in the ingrained system of race and racism in this country can all point to an incident at work, the affirmative action discussion, the mentor, the professor, the shooting of an unarmed Black man or the friend who opened our eyes to the deeply entrenched whiteness of this country. For me it was Dr. Joe Feagin and *The White Racial Frame*. *The White Racial Frame* took all of my experiences growing up Black in the housing projects, being underestimated by teachers, falling into the traps of the stereotype and emerging from a predominately White institution instead of prison and grounded those experiences in a framework that made sense of the systemic inequities growing around me like weeds and weighing me down like anchors. For educators, out there, especially White educators, struggling with the chasms opening in the their lives through the blooming recognition of systems of inequity and struggling to push through the guilt, the fragility and the privilege, this book offers hope. It offers theories, research, humor, honesty and practical ideas. If you read this far, and are still reading, then you do truly want a way through the murk, not only for you and your students, but for all of us.

Brother Flynn challenges us to look deep within ourselves for the humanity suppressed by years of racist rhetoric that demonizes some and canonizes others. The idea of White fatigue is essential. The National White Privilege Conference is grounded in the Moore Relationship Model and follows the tenets of Understanding, Respecting and Connecting. Reading through *White Fatigue: Rethinking Resistance for Social Justice* I felt his push, his tug, his hand, and his heart trying to move White educators to that final step. That understanding the inequities, the systems, the illogical ideology of racism and privilege is not enough. That respecting the literature and teaching Black History Month, that Columbus did not discover America, that California belonged Mexico not the other way around, and that this country is built on the back of an enormous number of women, members of the LGTBQ+ community, immigrants from around the world and others, is not enough. That you can't burn out or give up when you are sitting on the edge of the chasm staring into the manipulated racist system staring back. You have to take that final step. You have to connect. For humanity, for my children, for your children, for all of us. Don't let the fatigue win, don't let the racists win, we are better than that. Let's do it. #MakeItHappen #BeMooreCourageous #TogetherWeCan #WhiteFatigue.

sj Miller & Leslie David Burns
GENERAL EDITORS

Social Justice Across Contexts in Education addresses how teaching for social justice, broadly defined, mediates and disrupts systemic and structural inequities across early childhood, K–12 and postsecondary disciplinary, interdisciplinary and/or trans-disciplinary educational contexts. This series includes books exploring how theory informs sustainable pedagogies for social justice curriculum and instruction, and how research, methodology, and assessment can inform equitable and responsive teaching. The series constructs, advances, and supports socially just policies and practices for all individuals and groups across the spectrum of our society's education system.

Books in this series provide sustainable models for generating theories, research, practices, and tools for social justice across contexts as a means to leverage the psychological, emotional, and cognitive growth for learners and professionals. They position social justice as a fundamental aspect of schooling, and prepare readers to advocate for and prevent social justice from becoming marginalized by reform movements in favor of the corporatization and de-professionalization of education. The over-arching aim is to establish a true field of social justice education that offers theory, knowledge, and resources for those who seek to help all learners succeed. It speaks for, about, and to classroom teachers, administrators, teacher educators, education researchers, students, and other key constituents who are committed to transforming the landscape of schools and communities.

Send proposals and manuscripts to the general editors at:

sj Miller   sj.Miller@colorado.edu
Leslie David Burns   L.Burns@uky.edu

To order other books in this series, please contact our Customer Service Department at:

(800) 770-LANG (within the U.S.)
(212) 647-7706 (outside the U.S.)
(212) 647-7707 FAX

or browse online by series at:

WWW.PETERLANG.COM